# Call of the Game

## What Really Goes on in the Broadcast Booth

GARY BENDER

WITH MICHAEL L. JOHNSON

PARK LEARNING CENTRE
UNIVERSITY OF GLOUCESTERSHIRE
PO Box 220, The Park
Cheltenham GL50 2RH
Tel: 01242 714333

BONUS BOOKS, INC., CHICAGO

98   97   96   95   94                                   5   4   3   2   1

**Library of Congress Cataloging-in-Publication Data**

Bender, Gary.
   Call of the game : what really goes on in the broadcast booth /
Gary Bender with Michael L. Johnson.
     p.    cm.
   Includes index.
   ISBN 1-56625-013-7 : $19.95
   1. Radio broadcasting of sports—United States.  2. Sportscasters—
United States.  I. Johnson, Michael L.  II. Title.
GV742.3.B46  1994                        94-26463
070.4'49796—dc20

**Bonus Books, Inc.**
160 East Illinois Street
Chicago, Illinois 60611

*First Edition*

*Cover design by Jerry Durkin*

*Cover photo: Gary Bender with Keith Erickson (left)*

*Cover photo by Mike Moore, Phoenix Suns*

*Printed in the United States of America*

# CONTENTS

# *Acknowledgements*

*M*any thanks go to the following for their help in bringing this book to life:

Dayle Bakley for transcribing all my hours and hours of tape;

Monte Johnson and Linda Johnson for proofreading the manuscript and suggesting improvements;

Michael Johnson, the wordsmith who painstakingly poked and jarred from me the many memories of my career; and

My wife Linda, my best friend, who for over 25 years allowed me to travel and experience all we've written about.

\* \* \*

This book is dedicated to my sons Trey and Brett who are following in my footsteps.

Gary Bender

# *Prologue*

The date—December 28, 1975. The place—Metropolitan Stadium in Bloomington, Minnesota. The event—the play-off game between the Dallas Cowboys and the Minnesota Vikings to see which would face the Los Angeles Rams for the NFC crown.

What an exciting time for me. I was ending my first year with CBS. For a rookie to be assigned to do the play-by-play of such an important game was remarkable. Usually broadcasters had to work two to three years at the network level before they were given an opportunity to do a game of such significance.

The whole year had been the realization of a dream. During the season, I had been honored to be teamed in the booth with Johnny Unitas, one of the most recognizable people I've ever been around in my career. To prepare with a legend for a game that would be viewed by every football fan in the nation seemed more fun than work.

Still the pressure and excitement of the moment hit me. I couldn't sleep the night before. In fact, I got sick. The next morning as we were going to the ballpark, John—who never got rattled or frustrated by anything—turned to me and said, "This is just another game, Gary. Just treat it like that. Let's just have fun like all the other games we've done."

The weather was typical for Metropolitan Stadium. I had worked several Viking games in the past and it seemed that there was never anything but snow and ice and a wind that whipped across the parking lot. That day was no exception.

All day long the temperature hovered just below the freezing mark.

Before the game, I walked down on the field to get a sense of the conditions. Because they had covered the field with a tarp and warmed it with hot-air blowers to prevent freezing, the natural turf was muddy and wet. Snow that had previously accumulated on the field had been plowed off and piled beyond the end zones, right where the "NFL Today" crew was preparing for an on-site broadcast. Brent Musburger, Irv Cross, Phyllis George, and Jimmy the Greek were bundled up, walking through their pre-game, halftime, and post-game shows. I remember Phyllis complaining about how cold it was going to be on the air.

Though it featured Fran Tarkenton and Roger Staubach, the top two passers in the NFC that season, the game evolved into a defensive struggle. It was an intense physical match between the Purple People Eaters of the Vikings and the Doomsday Defense of the Cowboys.

Neither team could sustain a drive in the first half. The only score came in the second period after Minnesota was awarded possession on the Dallas four when a Viking punt was ruled to have hit Cowboy Cliff Harris on the back of the leg. Our replay showed the ball came closest to Bennie Barnes and the first report from the field said it was actually a Cowboy lineman who had touched the ball thinking it had already nipped one of his teammates. It was the first of several controversies we had to deal with that day.

Dallas tied the score at 7–7 in the third period after Staubach led a drive which featured clutch first-down passes to Preston Pearson and Billy Joe Dupree and a 15-yard roughness penalty against Minnesota's Wally Hilgenberg.

Midway through the final period, Tarkenton directed the Vikings' only sustained drive of the day, putting Minnesota in front 14–7.

Dallas countered, converting two third downs and a fourth down on the way to a 24-yard field goal by Toni Fritsch. The stage was set for one of the most exhilarating finishes in NFL history. The sequence of events came in such rapid succession it was difficult to describe each incident in full and we didn't learn some of the details and their impact until later.

Trailing 14–10 in the final two minutes, the Cowboys faced a do-or-die situation with fourth-and-16 on their own 25. Pearson took off on a corner route and beat Nate Wright, grabbing a 25-yard pass from Staubach, landing near the sideline.

Did he have both feet in bounds? Replays showed it was questionable whether Pearson got either foot in bounds let alone both. However, the official said, "Yes, both feet were in." The drive remained alive.

Two plays later on second-and-10, Staubach called a play he had saved for the most desperate of circumstances, one he felt sure would be open. He rolled to his right, set up, and fired a 45-yard bomb in the air. As Pearson made the catch, appearing to trap the ball on his hip, his defender Wright fell to the ground. Pearson was free to scamper the final five yards into the end zone with 24 seconds on the clock.

That pass, known now as the "Hail Mary," is a staple of NFL highlight films. Few remember the controversy that surrounded it, however, principally because of how we covered it.

Two points of view prevailed in the locker rooms after the game. The Viking version held that Pearson had pushed off against Wright, causing Wright to fall. According to Pearson, when Wright leaped to try and bat the ball away, he pinned the ball against Pearson's hip, giving Pearson that precious split second he needed to realign himself so he could pivot towards the ball and take in that historic catch while Wright fell.

What did happen? Was it offensive pass interference? The camera angle that we showed on the air was inconclusive. If we had used a different angle shot, maybe the controversy might have been resolved. But early in the broadcast, our director had decided the real story was being played out in the trenches. He elected to train the camera on the line of scrimmage. Consequently, the debate still rages.

After Dallas took the 17–14 lead, things became more complicated and even a little bizarre. With 18 seconds remaining, the Vikings had to start from their own 15-yard-line after the kickoff, a nearly hopeless situation. On the snap, Tarkenton rolled out and did what you might expect from the greatest scrambler in the history of the game—he scrambled, buying additional time to throw the ball.

Eventually he was sacked for a 14-yard loss. However, Tarkenton felt he had gotten rid of the ball, had thrown an incomplete pass, therefore, avoiding the long loss. He became outraged by the call. He ran over to referee Jerry Burgman, ripped off his helmet, and slammed it down on the field where it bounced across the gridiron.

Meanwhile, further up the field, one of the Viking fans, equally incensed by the call, threw a bottle from the stands and hit one of the officials, Armen Terzian. Terzian dropped and lay still.

In the booth, we were torn between two simultaneous actions. At one end there was Tarkenton windmilling his arms, pleading his case to Burgman while at the other end half the officiating crew had surrounded their motionless comrade who John and I feared had been killed by the bottle. (Terzian, who received a gash on the forehead which did not require stitches, later told me that he never lost consciousness, but was paralyzed by the shock of what had happened.) We later found out it was at this particular point that Tarkenton's dad, who was watching the game on TV with his other two sons at his home in Georgia, suffered a heart attack and died.

That Viking-Cowboy play-off game remains one of the high points of my broadcasting experience not only because of the historic "Hail Mary" ending, but also because of the lessons it taught me. Though it was sometime later before I knew the full ramifications of that broadcast, I realized for the first time what an immense responsibility a broadcaster has. You have to be accurate. You have to be prepared. You have to be able to capture the emotion of the moment. Though there is a tremendous amount of pressure because of rapidly unfolding events, you cannot lose your poise.

* * *

It's a long way from the Met in Bloomington, Minnesota, to a farm in eastern Colorado. But that's where my dream of becoming a sportscaster began.

My dad had been an outstanding coach at Dodge City (Kansas) Junior College, taking his team to the national tournament five years in a row. Being the son of a coach was the best of lives—sitting on the bench with my dad's team, traveling with them, feeling a part of everything that happened.

Then, suddenly, I was "farmed out." My dad was given the opportunity of taking over his father-in-law's farming business in eastern Colorado and left coaching.

My life changed completely. The farm was in the middle of nowhere. There were no real neighbors. I attended a simple one-room country school. There was nothing that was remotely connected to what I had previously experienced.

That first summer on the farm in my seventh-grade year was one of the most difficult times of my life. My daily routine consisted of getting up early to milk two cows before breakfast. I would then gas up the tractor and plow till lunch, come in and eat, gas up the tractor again, and plow till sundown. Each hot summer day unfolded the same. I was disappointed, unhappy, and bored.

Then I discovered a way to survive 12- to 13-hour days of plowing fields.

As soon as I settled into my daily routine on the tractor, I would make up a "Game of the Day." One day I would be in the Los Angeles Coliseum. Another day I would be in the Orange Bowl. I even had a network. I used to imitate the old Liberty Broadcasting System. I would sign on the air, sing their jingle, then say, "This is the Liberty Broadcasting System bringing you the Game of the Day. Today we're in Yankee Stadium where the New York Yankees will meet the Boston Red Sox." Besides doing the play-by-play, I also sang the national anthem and inserted commercials. My favorites were Gillette's "look sharp, be sharp" commercials. I got so I had them down pat.

I would do this hour after hour. If I had an extra round to plow or another hour to put in on the tractor, I would go into extra innings, sudden death, or overtime. By the end of the day, I would come in from the field hoarse from talking above the noise of the tractor, from the dust, and from all the confusion.

My dad wondered what was going on. So one day he contrived to plow the same field with me. After a while he stopped and pretended something was wrong with his tractor. He shut his tractor off as I was coming towards him and, as I plowed by, he heard me calling a game.

He asked me about it later, but not in a way that was embarrassing. In fact, he encouraged me by saying, "Whatever you decide to do, just try to be the very best that you can be." It may sound like a cliché, but at that time of my life, it was the kind of encouragement that spurred me on to thinking that it *was* possible for a farm boy from eastern Colorado to become a broadcaster.

Those many hours spent on the tractor had a great impact on me in a number of ways. First, my imagination had a chance to develop and to be outwardly expressed without the scrutiny and faultfinding of other people. Second, when I finally did enter the broadcasting profession, the nuances of the business, the terminology, the ways of expressing myself came to me naturally, having evolved from those long hot summers of practice. Finally, it was indelibly imprinted on my mind that this was what I wanted to do in life.

Many people in various walks of life have bucked the odds. They have made similar journeys from the meager possibilities of a farm in eastern Colorado to the American dream of covering a major sporting event before a national audience. Like me, they all have had one thing in common—they were given a chance.

That is the reason for this book. I want to express my gratitude to all those people who gave me the opportunity to succeed, who reached out when I needed help.

Early in my career I was the voice of the University of Kansas Jayhawks and one of my responsibilities was to teach. Unfortunately, I had little to offer. I had a Master's Degree in Radio/Television/Film and had been in the business for two or three years, but I really had little on-the-job experience. Often I was challenged. "Well, how do you know that?" I felt inadequate and embarrassed that I didn't have the answers. Now after more than 25 years as a play-by-play announcer, I feel I have something to give back to the profession, hopefully in an unselfish way.

So many young people come to me today and say, "I want to be a sportscaster. How do I begin?" That's what this book is about. It tries to show you how to begin. It is meant to encourage you, nudge you along. It is meant to challenge you to evaluate why you should or should not be in this crazy business.

Believe me, broadcasting *is* a crazy business. There have been times that I've been almost near panic. There have been times when I've shed tears. There have been times when I've been immensely disappointed. But nothing has overshadowed this fact—I'm probably one of the luckiest people in the world to have had the opportunity to experience what I've experienced.

# PART I

CHOOSING A CAREER IN SPORTSCASTING

# CHAPTER ONE

# *Why Sports Broadcasting?*

Most young people who pursue a sports broadcasting career enter the profession for all the wrong reasons. Consequently, they are doomed to experience disillusionment and failure.

What are the wrong reasons? The most common is to seek fame and fortune.

People who want to be sportscasters often use network level announcers as their gauge. They read in *USA Today* that Bob Costas or Pat Summerall has signed a huge contract and associate lots of money, fancy cars, and big homes as standard issue for the profession.

But the Costases and Summeralls and the rest of the network broadcasters represent less than one percent of the business. Most sportscasting jobs, especially entry-level ones, will be in small markets with limited resources. Those who graduate from college with a degree in broadcasting can expect to see their fraternity brothers and sorority sisters quickly pass them on the earnings scale. If you are ever tempted by big corporate bucks and company perks, take them. Sportscasting isn't for you.

Likewise, if you have a real need to be recognized, to have your name on a marquee, forget about becoming a sportscaster. The jobs you are likely to get in places like Jamestown, North Dakota, Great Bend, Kansas, or Twin Falls, Idaho, will not have high enough visibility to satisfy your ego. Your desire for fame will not sustain you when you drive 200 miles to cover a basketball game in the dead of winter, return home at three in the morning, only to get up at six to do the 7:00 a.m. sports show.

So what are the right reasons to choose sportscasting as a career? There is no 100 percent guaranteed answer.

Play-by-play announcers who achieve success, who are truly happy with their work regardless of whether their careers peak at the network, regional, or local level, seem to have one thing in common—they were destined to do what they do. They were always in or around athletics. They cut out pictures of sports heroes for scrapbooks or collected baseball cards. Whenever a game was broadcast on radio or television, they were captivated by the play-by-play; their heartbeats quickened; their palms got sweaty. They all have "tractor" stories to tell about how they made up ball games driving down the street or walking to school or how they sneaked into the press box to tape the announcers. They recognized early in life what they wanted to do and everything they did prepared them for that eventuality.

When you encounter young men and women who change their major to broadcasting in college or who decide on a sportscasting career after a couple of false starts at other endeavors, it is hard to be encouraging. How will they compete against the budding young broadcaster who is driven to describe sports on the air and has had that tunnel vision from an early age? Who is more likely to relish doing a 7:00 a.m. sports show on three hours of sleep?

# CHAPTER TWO

# *Broadcasting Skill Inventory Checklist*

*I*f your reasons for pursuing a career in sportscasting are well-founded, you may still wonder whether you have the ability. What skills do novice broadcasters need to have or develop?

Before listing skills you do need, let's review the attributes you do *not* need:

## You do not need a "radio" voice.

In May of 1923 in the early days of radio, Graham Mc-Namee killed time during a break from jury duty by walking into the WEAF studios in New York City and speaking into a microphone. He was hired on the spot. McNamee's magnetic baritone voice, which had been trained for singing on the stage, was the only criterion evaluated.

Like McNamee, who eventually worked for NBC announcing major events from operas and concerts to political conventions to sports, many of the pioneers of broadcasting were chosen to do their job solely because of their voice. If you could shake the foundations of a building when you spoke, you were a strong candidate for a job on the air.

Some people still place a strong value on a broadcaster's voice. However, in the reality of the business today, it isn't the tonal quality of your voice that is nearly as important as how you use it. Many successful sportscasters from the local to the network level do not have a classic "radio" voice. They have overcome a supposed "disadvantage" with superior writing ability, with excellent reporting skills, or with the ability to convey their personality on the air through their expression.

**You do not need to look like Mel Gibson or Cindy Crawford.**

Because of the influence of television, the public generally assumes it requires good looks to get on the air. Nothing could be farther from the truth for broadcast sports journalism. Just think for a moment. How many network sportscasters would qualify for the romantic lead in a movie based on looks alone? Very few. We're a rather ordinary-looking lot.

The reason looks are not that important, particularly for play-by-play and color analysis, is that there is little need for the broadcaster to be seen. When basketball, baseball, or football is televised, the people in the booth are rarely put on camera more than three times a game—for the introduction, for mid-game or halftime analysis, and for the post-game wrap up—and then only briefly. In other sports such as golf, a commentator's time on camera is even less.

Of course, radio broadcasters are not seen at all. Everyone can cite an instance of having faithfully listened to favorite radio announcers for years without ever knowing how they look. In fact, when you do finally see them, they look nothing like what your mind envisioned. The broadcasters created a persona you came to trust and enjoy. You continued to listen to them because of what they said and how they said it, not because of how they looked.

**You do not have to be an ex-jock.**

It's true that more and more former pro athletes are taking up the mike once their sports careers are finished. Their insight into the game is something the networks currently find invaluable since the sophistication of today's fan requires expert analysis during a sporting event.

But you do not have to be able to dribble a basketball and chew gum at the same time to be a successful sportscaster, especially when it comes to play-by-play. In my network career, I've had the dubious honor to have covered 29 different sports. No way have I personally competed in all 29. I had my bell

rung playing football in high school and college, but I was i
a gifted athlete. The ability to cover such a diverse array of
sports came from considerable short-term preparation and
years of long-term development of basic broadcasting skills.

Now let's look at the skills you *do* need to become a successful sportscaster. What follows is a checklist to help you
qualify your suitability for a broadcasting job. The list is not
all-inclusive nor in any order of priority, but does present
capabilities essential to the business:

### Do you have the ability to write?

A sportscaster is by definition a broadcast journalist. And
like all other journalists, sportscasters have to know how to
write. A majority of the time the copy you read is your own.

Everyone works differently. A few people are gifted enough
to simply get by with mental composition. Some have to write
it first to see what it looks like. Still others go to the extreme
of memorizing what they write out. All have to know the
basics of good writing.

Any time a sportscaster says something concrete that
deals with issues, you can be fairly certain the comment didn't
come out of the blue. The statement was at least thought
through mentally if not written down beforehand. Vin Scully,
whom many consider one of the most poetic announcers of all
time, composes much of what you hear on the air by putting it
down on 3-by-5 cards beforehand. I also fall in this category.
I've often said to friends that I have to go back to my room to
get ready for the next day's broadcast and write out my ad-libs.

Writing is also important when it comes to retaining information. If I write something down, I never forget it. But if
somebody tells me something, there is a good chance it will
slip my memory. It has been statistically shown that we retain:

> 10% of what we read;
> 20% of what we hear;
> 30% of what we see;
> 50% of what we see and hear;
> 70% of what we say; and
> 90% of what we say and do.

Just reading, seeing, and hearing are not enough. To really remember something, reinforce it by performing some physical action. For most sportscasters, the easiest action is to put it down on paper.

Writing for radio and television obviously is different from writing for print. A number of print journalists have crossed over into broadcast journalism and have had a rocky transition; their script tended to contain too much description, their sentences were complex and too long.

Writing for the ear requires simplicity and conciseness. Dr. Bruce Linton, the former head of the Radio/Television/ Journalism Department at Kansas University, once said, "Don't challenge your audience. Hand it to them piecemeal. Don't make them think. They've worked hard all day long and they don't want to have to think through what you have to say."

## Do you have the ability to read?

The initial reaction to this question is typically, "I have an education. Of course I can read." But there is a significant difference between reading to yourself for comprehension and reading aloud on the air.

When we first learned to read, most of us read aloud, word for word. We were then encouraged to read to ourselves. The effort was still word for word. Then as reading became second nature to us, our eyes and our mind worked together to filter out nonessential words in a subconscious effort to speed up the process. We no longer needed to mentally say every word to understand the thoughts and ideas expressed on the printed page.

This mental speed-reading works to the detriment of the on-air announcer who must not only say every word, but say them with emphasis and emotion. Try it. Read a couple of paragraphs from a magazine to yourself, then read the same two paragraphs aloud. You will find that you have to focus on every word, really screw your attention down, to keep from skipping a word. You may even find your tongue tripping over words or saying words that aren't there, because your eyes and mind are used to working together alone and not in concert with your mouth.

Reading aloud does not come naturally. Some are better than others, but every broadcaster has to work at it to develop discipline. This takes practice. Whether it's reading street signs while riding in a car or reading homework in front of a mirror, practice every opportunity you can. Reading aloud seems such an obvious and simple skill, yet it's one of the biggest stumbling blocks for a young sportscaster breaking into the business.

## Are you expressive?

In communicating a message from one person to another, studies show eight percent of the communication is verbal (what we say), 35 percent is emotional (our tone of voice), 55 percent is body language (how we stand, walk, or sit plus our facial expressions), and two percent is intuitive (the message transmitted beneath everything else). Even if the content of your message is thoughtfully constructed and powerful, it still needs the other 92 percent of communication to be made most meaningful to the recipient. This is why selling over the phone is more difficult than selling in person. Telemarketers only have control of 43 percent of the communication tools available to them: verbal content and emotion. The same also applies to sportscasters.

Everyone can read a poem, but not all can bring emotion to their interpretation. Everyone can recite lines of a play, but few can make those lines come alive into a real character on the stage. The difference is expression. It is the ability that sets the broadcaster apart from the average person on the street. Expressive people have the ability to convey their personality on the air. They can communicate or sell ideas. People want to listen to them.

Expression requires a sense of voice inflection, proper enunciation, correct pronunciation, and the use of good diction. All these can be developed through various activities mentioned later. But you cannot get by on technique alone. You must be believable. If your expression is phony, if it is manufactured not genuine, if you are not interested in what you are saying, it will become apparent to the listener sooner or later. You can fool people some of the time, but not all the time.

If your desire and passion to become a sportscaster comes through in your voice regardless of your words, then you are expressive.

## Do you have a sense of time?

Whenever he made his first trip with the Green Bay Packers under the great Vince Lombardi, a rookie football player or journalist invariably arrived late, regardless of his attention to punctuality. What he didn't know and what veterans of the team and the media took for granted was that there was regular time and there was Lombardi time. Lombardi time was always 15 minutes earlier. If you weren't there 15 minutes before a scheduled departure, the bus or plane left without you.

Some people have an instinctive sense of time; they are always aware of the year, month, day, and hour; they not only know what they will be doing 45 minutes from now, but what is on tap a week from Tuesday. For others, life is a freewheeling experience that cannot be constrained by time; arriving for a party 15 minutes early or half an hour late is of no consequence. The former will adapt to the demands of broadcasting very well; the latter will immediately fail unless they train themselves to be otherwise.

Whether it is being prompt for interviews or making sure you get every word on the card read in a 30-second spot, sportscasters must be constantly aware of time. It is crucial to the business. If you are not dependable and do not plan ahead, you will be of little value. There is *no* leeway. Arrive 15 minutes late for a live broadcast that has been sold to advertisers and see how forgiving the station manager is.

## Are you organized?

In the past, the broadcasting business developed a reputation for hiring sportscasters based on their gift for gab, their ability to sit down behind the mike and fly by the seat of their pants with little or no preparation.

With the proliferation of sports on television, especially in the last decade, an announcer can no longer afford to walk into the booth at the last minute and wing it. The business is too sophisticated, the fan too knowledgeable. If Tim McCarver makes an astute prediction or comes up with a witty line, most likely he didn't ad-lib it. He did his homework before the game, anticipated the situation might arise, and had his prediction or line ready just in case.

Today's announcers spend far more time in preparation for a broadcast than they spend on the air. By the time I create my spotting boards, do my pre-game research through phone calls and reading, do my memorizing, watch game tapes, and interview coaches and players, not to mention production meetings, I will have spent 25 hours of preparation just to broadcast a three-hour football game.

You do not always have the luxury of as much preparation time as you would like. During the 1987 World Series, I had to prepare for a Soviet-Milwaukee Bucks exhibition basketball game, a Purdue-Iowa football game, the Broncos-Vikings Monday night game, plus post-game interviews for the final game of the Series all on a contingency factor based on how many games the Series went.

The point is: you cannot wait until the last minute to do everything. You have to be organized and plan ahead. By being prepared you are less likely to be surprised on the air and more apt to say things that make sense. In fact, preparation is so vital to the business today that an entire section of this book has been devoted to the subject.

**Can you focus?**

Everyone knows the image: Jack Nicklaus lining up a putt; Dave Stewart glaring in at the catcher before a pitch; Charles Barkley eyeing the rim before a free throw; Mike Powell visualizing his run down the runway before the long jump. Athletes refer to it as "getting into a zone." It is the ability to command utmost concentration, regardless of distractions or pressure.

Sportscasters need the same ability. When you are in the booth, you cannot be a fan. You have to be above the emotion around you. You must remain in control and report the action accurately. You cannot lose your poise.

In 1983, Billy Packer and I covered one of the most explosive moments in collegiate basketball when Cinderella North

Carolina State upset favored Houston in the NCAA Final Four championship game, 54–52. When the game concluded on a last-second slam by Lorenzo Charles after an air-ball miss by Dereck Whittenburg, the University of New Mexico's University Arena erupted: fans poured out of the stands, swarming over the Wolfpack players. It was difficult not to get caught up in the emotion of that surprising finish. In fact, Billy jumped out of his chair, joining the pandemonium on the floor, leaving me alone to recap the ending for the audience.

While the Houston players pounded the floor in disbelief, the North Carolina State players jumped and yelled for joy, and Wolfpack coach Jim Valvano ran through the crowd in an attempt to find someone to hug, I kept quiet, letting our cameras show the drama. When the initial revelry subsided, I summarized what had happened and put an exclamation point to its significance, then reviewed the replay, accurately describing the miracle ending.

When we broke for commercial, I joined Billy on the floor to prepare for our post-game interviews. I asked him, "Where did you go?"

We both broke up laughing because for Billy to become that emotionally engrossed in a ball game was out of character for him. His longtime ties to the ACC and the unexpected nature of the game's conclusion simply got the better of him.

When the broadcast came back to us, we returned to business, concentrating on asking intelligent questions while everybody around us jumped and screamed and pounded us on the back.

Can you remain similarly focused regardless of the emotions and distractions around you? Try reading a magazine at a basketball game played before a cheering full house sometime. If you can remain focused on what you are reading despite the extraneous background stimuli, you may have a gift that is a necessity in this business.

**Are you curious?**

My wife used to laugh at me because whenever we drove anywhere, I would read every billboard along the way, notice things happening on the sidewalk, or point out people she hadn't seen. Sportscasters must be similarly sensitized to their surroundings. Like their journalistic brothers and sisters who have a "nose for news," they should always have their antennae out gathering new information. They should be intrigued by everything and have a desperate need to know more.

You must also be observant. You cannot rely solely on reading and interviews for information. When you are invited to watch practices before an upcoming broadcast, you need to be knowledgeable enough to see when a team is running out of a new formation or preparing a new play. The coach may not tell you. Dick Vermeil and I once watched a Bo Schembechler-coached Michigan squad practice the wishbone, a formation the Wolverines had never used. We knew that if they employed it in the upcoming game the other team would be totally surprised. Sure enough, in a key moment in the contest, Michigan ran from the wishbone. The opposition was not prepared. We were. The Wolverines scored a touchdown and won the game.

No data is useless. At some time it may be needed on the air.

I once interviewed Mike Gillette, a punter and kicker for Michigan, the day before a game. During our talk, the subject strayed from football to baseball. Gillette was a catcher for the Wolverine baseball team and one of the pitchers he caught was Jim Abbott. This was before Abbott won the Sullivan Award, led the U.S. to a gold medal in the Seoul Olympics, and then became a professional with the California Angels and the New York Yankees. I had heard about this exceptional young man who had overcome the challenge of being born with no right hand and was fascinated to know more. Gillette provided all kinds of details, including the observation that he had caught Abbott so much he no longer noticed the fact that Abbott had to switch his glove to his throwing hand after every pitch. None of our discussion had any bearing on the upcoming football game.

During the next day's broadcast, someone noticed Abbott in the stands. We set up a camera shot of him and I related some of the information I had received from the conversation with Gillette. It was a fill that worked beautifully.

## Can you adapt rapidly to change?

At the end of the 1965 NFL season, with a Western Conference play-off birth on the line, the Baltimore Colts faced a double dilemma: They had to beat the Rams in the Los Angeles Coliseum, and they had to do it without Johnny Unitas or Gary Cuozzo, their two quarterbacks who were out with injuries. Colt coach Don Shula had no choice but to turn to halfback Tom Matte who had played quarterback for Woody Hayes at Ohio State.

The week before the game, Matte was given a crash course, one that stressed only the fundamentals of the Colt offense. Since Matte had not thrown much under Hayes' three-yards-and-a-cloud-of-dust offense at Ohio State, the Colts focused on plays that put Matte in motion: roll-out passes, quarterback keepers, pitchouts. To help him remember, they devised a wrist chart they taped to Matte's forearm so he could refer to it in the huddle.

With about a minute left before halftime in the game in the Coliseum, Baltimore stopped the Rams on the Colt goal line, taking over on downs. Shula turned to Matte and said, "Tom, get in there and just kill the clock."

Matte replied, "What do you want me to run?"

Shula said, "Just be conservative. Just hang on to the football. Get it away from the end zone. Get some breathing room and we'll take what we have into the locker room. We don't want to take any chances."

Still perplexed as to what play to run, Matte asked in the huddle in the end zone, "What would Unitas call in this type of situation?"

All-pro offensive guard Jim Parker responded, "You're the quarterback. You call the play."

Matte made a selection and the team lined up at the line of scrimmage. Just as he was getting under center for the snap, Matte heard a voice frantically whispering from his backfield, "No way, man. No way."

Matte looked over his shoulder at Lenny Moore, his running back, and noticed that if they ran the play he called in the huddle, Moore would run into the goal post (at that time, the goal post was situated on the goal line rather than at the back of the end zone as it is now) before getting the hand off.

Matte was in a predicament: He could not run the play he called without forcing a sure safety; and he could not change the play at the line of scrimmage—there had not been enough time during the week to teach him how to audible.

Thinking on his feet, Matte yelled out, "Quarterback sneak. On two."

The Colt offensive linemen got up out of their three-point stance and looked at him in disbelief. Across the line, the Rams' Fearsome Foursome of Merlin Olsen, Lamar Lundy, Deacon Jones, and Rosie Grier, were chuckling. They, too, couldn't believe what they had just heard.

Undaunted, Matte repeated, "Quarterback sneak. On two." On the second count, the ball was snapped and Matte ran nine yards straight up the middle. The Colts eventually won 20–17.

Like quarterbacks who audible, sportscasters must have the ability to think on their feet and adapt to rapidly changing conditions. Rarely does a broadcast game plan go exactly as you expect. The disruptions come from everywhere.

For one, the event you are covering may unfold differently from how you prepared: an expected close contest becomes an early blow out; a brilliant star you have interviewed all week and have great material on is suddenly injured in the first minute of play, leaves the game, and is not a factor thereafter.

The disruption may be technical: your mike goes dead; the TelePrompTer fails to operate; the network loses the picture, but not the audio.

Often the disruptive element is a simple by-product of the business' complexity. For example, when doing television, the play-by-play announcer wears a headset that enables three people to give instructions regarding the broadcast: the director tells what shot will be next; the producer is in charge of the overall picture and reminds when the promo for next week's game should be run; and the associate producer counts down to the next commercial. A typical scenario might be: the director calls for a sideline shot of Don Shula after Miami's point-after-touchdown is kicked; the producer interrupts to remind you to promote next week's game between the Washington Redskins and the Dallas Cowboys; the associate producer begins the countdown to commercial; and you begin your lead-in to break. At this point your natural inclination might be to panic since there are 10 seconds to commercial. But the director, the producer, and the associate producer are not on the air—you are. You must instantaneously sort through the audio input, make the proper mental adjustment and verbal response, and all without having a train wreck.

Though the natural human reaction to unexpected change is distress, some people become disoriented while others have an innate ability to switch gears and rapidly adapt. Having just witnessed a terrible traffic accident, the former will relate the details in rapid fire, in no chronological order, distorting the details, while their emotions run rampant. The latter will calmly catch their breath and coolly describe the accident in a sensible, well-constructed way, holding their emotions in check.

I once had to cover an away football game on radio at a high school that had recently been built. It was the first game played on their football field and the drop box for the phone line had not been hooked up yet in the broadcast booth. Of course, I didn't find this out until just before going on the air.

Like anyone else who might be placed in the same situation, my initial reaction was, "Oh, no! Can you believe this?" It felt like all the blood had drained from my head. Under the circumstances, I could have thrown up my hands, dropped the broadcast, and would have had my explanation for doing so readily accepted by the station manager. However, it was one of my first assignments. Instead of looking at the situation as an obstacle leading to failure, I saw it as an opportunity for success.

The broadcast went on the air. How? I strapped the amplifier to my waist, climbed the telephone pole located at the 50-yard line, hooked up to the drop box connection, and did the play-by-play for the entire game from atop the pole.

If you avoid stressful situations because you are unable to adapt readily to change or if you do not see unexpected obstacles as challenges, do not choose broadcasting as a career. Otherwise you will not be able to rise to the occasion when things really get scary as Jim McKay did during the terrorist hostage crisis during the 1972 Munich Olympics or as Al Michaels did amidst the havoc and destruction of the earthquake during the 1989 World Series.

## Do you get along well with people?

The broadcasting business is populated with egos. There is a well-known play-by-play announcer who finds fault with everything: lighting, sound, airplanes, meals, hotels, you name it. He is universally recognized as a pain to work with. But, because he is considered a gifted superstar, his co-workers grin and bear it.

Not everyone is a superstar, though. Since putting a show on the air requires teamwork, you will have a better chance of success if you treat people well, see their value, and appreciate them. You will often find that their strengths support your weaknesses. Consequently, when things become rough in the booth, you will not have to handle the situation alone.

If, on the other hand, you are the type of person who doesn't interact well with people, you had better be a superstar. Otherwise, at some point in your career, your lack of good working relationships will subtly affect your performance on the air. At that point, you will be through in the business.

CHAPTER THREE

# *How Broadcasting Skills Are Used*

$T$o illustrate how the preceding skills come into play during a broadcast, let's look at an incident that happened early in my network career, then go point-for-point through the skill inventory checklist.

In my first year at CBS, I was a part of the crew that covered Super Bowl X between the Dallas Cowboys and the Pittsburgh Steelers held in Miami's Orange Bowl. My assignment was simple and brief. Johnny Unitas and I stood in front of the Pittsburgh Steelers locker room and did a pre-game analysis to help set the stage for the upcoming game. Afterwards, we, along with Sonny Jurgensen who was also a part of the pre-game crew, went to our seats in the stands, while Pat Summerall and Tom Brookshire called the game.

When we got to our seats, they were taken. The Orange Bowl had a major problem that year with bogus tickets. There were thousands of fans with duplicate seats. Instead of raising a fuss, we decided to use our press passes to go down to the field.

You can imagine the thrill it was to walk the sidelines, watching the game with and hearing the observations of two of the greatest quarterbacks in the history of the National Football League. It was also a memorable experience because they were filming the movie *Black Sunday* using the Super Bowl as a backdrop. At one point during a time-out, Robert Shaw, the star of the picture, ran across the field in front of the full stadium with the cameras rolling.

The game was a tight defensive struggle and at the end of three quarters, Dallas led 10–7. At that point, I decided to go back to the press area behind the stands to watch the final period on TV in order to learn from Summerall's and Brookshire's call of the game.

As I was about to leave the tunnel leading under the stands, Chuck Milton, our executive producer, came running up and grabbed me by the shoulders. "You're doing the losing locker room."

I looked at him and said, "Excuse me. What are you talking about?"

Milton then explained that during our production meeting they had neglected to tell Johnny Morris that he was supposed to do the post-game interview in the loser's locker room. Morris and his wife had, therefore, gone back to their hotel. With the traffic tie-ups there was no way he would be able to make it back in time.

I went back to the sidelines to watch the game more intently than I had before. And there was plenty to watch. In the final period, Pittsburgh surged ahead on a safety, two Roy Gerela field goals, and a spectacular 64-yard touchdown pass from Terry Bradshaw to Lynn Swann with four minutes left. Trailing 21–10, Roger Staubach engineered a 67-second drive capped by a 34-yard touchdown pass to Percy Howard. Then with 1:28 remaining, the Cowboys took over on downs, setting up the possibility of another miracle finish similar to the "Hail Mary" ending Staubach and Drew Pearson had pulled off just a few weeks earlier against the Vikings in the play-offs.

As the Cowboys made their way toward the Pittsburgh goal in the final seconds, we still did not know which locker room we would have to go to. Consequently, Milton, myself, and a cameraman stationed ourselves behind the Steeler end zone, the one nearest the locker rooms. On the last play of the game, Pittsburgh's Glen Edwards picked off Staubach's pass in the end zone, preserving the Steeler win. We immediately rushed to the Cowboy locker room.

We were among the first to arrive, but soon the hallway was crammed sardine to sardine with reporters who were waiting for their invitation inside, trying to stay out of the rush of Dallas players disappearing into the haven of the locker room. The door closed momentarily, then reopened. Some unfortunate soul who had snuck inside was passed bodily out of the dressing room above our heads. In frustration, one of the Dallas players had apparently knocked him out.

The whole scene was very intimidating, particularly since I had been thrown into it at the last moment. I had covered a number of different sporting events before, but nothing nearing the magnitude of the Super Bowl. When we were finally allowed inside, the range of emotional extremes I witnessed caught me off guard. Some players sat in the corner crying. Some were violently angry, yelling expletive after expletive, slamming lockers. Others were totally silent, sitting motionless in a state of shock. My only thought was, "Who in the world is going to talk to me in this situation?"

The press immediately crushed around Staubach. With time running out, I pushed my way through the crowd and said, "Roger, would you be willing to go on our post-game show with me? We'd like to talk with you."

Pittsburgh's Steel Curtain defense had sacked Staubach seven times. His arms looked like hamburger from having been pounded into the Orange Bowl's artificial surface. He was utterly exhausted. He was in obvious pain. I had never seen anyone so drained emotionally, physically, or spiritually. He was the epitome of the fallen warrior who had given everything on the field of battle. I'll never forget the look he gave me, his eyes saying, "Do I really have to do this?" Being a class person, Roger said, "Yes, I'd be glad to go on with you."

I breathed a sigh of relief. Under the adverse conditions, the show went well.

\* \* \*

Now let's go through the skill inventory checklist to see how each skill was utilized.

**The ability to write:**

Almost every pre-game performance on camera is written beforehand. In this particular situation, we discussed in production meetings what approach we would take in our analysis of Super Bowl X. Then I wrote set-up questions to ask Unitas.

Before going live, Unitas and I rehearsed to see how he would react to what I'd written. We then made additions and deletions.

This might appear to be the only writing that was necessary in this illustration. But in fact, all during the final quarter, I was jotting down notes about the game and developing potential questions to ask in the post-game interview. Even up until the final moment when Staubach and I were on camera, I was mentally composing the questions I would ask him.

## The ability to read:

This is the one skill in the checklist that I did not use in this illustration. Occasionally a pre-game analysis might be done in a studio situation where a TelePrompTer might be used. In that case, the broadcaster's ability to read comes into play.

Usually the only reading aloud done at a remote location for television involves the reading of network promotions and leads to commercials. Since this was the Super Bowl, Pat Summerall did a fair share of reading on the air.

## The ability to be expressive:

This skill is used every time a sportscaster goes on the air. How you say things dictates the tone of the broadcast. In the case of the pre-game analysis of Super Bowl X, I had to convey a sense of excitement about the upcoming event, to make the viewer want to stay tuned to what followed.

The post-game interview was entirely different. I had to reflect the mood in the Cowboy locker room without seeming intrusive. Had I conducted the Staubach interview with the same upbeat tone as the pre-game show, my body would have been the second carried out of the dressing room. Talking with someone who has just lost a major sporting event is one of the most difficult interviews to do. You have to be a good journalist, ask the tough questions, and at the same time, be sensitive to the feelings of the person you are interviewing.

In both the pre-game and post-game work I did on the air, the emotions I expressed were genuine and easy to convey. It was my first Super Bowl. If I couldn't get excited about that, then I did not belong in broadcasting. As for my interview in the Dallas dressing room, I knew Staubach personally and respected him greatly. I truly empathized with his sense of loss.

**Sense of time, the ability to organize, and the ability to focus:**

These three abilities go hand in hand in the broadcasting business and have no better illustration than how they were used in my preparation for the post-game interview. Before I learned of my assignment, I had watched the game as a fan, lazily enjoying the spectacle, paying only token notice to its details. After I was notified, I had essentially one quarter to put the game in perspective, make notes on the highlights, and prepare general questions that would have relevance to what had happened. From the final gun until the time I went on the air with Staubach, I had between 10 and 12 minutes to line up the interview and compose the specific questions I would ask. In both instances, I had no time to waste. Because I was aware of my time constraints, I focused my attention, watched the game from a more detailed perspective, and organized my thoughts accordingly so the questions I asked had a degree of intelligence.

**A sense of curiosity:**

Even though I watched the first three quarters of Super Bowl X as a fan, I still had my antennae out and it paid off. Throughout, I listened to the comments of Jurgensen and Unitas and was fascinated by their view of the game through a quarterback's eyes. Since Terry Bradshaw and Roger Staubach were instrumental to the outcome, most of what they said had relevance when my role switched from observer to broadcaster.

In particular, they were intrigued with how Pittsburgh's "Mean" Joe Greene lined up in a slanted position at his nose tackle rather than facing the center head on. By stunting off the slant, Greene was able to get great penetration. When I saw how beat up Staubach looked, it immediately triggered the observations of Jurgensen and Unitas. Consequently, one of the questions I asked Staubach regarded the penetration of the

Steelers' Steel Curtain and how it felt to go behind center and see big No. 75 staring across from him every time.

## The ability to adapt rapidly to change:

If I had panicked at the news of my last-minute assignment or if I had balked when Chuck Milton gave it to me, two things might have occurred. First, my attention would have been split between the tasks at hand and the fear that I would not be prepared to do what I'd been asked. Second, I would very likely not have been accorded the opportunities I later received at the network level.

Once I understood my assignment, I relished the challenge. I shifted gears, first slowing to collect my thoughts and plan a course of action, then building momentum, kicking into overdrive once the final gun sounded. In spite of the pressure, it was more fun to be a part of the live broadcast from a Super Bowl locker room than it was to be a bystander on the side lines.

## Getting along with people:

The primary reason my interview with Staubach came off so smoothly was that I had previously established a relationship with him away from the football field in our work with the Fellowship of Christian Athletes. As a result, when I shoved my way to his side through the crush of press, I didn't have to tell him who I was. In addition, he had a positive perception of me and had confidence that I wouldn't embarrass him with stupid questions.

# CHAPTER FOUR

# How to Develop Broadcasting Skills

*T*he best way to develop basic skills that can be used in a broadcasting career is to get a good education. I am very proud of my master's degree. Getting it helped broaden and mature me. It also put me in contact with people who served as positive career role models both on and off the air.

Though there is no such thing as too much education, not everyone needs to receive a graduate degree to enter the broadcasting business. In fact, broadcasters who have attained an advanced degree are the exception rather than the rule. However, it *is* imperative that you earn a college diploma. Because of the intense competition for the available jobs in the industry, a college degree has become almost a prerequisite for any entry-level position.

The type of education you receive should be planned with your ultimate goal in mind. Regardless of how the university you attend classifies its broadcasting degree, you should seek a well-rounded liberal arts education. There should be emphasis on those courses that develop communication (writing and speech) and performance (drama and music) skills and laboratories that give you hands-on training in basic radio and television station operations.

You should also participate in extracurricular activities that will help broaden your skill base. When I was in high school, my sole focus was to become an athlete. Fortunately, my mother saw to it that my interests were not so limited. I participated in debate, drama, and even took private singing lessons. I was often dragged kicking and screaming to some of those activities, but their value to me today is immeasurable.

Finally, if your ideal is to become a sportscaster, you should become active in sports. This does not necessarily mean you must be a direct participant. You can be a team manager, work on the school newspaper covering sports, or simply be an avid fan. The point is you must live and breathe sports.

Many of us in the business cannot tell you how we learned certain things. Like plants that obtain nutrients from the soil through osmosis, our subconscious absorbed untold pieces of information we found valuable later. I'm certain the fact that I was a coach's son and participated in athletics gives me insight into the feelings of athletic participants and subtly creeps into my interpretation of a game.

Now let's look at the skills in the preceding checklist and suggest specific ways to develop each.

## The ability to write:

A broadcaster describing a sporting event is much like a jazz musician improvising a solo during a jam session. Each is able to construct meaningful statements or passages on the spot with little conscious thought.

This ability did not happen overnight. The jazz artist spent years learning notes, scales, chords and the other building blocks of music, practicing hour upon hour, playing piece after piece, then writing piece after piece, before finally reaching a point where the basics became second nature, allowing the musician the freedom to be an impromptu composer.

Likewise, to be able to communicate thoughts and ideas extemporaneously on the air as though they had been composed on paper beforehand, a sportscaster must first learn the mechanics of writing. If you can't write it, you can't say it. Therefore, take as many composition courses and engage in as many writing activities as you can to develop your basic writing skills.

In addition, read. Don't just read the sports page in the newspaper. Read contemporary literature, the classics, anything outside your field of endeavor. You should have a book in your hand whenever possible. The experience will not only develop your vocabulary, but also broaden your information base.

Also learn to type. It is a real handicap to be a hunt-and-peck artist on the keyboard in this age of the computer.

Finally, here is an exercise that will help you learn spontaneous composition and prepare you for a job in the booth. First, set up your VCR to record a game you are about to watch. Then, while the game is in progress, turn the sound off and type out descriptions of the plays as they happen. This will force you to think and compose quickly and concisely. You can measure how well you've done by replaying the tape and calling the game yourself, using the script you've written.

## The ability to read aloud:

The obvious way to learn to read aloud is simply to practice doing so. Unfortunately, even professionals who have been in the broadcasting business for years occasionally go into cycles where they have trouble reading.

One way to get your mind to overcome its tendency to speed read is to read something more complex than you're used to reading, something which requires conscious thought to understand. For example, try a book on the philosophy of Nietzsche, a collection of Elizabethan poetry, a classic novel like *Moby Dick,* or a Shakespearean play—anything which cannot be skimmed but must be read word for word to be understood. You will find yourself concentrating on specific words and complete thoughts and reconditioning your eyes and your mind to focus accordingly.

## The ability to be expressive:

There are a number of activities that will develop your ability to convey ideas and emotions while at the same time improving your diction.

Any form of music will be helpful in developing your ability to be expressive, but singing is the only form that uses the same instrument you will use in the sportscasting booth—your voice. Besides having to hit the correct note, singers must also learn voice and breath control and proper enunciation, all essential to broadcasters.

In debate, you will learn how to speak clearly and concisely under the duress of a time frame. You will also learn to sell yourself and your ideas to strangers, much like the announcer does to his audience.

For those who eventually want to be in front of a camera, drama will give you a better physical perception of yourself. You will learn how to control your body movements, what gestures to make, how to stand, how to sit. Of course, drama will also improve your voice inflection and projection.

Finally, any time you can get up and express yourself in front of a gathering, whether its running for a student government position or participating in the functions of clubs and organizations, you will be practicing for a job in the broadcasting booth.

**Sense of time:**

Some people are born with a built-in mechanism that makes them aware of time. These people have a great advantage if they choose to go into broadcasting.

However, people who do not have an inherent sense of time can develop one.

When I worked with Bob Costas at KMOX radio in St. Louis before his climb to the network level, Bob never wore a wrist watch. He never knew what time of day it was. He also turned down his phone at home so you couldn't call him. If Bob was due on the air shortly, someone in the office would invariably say, "Where's Bob? Somebody better go get him." You never knew whether he would show up on time.

Obviously, Bob corrected this trait or he wouldn't be where he is today. Anyone who can host "NFL Live," keep up with every game in progress, and inform viewers during the frequent breaks to the different regional broadcasts across the nation, has to have a good sense of time.

A sportscaster needs two kinds of time awareness: short-term and long-term.

For short-term awareness, you need to learn exactly how long 30 and 60 seconds are. You have to know how much to write to fill that amount of time and you also have to know how to pace your delivery when reading to fill that amount of time. You do not want to be caught with nothing to say (i.e., dead air) nor do you want to be caught at the last second with a sentence unfinished. Practice by reading copy while glancing at a stop watch. Practice until you can feel when 30 or 60 seconds have elapsed without having to refer to the watch.

To gain long-term awareness of time, create a daily ledger and log what you do during the day and when. Writing down your activities will force you to be conscious of time.

## The ability to organize:

To be organized you have to be able to budget your time. And to budget your time you need to develop a routine. Once you know what has to be done and how long it will take, you can schedule your time accordingly.

For example, I have a set routine for preparing for a weekend college football or basketball game. By noon on Monday, I try to have all the material I need on both teams either in hand or on its way by fax or Federal Express. On Tuesday, I prepare for one of the two teams, creating spotting boards and organizing material so it's easily accessible and ready to go on the road. I prepare for the other team the same way on Wednesday. Thursday is a travel day and I use what otherwise would be wasted time on the plane to memorize facts, figures, names, and numbers. On Friday, I interview players and coaches. Saturday is game day.

Since I have followed this routine for years, I know how long each activity should take, and if I haven't finished that activity by the time scheduled, I know I have to make up the time elsewhere.

You can do the same type of planning when organizing your study time during the week. Purchase a day-timer and log when assignments are due. Then determine how long it should take to do the assignment and allocate the time in your schedule.

## The ability to focus:

There are two aspects to focusing. You must first block out unwanted stimuli. At the same time, you must amplify your concentration on the stimuli that count.

Blocking out extraneous noise is simply a matter of familiarizing yourself with your surroundings and developing a routine; your subconscious will take care of the rest. If you have ever stayed overnight at an unfamiliar house with a large grandfather clock that bongs on the hour, there is a good chance you awakened every hour on the hour. However, if you lived in that same house for any length of time, you would eventually sleep through the night. Your mind would become used to the pattern, shut out the bonging every hour, and allow you to continue sleeping.

Former Philadelphia 76er Doug Collins, who later became a colleague in the booth, is a firm believer that routine helps you focus. By going through the same motions every time you stand at the free throw line—pulling up your socks, brushing your hair away from your eyes, hitching up your shorts, spinning the ball in your hands, bouncing the ball so many times—it conditions you to concentrate when you finally take your shot.

To prove his point, Collins cites his experience in the gold medal match of the 1972 Olympics when the Soviet Union handed the United States its first loss in Olympic competition. With three seconds in the game and the U.S. trailing 49–48, Collins was undercut by the Soviets' Sako Sakandelidze. Collins was knocked momentarily unconscious and was still groggy when he stepped to the line to shoot two crucial free throws. By going through the same pre-shot routine he'd always used, he was able to fight through the haze, concentrate on the basket, and pull the trigger twice, giving the U.S. its only lead of the game.

Here are two exercises designed to help you learn to focus:

First, carry on a conversation with a friend while listening to two other friends carry on a separate conversation next to you. See if you can remain focused on the details of both concurrently.

Second, set up two televisions side by side and watch two different games simultaneously, keeping a play-by-play account of each, picking out highlights you might use to summarize each on the air.

The principle behind these two exercises is simple: If you can focus on two things at once, you can focus on one.

## A sense of curiosity:

For each skill in this checklist, there are individuals who have the ability innately and others who have to develop the ability through training. The people who come by the skills naturally have a distinct advantage. Everyone can learn to dribble and shoot a basketball. But the skill level attainable is limited to the inherent physical ability you were granted at birth. No amount of training can turn you into a Michael Jordan unless you share the same God-given physical abilities he possesses.

Curiosity is the one skill in the list that is the hardest to develop if you do not already have it. How do you train someone to love investigation, to be perpetually inquisitive? If you do not have a sense of curiosity now, you will most likely never develop one.

Lacking a sense of curiosity will not preclude you from being a sportscaster. However, having a probing mind will set you apart: You will be capable of performing a Michael Jordan, 360 dunk in broadcasting while others barely touch the rim.

## The ability to adapt rapidly to change:

Adaptability comes down to one factor—attitude. If you do not have an I'll-try-anything attitude, you will not be flexible when changes require it.

Often your attitude is the product of successes or failures in your past. A person who tries various endeavors and succeeds develops confidence and is more willing to try new things. Let me illustrate with an example from my past.

When I entered high school, my mother saw to it that I took singing lessons. The choice was not mine and the experience was often painful to me, particularly when it came to competition.

Before one such competition, I prepared by singing "He Smiled Upon Me" at every opportunity from church socials to gatherings of friends. I knew the song backward and forward.

When it came my turn to compete, George Wolf, my singing instructor, began playing the song and I started my solo—by saying the wrong word. Mr. Wolf kept playing. I froze. Sitting in the front row were my mom and dad, my grandmother, and my friends.

Mr. Wolf stopped, turned to me, and said, "Do you want to start again?"

I took a deep breath and replied, "Yes."

Mr. Wolf began again. I sang the song all the way through with no further problems.

As I left the stage, I was devastated. My friends and family tried to encourage me, saying, "Boy! What a great job you did that second time." I could only see the gross error I'd made the first time.

We left the competition, visited with friends, then returned to the school later to see the posted scores. My score was a "1" which meant I qualified for state. I was dumbstruck.

I tracked down the judge of the competition and asked him why my score was so high. He said, "I'll tell you what. I was embarrassed for you when you flubbed the song. But you showed me such ability to recover, such poise to come back and sing well the second time, I thought you deserved a '1' and I forgot about the first time."

If that judge had been less understanding, who knows, maybe I wouldn't be in broadcasting today. But the fact that he recognized my effort gave me confidence. It was comforting to know that an occasional error does not always lead to failure.

The point is—you must continually challenge yourself in front of people. There will be times when you succeed and times when you fail. But the more you try, the more you will experience success. At the same time, you will also be cultivating the type of attitude that will accept change, thus preparing you for the volatile life of a sportscaster.

### Getting along with people:

To get along with others you must first learn to value them, to care for them. To understand the value of people, you must be involved. If you isolate yourself from others, chances are you will have difficulty relating.

The best way to develop social skills is through social interaction. The more you come in contact with people, the better the odds you will learn to get along with them.

You also need to learn how to work in a team environment. Participating in team sports where the goal is to pull together to win or working within clubs or organizations to accomplish a specific aim, like building a homecoming float, are excellent ways of learning the give-and-take required for a successful team effort in the broadcasting booth.

# *How to Get That First Job*

$T$he first broadcasting job for NBC's Bob Costas was at KMOX radio as the voice of the ABA's Spirit of St. Louis. He earned the position straight out of Syracuse University by submitting a demo tape on a lark, thinking he had no chance at all. However, station manager Bob Hyland spotted Costas' fresh style and unique talent and hired him virtually sight unseen.

The chances of someone else getting their first job with the same apparent ease are astronomical. In fact, if you choose sportscasting as a profession and remain in the business for any length of time, you will eventually look back and realize that getting that first job was the most difficult step along your career path. There are two reasons why.

To begin with, significantly more people seek positions than there are positions available. In 1988, just under 9,100 radio stations and 1,400 television stations were in the United States. That's less than 10,500 places where a potential play-by-play job existed. Consider that the radio numbers included formats varying from religious to rock and the television numbers included those devoted exclusively to education and the number is significantly reduced. Say 25 percent (a generous figure) of all radio and television stations did local origination sports broadcasts. That would leave a little more than 2,600 stations where a sportscaster could find play-by-play opportunities in 1988.

In the spring of 1991, the California Angels' short-season Class A team in Boise, Idaho, advertised for a play-by-play announcer to act as the radio voice for the team. Though it is the largest city in Idaho, Boise is not a major metropolis. The job, too, was not major league, lasting only from June to September, covering the Hawks' 76-game season. Still, Hawk General Manager Ken Wilson received over 100 audition tapes.

To even have a chance at any opening, you must have talent. You can count on the fact that the candidates you will be competing against will be as capable as you, if not more so. Consequently, you must also be aggressive.

Second, when stations look at candidates, they are more likely to opt for experience over inexperience. Nearly every novice broadcaster faces the same catch-22 situation: I can't get a job because I have no experience and I can't get experience because I have no job. How do I break the vicious cycle?

Unfortunately, though you may have all the talent in the world and are aggressive in your pursuit of a sportscasting position, getting your first job will most likely come down to two factors:

(1) who you know; and
(2) timing.

In the spring of 1964 as I was preparing to complete the requirements for my graduate degree at the University of Kansas, I could have killed for a job. I had no prospects.

Then one of my professors, Tom Hedrick, who was also the voice of the Jayhawks and the Kansas City Chiefs, told me of a potential opening at KWBW, a 1000-watt station in the south central Kansas city of Hutchinson, population approximately 40,000. According to Hedrick, who had gotten his start at the same station, Fred Conger, the owner, did the play-by-play on his own local sports broadcasts and was contemplating stepping down.

Without knowing for sure whether there truly was an opening, I drove to Wichita, where a state radio broadcasters' meeting was being held, in hopes of talking to Conger. I had no resumé, no demo tapes, nor any practical experience. The only live play-by-play I had done was as a student at Wichita State University where I covered some football and basketball games for KMUW, the university's radio station. All I had was an all-consuming desire to be a sportscaster.

I waited impatiently outside the conference room doors until the meeting broke then virtually tackled Conger to plead my case. Naturally, he asked, "Why should I hire you?"

I recited the typical litany of someone desperate to enter the profession. I also mentioned how hard it must be for him to cover games while running a station and how he might enjoy a change. Nothing appeared to persuade him.

Then Conger asked, "What does your wife do?"

I told him that Linda had worked the past year as an elementary school teacher in Kansas City while I completed my degree work.

Conger suddenly broke into a smile from ear to ear. "I tell you what. I'm also the president of the school board. We're looking for a teacher. We may just hire her and let you tag along."

Conger eventually did hire both of us; me after a successful audition at the National Junior College Basketball Tournament and Linda after interviewing with the school board. Linda's salary was larger.

Fred and I are good friends and we now laugh about how he got "two good people for the price of one," but the truth is: I would probably not have gotten the job if (1) I hadn't had the input of Hedrick, and (2) the Hutchinson school board hadn't needed a teacher.

Young people today who embark on a career in sportscasting have several advantages over those of us who started out 25 years ago. First of all, they have been exposed to the concept of networking: the more people you come in contact with, the more people might remember your name, your face, or something about you when a potential job situation arises. Even the briefest of encounters can lead to a job opportunity. Word of mouth has precipitated more than one hiring in the broadcasting business. Take, for example, my first job at the network level.

I was working for WKOW-TV in Madison, Wisconsin, doing Green Bay Packer games for WTMJ-TV in Milwaukee and Big Ten football games for the TVS network, when I received a call from Bob Rosen, an agent from New York City. "I understand you might be network quality. Could you send me your tape and resumé?"

I had tried for years to make the jump to a network. Obviously, I was ready to do anything and immediately fired off a demo tape and resumé. Four days later Rosen called back and asked to represent me. After talking with Jim Simpson, another of his clients, I signed with him and three days later I was hired by CBS.

How did I get the job so quickly? Before initially talking to me, Rosen had been having lunch at a New York delicatessen with Bob Wussler, the president of CBS Sports. As they got up to leave, Wussler said, "By the way, I found out today we're losing Jack Buck. He's going to NBC to do "Grandstand." Do you know anyone who has network potential?"

Rosen had no one in mind. However, a gentleman sitting at the next table came over and said, "Excuse me. I don't mean to interrupt or be nosey, but I couldn't help overhear your conversation. I have someone to recommend. Gary Bender. I think he could do a great job at the network." The gentleman who gave the recommendation was Alan Lubell, a producer with TVS who had worked several games with me.

Another advantage young people have today is that they have more avenues of access to the "giants" of the broadcasting business. When I was in college, I had the unique privilege of sitting in the booth and observing people like Ernie Harwell and Monte Moore at work. However, there was no interaction. Whatever I learned, I picked up from simply watching and listening.

Now high school and college students can attend seminars around the country such as those put on by Sports Careers. These seminars cover every aspect of the sports industry from marketing to player representation to broadcasting. They allow young people with dreams of a sports-related career to ask tough questions about the business from those who are in it. These seminars not only eliminate illusions about the job, but also about the people who do the job. One of the big hurdles in the career of any sportscaster is crossing that fine line between being in awe of the people you work with or see perform and being impressed by them. Having eye-to-eye contact tends to take idols off their pedestals.

Probably the biggest development young people can now take advantage of is an internship. There are two ways to become an intern. One is in conjunction with a university or college where professors select the most worthy individual from their program to work as an intern for a period of time at the local radio or television station. You can also become an intern through the recommendation of someone at the station, such as the station manager or someone in the sports department.

There are different types of internships. Some pay nothing while others pay a minimum wage. Some internships actually utilize the interns, making them a part of the day-to-day operation, giving them assignments to go out and help cover a story, edit a tape, or sometimes even write a story. Other internships turn the intern into a glorified gofer who runs for coffee. In these cases, there are few opportunities for on-the-job training. Learning comes from observation or from experimentation on your own time when the station allows you to use its equipment.

The value of an internship is directly related to the type of rapport you are able to establish with the sports director. You must realize that from the sports director's standpoint, training an intern takes time that could be used more productively elsewhere. You are not yet a member of the fraternity of broadcasters. You are still an outsider looking in. It is also sometimes difficult for savvy veterans to tell 19- or 20-year-old kids what they think. It will be up to you to cultivate the trust necessary to be considered part of the station's everyday work force.

To make it worth everybody's time in the sports department, you must create a useful niche for yourself. You should be like a puppy dog who latches onto someone's pant leg and won't let go for dear life. Every time someone jumps into a car to cover a story, you should be in the back seat riding with him. Every time someone edits a tape, you should be looking over her shoulder. You should not become an irritation, but you must convey that you want to learn more and are not content to be just a part of the office furniture.

I have had interns who were content to sit and watch, others who constantly wanted more to do, and still others who were overwhelmed with the assignments I gave them. An internship is the best time to test your limits. You do not want to accept your first job and then discover that it is more than you can handle, that you wish you had learned more as an intern. A good internship can be a valuable experience. It can give you an edge when your resumé is reviewed for that first job. If you have done an impressive job during your internship, it's even possible you will be hired by the station with which you interned.

Most college graduates who are seeking sportscasting positions want to start out working in Phoenix, Seattle, Kansas City, or other large markets. Their chances are not realistic nor strategically practical from a career standpoint. If your goal is to become an in-studio anchor, it makes sense to seek employment at a television station in the largest market possible. But, if your long-range goal is to be a play-by-play announcer for a major market or for a network, you have a better chance of reaching your goal if you start out working for a radio station in a small market.

First of all, there are limited opportunities in a major market. Even if you can land a job at major-market station, your chances of immediately doing play-by-play are nonexistent. The people who hold those positions are veterans who have been in the business for at least a decade. You will end up doing weekend reports, putting together packaged sports reports, or doing background work for stories covering the local pro and college teams. It may be years before you have a chance to get any play-by-play experience. By the time a position does open, the fact that you haven't had experience will work to your detriment, particularly when competing against someone who has logged five years of continuous work in various venues at a station in a smaller market.

Working in a small market allows you to hone your skills, smooth out the rough spots before you come under the critical eye of a much larger audience. You can also establish your credibility quicker. Because most smaller markets have less competition, your name can become associated more readily to sports in the community. In other words, you can become a big fish in a small pond, the expert.

As for whether to look for a job in radio or television first, choose radio if you want to do play-by-play. Until you have learned the nuances of describing a sporting event on radio, of painting vivid pictures in the listener's mind, you will not have developed the abilities to do the same job on television. Radio is the cornerstone of a play-by-play career.

One word of caution: Do not accept a position at a station that does not have a tradition of carrying sports in hopes that you can eventually convince management to do so. Even if the station has had a limited history of covering sports, there is a chance to make inroads. But if you hire on as a disc jockey at a station that has always had a music format, expecting to turn it into a sports station in six months, you are not being realistic.

Choosing to work in a small market will be a gut-check decision for some people. Not everyone relishes the thought of going to the Hutchinsons of the world. Such a move likely means leaving family and sweetheart. It will most definitely mean leaving the bright lights of pro and major college sports for the relative obscurity of high school, junior college, and small college sports. It will mean less than first-rate broadcasting facilities, little or no information, no time to do all you want to do, and less pay for what you do.

When I hired on at KWBW as the "sports director," sportscasting played a very small part of my day-to-day activity. I was a disc jockey. I did the news. I wrote, produced, and sold spots for my own broadcasts. I even co-hosted a country-and-western show titled "Big Ben and Ed the Redhead" which lasted until the wee hours of the morning. The job was not easy. At times it was even threatening because there were some tasks that I did not perform well. I was the worst disc jockey that has ever been on the air.

I persevered because there were also times when I sat behind the mike, describing sporting events. Initially, all I covered was Hutchinson High basketball and football games and the National Juco Tournament. But, as I developed credibility within the community by speaking to quarterback clubs and civic organizations and by going out on sales calls with our salesman, I eventually added Hutchinson Junior College football and basketball and American Legion baseball.

It often required initiative, inventiveness, and sacrifice on my part to cover some sports. For example, though it had

established a rich tradition, the local American Legion baseball team had never had its games covered unless they were in
regional and state tournaments. The station couldn't afford to
do the games because no one would buy commercial time. I
suggested how we could do it with no expense to the station.

To begin with, we used Marti equipment to provide line-
of-sight transmission, thus avoiding the cost of a phone line.
The way it worked was very simple: you hooked your amplifier into the Marti unit; you put your antenna up behind the
press box atop Bud Detter Field south of town; you lined up
the antenna to the station in the north end; you called over a
phone line to see if the station was picking up the signal; and
then you broadcast the game. If we were fortunate to sell
a spot, we considered it a bonus. Otherwise, we carried the
games as a public service. There was one additional kicker:
I did the games for nothing.

I had no qualms about not being paid to do those games.
My reasoning was selfish: I *wanted* to do those games. As far
as I was concerned, there was nothing greater in the world
than to be sitting in Bud Detter Field's old rickety press box
overlooking home plate, watching and describing baseball. I
was committed. I had tunnel vision. Being a play-by-play
announcer was all I wanted to do.

If you choose sportscasting as a career, you can expect
similar experiences, particularly when starting out. Others got
their start in the Hutchinsons of the world. In fact, Tom Hedrick, former voice of the Kansas City Chiefs, the Cincinnati
Reds, and the Kansas Jayhawks, also began his career in
Hutchinson. Monte Moore, former television voice of the
Oakland A's also worked in Hutchinson after getting his start
in Lawton, Oklahoma. Merle Harmon, past voice of the Texas
Rangers, began in Wichita Falls, Texas. Bob Starr, one-time
voice of the Boston Red Sox and the California Angels, started
in Peoria, Illinois. Bill King, radio voice of the Oakland A's and
the Los Angeles Raiders first worked in Pekin, Illinois. Unless
you are flexible enough to accept something less than ideal,
your dreams may never be realized.

# PART II

BEFORE ENTERING THE BOOTH

# CHAPTER SIX

# *The Importance of Preparation*

*T*he red letter day comes. The phone rings. You pick it up and on the other end someone is offering you your first job as a sportscaster. You celebrate, pack, say your good-byes, and move. Even before you settle in, you receive your first assignment. Maybe it's to cover the local high school's first football game of the season. The adrenaline is pumping. You're itching to get in the booth. You're confident you can do the job.

Then it occurs to you—"I don't know anything about the teams playing. I know nothing about the league. What's the tradition? What do I do now?"

How would you feel if you were about to enter the operating room for major surgery and discovered the surgeon who was about to use a scalpel on you had not read your charts, had not looked at your x-rays, had not consulted with your family physician, knew nothing about you?

Play-by-play announcing is not as exacting as surgery. Still, like most professions, the key to success is directly correlated to how well you prepare. If you ever find yourself in a position where you walk into a booth and attempt to fly by the seat of your pants, it will catch up with you. The audience will know it. If your job leaves you with no time to prepare, you have to fight to create that time. It will not happen suddenly. As John Wooden put it, "The failure to prepare continually means preparing to fail."

The need for preparation never stops. It is a process that has to be steadily maintained. Even if you've covered a team, a league, or a sport for 20 years, you must continue to exercise discipline in your preparation. The play-by-play announcers who become settled in their jobs and shortcut their preparation, relying only on experience, will soon be retiring. The sports scene changes rapidly. Players come and go. Injuries and illnesses occur. Why a team is winning or losing varies from game to game. If announcers do not keep abreast and rely solely on the wealth of historical knowledge they've accumulated over the years, their comments become dated and not apropos. Soon the audience will start tuning out.

Vin Scully once told Bob Costas on his NBC program "Later," "I remember reading a line years and years ago from Sir Laurence Olivier. He was being interviewed and someone said, 'What does it take to be a great actor?' He thought about it awhile, and he said, 'It takes the humility to prepare and the confidence to bring it off.' And, I know, when it comes to doing an event, I am terrified of looking like a horse's fanny. So I prepare out of fear, and then I hope to get all those things across."

I have received my share of criticism over the years. In discussing one critic's comments with NBC's Bob Costas over lunch, Bob said, "Gary, one thing I can't understand is that every once in awhile he says you're inaccurate. How can that be? You are a veritable textbook of preparation."

I value that compliment. There are a myriad of variables that can affect the coverage of a sporting event, most totally outside your control. The only variable you *do* have complete control over is the background knowledge you carry with you into the booth. Consequently, thorough preparation will give you confidence because you know you are ready for any contingency.

By being so prepared, you will also experience a certain amount of frustration because only about 10 percent of what you prepared will be used on the air. After every game, you will sit back in the seat of your car or the plane, and say to yourself, "I wish I could have gotten this on the air," or "It would have been nice to use that." However, by preparing thoroughly, the odds are greater that the 10 percent that *did* make the airwaves had significant relevance, thus strengthening your broadcast.

There have been many stories about the late Bill Stern, one of the legends of sports broadcasting. Several deal with his inventions on the air. If Stern discovered that he had named the wrong man as the ball carrier during a radio broadcast of a football game, he simply described the ball carrier "lateraling" to the correct man. Few were the wiser.

The advent of television has created a more sophisticated sports fan who demands greater accuracy from the broadcaster. As Carl Klages said in his book *Sportscasting,* "A sportscaster's corrections never seem to catch up completely. He must say it right the first time." It may sound trite, but microphones don't have erasers. Though it's virtually impossible to spend two to three hours on the air without making mistakes, they can be reduced significantly. Good, solid preparation leads to accuracy.

Another by-product of preparation is the respect of your fellow workers. The people who work in the pressure-packed environment of the broadcasting booth develop a mentality similar to soldiers in a foxhole: Everyone has to do their job effectively for the whole to survive. If your co-workers have seen you prepare, have seen you talk with the coaches and players, have seen you work with the crew in production meetings to set up possible camera isolations, and have seen you spend time with the graphics people, openly sharing information with them, their confidence in you is elevated. The example of your commitment to the team effort can only help improve the quality of the broadcast.

Everyone has their own comfort zone regarding preparation. My method is very detailed. I compile my information and write everything down so that it is easily accessible. The procedure helps me memorize. Also, writing information down in an organized way so I can later refer to it provides mental security: I know the information is available at a glance if it should slip my memory in the pressure cooker of the booth. Finally, because I approach preparation in a detailed step-by-step manner, I slow down my thinking, allowing myself time to digest the facts and maybe to uncover new questions which need further research. I enjoy the whole process, the digging for new data, the reading, the interviewing, everything that readies me for entering the booth. I have the same enthusiasm for the work today as I did when I first started out in the business. It truly is a labor of love.

Not everyone prepares the same way. When Costas and I worked together at KMOX radio in St. Louis, he drove me crazy. I used the same diligent approach to preparation I use today and would walk into the booth carrying a briefcase-worth of detailed work. On the other hand, Bob would sit down with a flattened-out napkin on which he had scribbled some notes and would still do a great job on the air. It wasn't that Bob hadn't prepared. He simply didn't need a lot of prepared materials by his side. Whether he realizes it or not, Bob has a fantastic memory and remembers nearly everything he reads or everything someone says in an interview. It is an ability I envy.

Most likely your comfort zone will fall somewhere between Bob's and mine. Knowing your strengths and weaknesses will determine what type of preparation you should physically bring to the booth with you. To give you some guidelines on how to prepare for a game, the following three chapters describe the process I use. Because my method represents one extreme, it may not be exactly suited to your needs. Even so, because it is an extreme, it does touch all the bases.

In illustrating my preparation procedure, I will show how I get ready for a college or pro football game on network television. Calling football for a network also represents an extreme in sports coverage. There are announcers who are very successful in other venues who would prefer not to attempt football. The reasons are fourfold: (1) the number of people involved in the game which increases the amount of information you must prepare; (2) the intricate and varying sets of rules that govern the sport from high school, to college, to the professional ranks; (3) the distance from the field that most booths are situated; and (4) the weather. The difficulty of every other type of coverage is scaled down in comparison based on the medium, the market size, and the sport. This doesn't mean you are less professional if you are covering a high school basketball game for a 1000-watt radio station in Hutchinson, Kansas. It simply means you have fewer factors for which to prepare (i.e., there are only 10 players on the field of action in basketball in contrast to 22 for football; you have less technical preparations for radio than for television; and there are reams of information available about the professional ranks as compared to the high school ranks).

# CHAPTER SEVEN

# *Off-Site Preparation*

*I* work out of my home in Phoenix, Arizona. But whether you work out of your home or out of an office at the station, one of your first purchases should be a filing cabinet. You have to have someplace to put all the information you will accumulate. I'm certain the delivery person at the post office must hate me. Even though I have an oversized box, if I don't remove the contents every day, there is no way to stuff in a second day's worth. It's almost a full-time job just to keep up with my mail.

What kind of information will you be amassing? Anything that might pertain to the sport or sports you cover.

More specifically, you should subscribe to all the local newspapers and have occasional access to the largest major newspaper in your area. I subscribe to both Phoenix papers (the *Arizona Republic* and the *Phoenix Gazette*) and *The New York Times*. I also occasionally pick up the *Los Angeles Times* and any local newspaper when I'm on the road. A subscription to *USA Today* is also beneficial because it provides a good national focus on all sports daily.

You should subscribe to all the general sports periodicals such as *The Sporting News, Sports Illustrated,* and *Sport Magazine* and all the specialized periodicals such as *Pro Football Weekly, Pro Football News, Basketball Weekly, Basketball Times, Basketball Digest, Baseball Digest, Baseball America,* etc.

You should obtain scouting reports such as Bob Gibbons' *All Star Sports* for basketball. You should also be on the mailing list of every team you are likely to cover so you can receive the media guides and all the releases from the sports information office (college) or the public relations office (pro). It is not enough just to obtain information for the team or conference you cover, you need to also have information from all potential non-conference opponents and their conferences. Though you may not need to refer to them immediately, you never know when you *will* need them.

I have a file for every major college football conference school. I also have a separate file for each school for basketball. I am constantly updating the material in the files, adding brochures, media guides, news releases, and clippings from newspapers or periodicals. I even file notes and spotting boards for games that I've covered. I rarely throw anything away. Keeping media guides for past years gives you a good historical perspective for any team.

Special mention should be made here about developing a filing system for baseball. There are two aspects to baseball that make preparing for it unique.

First, unlike football where games are played once a week or basketball and hockey where games are played two or three times a week, baseball is virtually an everyday sport. Preparation has to be an ongoing process. There is no time to catch up.

Covering baseball is peculiar in that it is often the cumulative knowledge that is more important than the individual pieces. It is similar to taking a course in theoretical math: Because one theorem is used to prove another, you must study every day to gain understanding. If you wait until the last minute to cram for the final, you will find you have too much to learn. You may be able to memorize the material, but you will not have the understanding to apply it on the test. To be the most effective, play-by-play announcers who cover baseball have to be involved with the sport daily. Just seeing one or two games or even a series will not give you sufficient perspective regarding a team's strengths and weaknesses if for no other reason than you will not be able to see a team's entire pitching staff in action.

Second, baseball coverage is driven by statistics. Public relations people at the major league level can inundate you with statistical material. It still will not be enough. Knowing what a batter did against a certain pitcher early in the season may have a direct bearing on what you say when the match-up recurs during the seventh game of the American League Championship Series. Unless you have made note of that fact yourself and have it readily available you will have missed an excellent sidebar.

Consequently, the filing system you devise for covering baseball should meet three criteria: (1) it should be flexible enough to be updated daily; (2) it should have easy accessibility so that when a situation arises you can get to the needed information quickly; and (3) it should be portable.

The next time you see a baseball announcer carrying one of those flight kits pilots are always seen with, you'll know why. In fact, Kevin Cremin, the producer/director for KIRO radio broadcasts of Seattle Mariner baseball games, helps out the announcers by bringing along a huge metal case that contains the media guides for every major league team and a small library of books, including *Total Baseball, The Dickson Baseball Dictionary, The Baseball Encyclopedia, The Elias Baseball Analyst,* Bill James' *The Baseball Book,* and *The Sporting News' Baseball Register* and *The Complete Baseball Record Book.*

You will accumulate far more information than you will have time to digest. Therefore, you have to devise a system of prioritizing what you read. I start off the week on Monday by getting caught up on sports in general. I scan *Sports Illustrated* or *The Sporting News* for the overview of what's happening. I don't read every article word for word unless it has a particular personal interest or has a bearing on a game or sport I might be covering. Generally, I have a good handle on which games I will be assigned and keep up-to-date for those teams accordingly. The rest I just cut out and file so they are at my fingertips for future reference.

I also check out *USA Today* for weekend results of who won what. I approach my reading as though I were preparing to do the studio scoreboard show next weekend. When a score pops up on the screen, I want to be in a position to say whether the game was an upset or not, the significance it has for either team, and what bearing it has on the conference race or national rankings. By having that kind of knowledge in the booth, you have the ability to comment on games elsewhere when their scores flash across the screen during your broadcast. Sometimes you may even have an opportunity to add good sidebar information such as "That loss by Columbia [Columbia—0, Princeton—38], by the way, is an all-time record for consecutive losses."

The principal point you should keep in mind when doing your reading is you cannot prepare in a vacuum. You have to know how the game you are covering fits into the conference picture and the national picture. To do so, you have to know what is going on elsewhere in the sport.

When I have an overall feel for the sport, I then begin preparing for the specific game I will be doing next. I first read through my files for each team and see if anything is missing. No matter how meticulous you are in your filing, no matter how prepared you think you are, there is always a chance of something falling through the cracks: you never received the media guide; the stat sheet for last week's game didn't arrive; the depth chart changes because of injuries in last week's game. There is nothing more frustrating than to be on the road to the game site and discover there is some area of research you neglected. If you wait until you arrive at the game site to finish compiling your files, you will find you are overwhelmed by the on-site preparation you have to do. The sooner you know what information you have, the sooner you can react and request supplemental information.

After assessing my files, I phone each team's sports information director (college) or public relations director (pro) and request last week's game tape and anything else I need. They then fax or FedEx everything to me immediately.

The best friend of a play-by-play announcer is a team's sports information director or public relations director. They love the fact that you show interest in their team and will knock themselves out for you. Some are better than others. Some have more information than others. But for the most part, if there is something you need, they will do anything in their power to get it for you. Some, like Seattle Seahawk public relations director Gary Wright, are so thorough they send you everything you need and more. It's a challenge to get through everything Gary sends me.

All you need to do is to tell the SIDs your expectations. They may not be able to meet all of them, but usually all they need is some guidance and direction and they will jump at it. They will even go to the extent of sending you a complete set of clippings from the local newspapers for the entire season.

After you have developed a relationship with a particular sports information department, you may even find you do not have to call to request anything. When Auburn University received notification that the Tigers would be playing in the 1990 Peach Bowl, David Housel, the SID, had everything he knew I'd want in the mail almost the next day. I had worked with him previously, stated my likes and dislikes, and he remembered and took the initiative accordingly.

When I make the call asking for additional information, I also make it a point to determine the lay of the land. By using the SID's eyes and ears, I try to find out how the team has been playing lately, if any problems have arisen, what the emotional climate is on campus regarding the upcoming game. By finding out the key issues, the interview questions I develop for the head coach later that week will have more relevance. Instead of asking general questions such as, "How has your team been playing lately?" I can be specific: "I understand your quarterback has a sore ankle. How is it going to affect the game?" "What happened last week when your team was called for so many penalties?" "Why is your secondary giving up so many touchdowns?" By speaking in specifics rather than generalities, you show the coach you have a genuine interest in his ball club. He will then be more inclined to show an interest in helping you.

The next step in my off-site preparation is to thoroughly read the material I have for each team, taking notes and building my spotting boards as I do so. I usually allocate Tuesday to one team and Wednesday to the other.

Spotting boards are the most personalized of all your preparation materials. No two broadcasters do theirs the same way (see the spotting board illustrations following the photo insert). Because of the number of players involved, spotting boards are a necessity for football. But for other sports, some play-by-play announcers can even do without them. I tend to be a perfectionist. I often include very average stats just so I can get a complete picture of the player in question. Not everybody will need to be as detailed as I am. You have to find your own system.

There are certain essentials that appear on all spotting boards. The keys to being able to "spot" a player quickly are number and last name. These are usually highlighted in some manner for instant recognition. The other essentials are: first name, nickname, height, weight, number of years in the league (or year in college), and the college(s) they attended (or their hometown for college players).

The rest of the information on the spotting boards is left up to personal need. The data can be any kind of stat, quote, or story that might be usable on the air. Their representation on the boards depends on your taste. Some systems use a combination of multicolored pins stuck in the boards. Others use colored pencils or pens with each color having a different meaning. Some use brackets, parentheses, and circles to signify different facts. For most systems, placement on the boards is important (i.e., the upper right-hand corner means one thing, the upper left another), but the meaning of the placement varies from system to system.

Experiment to see what works for you. I do my football boards pretty much as I have since I first started in the business, but my basketball boards changed as my needs changed. The key is to develop a system of codes, symbols, abbreviations, and placement that will create instant accessibility for you in the event that a certain fact slips your memory in the booth.

I derive the information on my spotting boards from five source areas. These are represented in the following preparation resource checklist that I use when I review my team files on Monday, looking for missing items to request from the SID:

> (1) a current depth chart (the starting lineup and backups by position);
>
> (2) the previous game's speed card (a quick-reference roster);

   (3) the previous game's stat sheet (a summary of game stats);

   (4) the previous game's play-by-play sheet (a chronology of plays and their results); and

   (5) the media guide, all the team's weekly releases, and any appropriate newspaper and periodical clippings.

A team's current depth chart is by far the most important item in the list because without it, I cannot begin my spotting boards, the fulcrum of my preparation. It is imperative that I know the starters at each offensive and defensive position and their immediate backup. In the skill positions, I prefer a three-deep chart.

The speed card is made of reinforced paper or cardboard and contains a team's offensive and defensive starting lineups, the depth behind each position, and alphabetical and numerical roster listings. Sports information departments routinely provide the media with them for quick-reference use in the booth. Since I know my spotting boards so well, I rarely have a need for a speed card. I keep it so a spotter can refer to it when unable to find a player on my boards. I include the speed card in my preparation resources list because I occasionally use it as a fallback for creating my spotting boards if I don't have a current depth chart. There is a danger in relying on speed cards for depth, however. They are at least a week old and do not take into account recent changes in the lineups.

The stat sheet is fairly standard at the college and pro level and provides almost any piece of statistical information you could want about a game. The National Football League Game Summary includes the date, the weather, the attendance, the officials, the starting lineups, the substitutions, those who didn't play, a summary of scoring plays, team stats, individual stats, defensive stats, and a ball possession and drive chart. I use the stat sheet to note individual totals which should go on my spotting boards. I also note important team totals on a separate legal pad.

The play-by-play sheet is detailed enough that with it, you could do a recreation of the game. I pay particular attention to any outstanding individual plays (such as a 90-yard run from scrimmage) for potential inclusion on the spotting boards. I will also make notes so I can later request the plays on tape.

Finally, I use the media guide to cull basic background information on each individual and the team and the weekly release to update everything.

As you do your reading for each team, you should be on the lookout for three types of information that can be used on the air:

> (1) instant information—This is information that has to be committed to memory in order for it to be useful at any given moment. For example, say the Dallas Cowboys' Troy Aikman comes out next weekend against the Washington Redskins and throws an interception on the first play of the game. Without looking at my spotting boards, I would immediately say, "That is the first interception Troy Aikman has thrown in the last 74 passes." If I didn't have that fact in the back of my mind, if I had to look down at my spotting boards to find it, very likely the next play would get under way and the fact would lose its impact.

> (2) sidebar information—This information is usually non-statistical, a story or a sidelight on a person that can be fitted in anywhere in the broadcast. It is used when there is a shot of someone away from the action such as during a free throw or after an incomplete pass when the camera focuses on an individual. You might say, "Brownley is the first person in 20 years to do both place-kicking and punting for Washington," or "The coaches say Taylor is sort of a 'street-fighter' for this team. He's out of Great Falls, Montana, and has been playing hurt all year long."

> (3) referable information—This is information pertaining to the game or a team that you may "refer" to during dead moments of the broadcast such as commercial breaks or when an injured player on the field causes a delay. The break allows you time to glance at

your notes without fear of losing sight of action on the field. You can then make a detailed observation about the game or reinforce something your analyst has said. For example, when covering a University of Miami football game, I write notes on a legal pad setting up the school's rich tradition at quarterback, giving the current Hurricane squad an historical perspective.

The final step in off-site preparation is memorization. The more information you can commit to memory the better. Looking down at your notes to find a certain fact can destroy spontaneity. Constantly referring to notes can also lead to the dangerous situation of taking your eyes off the field or your monitor at a critical moment. You never want to be caught thinking, "What just happened?"

I use a two-step process to become familiar with my material: I memorize as much as I can before arriving at the game site; then I reinforce that memorization with a final run-through the night before the game.

In football, the key to your mental filing cabinet and to your spotting boards is being able to associate a name with a number. There are any number of ways to accomplish this. Dick Vermeil writes the names and numbers he's trying to memorize on a sheet of paper and carries it with him wherever he goes. If you ride with him in his car, eat with him, or watch a practice with him, you will notice Dick constantly referring to the sheet, trying to reinforce the names with the numbers in his mind. I familiarize myself by watching a team's latest game tape. After I have completed my spotting boards, I watch the tape, using the boards to identify players. I prefer this method because I associate players with their numbers more readily if I see them as human beings and not just items on a list. This exercise also helps me learn a player's location on the boards by simulating their use during a game situation.

I further familiarize myself with my boards when I fly to the game site. I try to memorize verbatim at least two or three facts (either instant information or sidebar information) per player. The rest of the material I may not know specifically, but I know it well enough to find it at a moment's notice on my boards.

Some play-by-play announcers think that you are better off knowing one good fact than three average facts. If you hammer at that fact during the course of the game, fans are more likely to remember it. Though this is partly a matter of individual style, the argument has some logical merit. There are times when I attempt to memorize too much and encounter a mental gridlock. I've become so burdened down with minutia that it doesn't register when I need it. You have to know yourself and your limitations regarding memory. ABC's Roger Twibell has said he can't memorize anything until game day because he would forget it otherwise. On the other hand, there are other announcers whose memories never shut down. When talking about No. 75 this week they may actually relate information about last week's No. 75. Everyone is different.

CHAPTER EIGHT

# *On-Site Preparation*

*W*hen a network covers a football or basketball game on Saturday, the Thursday before is generally a travel day. If possible, we try to arrange our schedules so we reach the game site in time to watch the home team practice Thursday afternoon.

I view any team practice the same way I watch a game film, using the opportunity to reinforce my ability to associate names with numbers. I also look for any idiosyncrasies that might make a player immediately recognizable from the booth. For example, Jeff Graham, a former wide receiver for Ohio State, put tape on his red football shoes in such a way that it appeared he was wearing spats. You didn't need to see his number to identify him on the field.

Looking for unique physical characteristics for players at practice is especially important when covering basketball or hockey because the action during the game happens so quickly. Anything you do to keep your eyes on the court or the rink will improve your play-by-play description. When covering these sports, you should learn to recognize players based on their physical appearance rather than having to continually refer to their number. Also, keep in mind that a player looks considerably different in uniform.

While watching a practice, I prefer to have the team's SID standing next to me. Often a player who is supposed to be a starter is not working with the first team or another player appears to be running with difficulty. The SID can quickly answer any questions regarding potential changes in depth and save you from having last-minute line-up headaches before the game. You can also pick up tidbits that can be used on the air.

Another important item I get from the SID is the correct pronunciation for each player's name. I've learned from experience to rely on the SID rather than the coach for correct pronunciations. Coaches are the worst at pronouncing names.

Correct pronunciation is critical for the play-by-play announcer. One way to ensure irate telegrams and letters from fans is to mispronounce someone's name on the air. Foreign names can be especially challenging. Once when Dick Vitale and I covered a game between the Soviet national team and the Bucks in Milwaukee, we were sent all the phonetic pronunciations for the Soviet players a week ahead so we could practice. The day before the game, the interpreter traveling with the Soviet team looked at our list of pronunciations and said, "Nyet," and gave us a completely different pronunciation for each name. As is his nature, Dick went crazy for about 30 seconds, then calmed down and started re-learning each name.

In the past, that last-minute correction would have blown me away. I used to be terribly overwhelmed by Chinese and Soviet names. To overcome this intimidation, I have developed a system where I first write the name phonetically so I can see the sound of each syllable. As soon as I know the sound of each syllable, I go back to the name as it is really spelled. You cannot read the name phonetically, syllable by syllable, because it will sound piecemeal. You have to put the sounds back together. I do this by picking out a key sound to get me into the name. For example, Ernest Nzigamasabo, a forward for the University of Minnesota basketball team, pronounced his name ZIG-AH-MAH-SAH'-BO. The pronunciation trigger for me was simply "Zig." For the Hungarian swimmer Krisztina Egerszegi (EGG'-ER-ZEG-EE), the key was "Egg." For former University of Arizona wide receiver Olatide Ogunfiditimi (OH-GUN-FIH-DIT'-IH-MEE), it was "Gun."

Some people cannot work with visuals and have to learn by hearing someone else say the name. Dick Vermeil could not say Ogunfiditimi until he heard me repeat the name a few times. He then parroted the sounds.

Regardless of the method you use, you must practice difficult names until your pronunciation of them is second nature.

Nothing breaks your confidence and concentration more than stumbling through a pronunciation. It's the tail wagging the dog; you become so intent on getting the name right, you lose sight of everything else. I have had instances where I was so determined to get the last name right, I completely blew the easy first name.

After practice, I spend a very brief period chatting with the head coach. Nothing detailed. No x's or o's. Just a little, "Have you had a good week of practice? Any surprises?" At most, I get a general overview of the team's situation, and I try to build rapport in preparation for a more specific interview the following day.

On Thursday evening, the producer, the director, the analyst, and the play-by-play announcer usually have dinner together. This is as much a social gathering as a working session. We enjoy the meal and learn what's in the rumor mill at the network or how each other's family is doing. If you are working with the same crew, you find out how the brass viewed last week's game and what areas need improvement.

Of course, we also talk football. Since the analyst and I have homes in other parts of the country, we have a good mix that leads to a better overall picture of what is happening nationwide. As far as the upcoming broadcast is concerned, we have individually developed opinions about the keys to the game and how they might be drawn into the broadcast, beginning with the opening. However, this is our first chance to exchange those views as a group. We ask each other questions such as, "How does this game fit into the conference picture? Does this game have any national implications? How has the network been promoting the game during the week?" As a result of our discussion, we are closer to establishing a common theme that can serve as a thread throughout the broadcast. Based on everyone's input, the analyst and I are also provided with definite avenues to explore during our interviews the next day.

Friday morning is reserved for talking with the home team's offensive and defensive coordinators and the head coach. The interviews are conducted separately rather than all at once. In a collective interview, the individuals tend to be more guarded: The assistant coaches may be inhibited by the presence of the head coach or the two coordinators may have an intense rivalry and won't open up in front of each other. There is nothing worse than having a group interview when the offensive coordinator says the defense is not doing as well as it should or vice versa.

When the analyst and I talk to each coordinator, we start with x's and o's. The coordinator will stand at a chalkboard and diagram the team's basic offensive or defensive sets. They are generally trusting enough to tell us what they think are their strengths and weaknesses. They also explain how they will try to combat the opposing team's strengths and exploit its weaknesses.

Coaches even advise us of new wrinkles they've devised specifically for this game. One time the Indiana coaching staff apprised us of the fact they had put the halfback option into their game plan after discovering running back Anthony Thompson was an excellent passer. Since Thompson was left-handed, we were particularly observant every time he ran to his left. Sure enough, after several runs in that direction, Thompson ran left, stopped, cocked his left arm, and threw for a long gainer. We were on top of the play all the way.

After the crash course in team strategy, we then ask the coordinator for a thumbnail sketch of each of his players. The questioning is done much in the manner of a psychiatrist conducting a word association test where the initial response is the most important. I might ask, "What about Joe Jones?" and the coordinator will say, "You know, this kid has got the biggest heart in the world. He's not a great athlete, but he plays his guts out every game." I listen for significant comments like this, make note of them, and then add them to my spotting boards later that evening. They make excellent sidebar information during the course of the game.

In our interview with the head coach, we dispense with x's and o's and information about individual players and focus on broader issues: How important is this game to your program? How key is this game in terms of your schedule? What did you tell your team? Is this a do-or-die weekend for you? Because of our prior research and the input from the SID and the assistant coaches, we are very specific in our questioning. Our goal is to capture the emotion of the upcoming contest through the coach's eyes. Often we can do that with one simple request: "Put this game in perspective for us." Frequently, we elicit a one-line quote that can be used on the air. After coming off a big 29–28 upset loss to California in the 1988–89 season, Arizona head coach Dick Tomey told us before the game against USC the following week in Tucson, "You know, this will be a great gauge for us as to how far our program has come or how far it has to go." The statement was key to our broadcast. By the time Arizona lost 24–3, we were able to show that the Wildcats had a ways to go before reaching the level Tomey desired.

After our morning interviews, the analyst and I head for the film room to review videotapes. We watch tapes of the home team's last game or of previous opponents who the coaches think have had an offense or defense closely resembling the team they will be playing this week. We also view tapes of the visiting team.

We have several objectives in watching game tapes. First, I am concerned with player identification, particularly in respect to the various sets the offensive coordinator has shown us. I watch all the skill positions in each set until I am able to tell which side of the field a wide receiver is split to based on the formation. Second, we watch for things the coaching staff has told us regarding special sets or plays or individuals they think are key players. Third, we watch for outstanding individual efforts that we *haven't* been tipped off to, something the average fan might not see. Finally, we look for telltale signs that might alert us to what play will be run next. Meeting the latter two objectives generally falls under the responsibility of the analyst. Analysts who are ex-coaches are excellent at picking out a player who telegraphs his move such as a guard leaning the same way every time he pulls to block.

Once in a while during my off-site reading, I will make note of an outstanding play and request the SID pull the tape so we can also see it. I once worked a University of Minnesota game with Dick Vermeil the year after Darrell Thompson ran 98 yards for a touchdown against Michigan, the longest run in Big Ten history. Since I had covered that game with Lynn Swann in the Metrodome, I made sure Dick had a chance to view the tape of that play. I wanted Dick to see the potential of

Thompson who was no longer playing well. During the broadcast, Dick said, "Darrell Thompson is not the Darrell Thompson who played last year, Gary. I saw the tape of his 98-yard run against Michigan last year and I tell you it's just not the same Darrell Thompson out there."

One of the more exciting things during the preparation process can be watching tapes with an ex-coach such as Dick Vermeil or John Madden. If you let them run the tape machine, they will continue to back up a play as many as 30 times until you wonder what they're looking for. Then they'll say, "Look at this pick," and they'll explain how a team has disguised an illegal pick where two receivers run through the same area so that one screens the defender off the other. Or they might say, "Look at this guy. This guy is a load. They talk about the other tackle, but this is the better player." Such an observation usually makes it on the air.

Reviewing films with ex-coaches can truly be an educational experience. They have heightened my awareness of various coaching techniques and philosophies. For example, Dick Vermeil has said many times, "I think coaches hang their quarterbacks out to dry." He thinks what coaches ask the quarterback to do looks better on the blackboard, philosophically sounds great, but on the field, the percentages say it isn't going to get done. A lot is expected of a quarterback that he isn't prepared to do.

These expositions may not make it on the air, but they often lead to discussions that do lead to usable material. Sometimes the analyst and I will stop the tape and talk about philosophies or the football season in general and as a result, the analyst will say, "You know, I'm going to use that in my opening."

Not every analyst has the same passion for intense preparation. One analyst, whom I dearly loved as a person, never prepared one iota. He hated it and it eventually killed him in the business. During the game, he watched only the quarterback. It was his only interest. He never used spotting boards nor memorized anything. Whoever worked as a spotter for the game deserved combat pay for constantly having to point people out on every play. It was like a game of checkers with the spotter bouncing all over the place. Though the analyst and I would talk football morning, noon, and night, we never once watched tapes together.

In the cases where you are teamed with an analyst who does not like viewing tapes, you should still use the time to refine your identification of players and your familiarization with basic formations. If nothing else, by watching a terrific play on tape, you can always say something on the air such as, "I saw a tape of last week's game and that same play went for 70 yards instead of a sack."

In the afternoon, we watch both teams go through brief workouts at the stadium. We view these walk-throughs the same way we watched the home team practice the afternoon before, concentrating on identifying players. This is sometimes complicated by the fact that, during these light workouts, players are often dressed in sweats without jersey numbers.

Sometime during the afternoon practices, we also schedule time to do sound bites—15- to 45-second taped segments that can be inserted into the broadcast at appropriate moments during the game. At the beginning of the week, I will talk to the producer and the two of us will decide on two or three players from each team to interview on tape in addition to the head coach. I will begin thinking about potential questions to ask and, when I'm on-site, discuss them with the producer prior to taping. I usually have four or five questions scratched out on a card or memorized.

Before the taping, particularly with young college athletes who are not used to being on camera, I engage in small talk to help them relax. I visit with them, asking questions I won't be asking later, so they have a chance to get to know me better. I also give them three instructions: (1) "We are doing the interview as though it were the day of the game so don't refer to the game as happening 'tomorrow.'" (2) "Be concise because, if your answers are too long, we won't be able to edit them down for use between plays or coming out of commercials." (3) "Look at me and react to me or, if you don't want to look at me, look at the camera."

Whether it's at practice or during scheduled interviews, I enjoy talking to the athletes. I make a point of meeting the quarterback, a linebacker who had two interceptions last week, or anybody who has been playing well and might have an impact on the upcoming game. Often the players, both pro and college, will come over themselves to talk. Our discussions usually have nothing to do with football. We'll talk about their hometowns, their families, or their parents and whether their family will be attending the game. You'd be amazed at the kind of information and stories that can come out of simple impromptu conversations.

One of the things you discover during these one-on-one chats is a player's true temperament or personality. When I talked with Indiana University's Anthony Thompson during the 1989–90 season when he was one of the leading contenders for the Heisman trophy, I found that winning the honor was important to him, but not overwhelmingly so. In our discussion, he revealed his mother was a God-fearing, Bible-toting, single parent who had raised him very strictly. Consequently, he was a no-sir, yes-sir person. I used that description on the air to show his character and how he had other priorities in life beyond football and the Heisman trophy.

Often you uncover information that heretofore has not been common knowledge. Before the 1983 Final Four, most people had become familiar with the facts surrounding Hakeem Olajuwon's migration from Nigeria to the University of Houston and his amazing physical capabilities in basketball. However, few were aware of his overall athletic prowess and that he was also an outstanding soccer and tennis player. When we talked before the semifinals, I kidded him that maybe the reason he was successful at soccer was because, as a 7' goalie, there was no goal mouth at which to shoot. He laughed. On the air, Billy Packer made the comment, "Can you imagine having to lob the ball over him on the tennis court?"

One of the more powerful and timely stories I developed came during the 1990 football season when I was preparing for a game between the Universities of Miami and California. In the preceding week, the Berkeley campus had experienced a fatal fire at the Kappa Sigma house. Five of the Cal players were members of the fraternity, including All-American punter Robby Keen, whose best friend had been among those who died in the blaze. Distracted by the funeral and his grief, Keen did not punt in practice all week before the Miami game. When I talked to him the day before the telecast, Robby said he was going to play the game for his friend, but admitted he was having trouble focusing. During a critical point in the contest, Keen mishandled the snap while standing on his own two-yard line. It was the first time in his career that he had dropped a snap. Miami recovered and went on to win the game. The misplay was the turning point and, because of my talk with Robby, I was able to put it and the game into a larger context.

The visiting team usually stays in the same hotel where our production crew is housed. After practice, we follow the team back to the hotel, then talk to the offensive coordinator, the defensive coordinator, and the head coach as we did with the home team that morning.

That evening the broadcast crew holds a production meeting. Everyone from the production assistants to the director are in attendance. The producer runs the meeting, going chronologically through the broadcast, noting everyone's responsibilities. He explains how we intend to open the show, what graphics or visuals will be used and when, what tapes are available, when we will go to commercial, and what promotions need to be inserted. Anything having to do with the broadcast is presented. Everyone listens and if there are any questions or problems they are discussed and resolved.

During the meeting, I take my copy of the production sheet—a blizzard of information on a stack of paper several trees died to produce—and note the items that pertain to me such as commercial lead-ins and voice-overs. I want to be aware of all segments of the broadcast, since I will be the one introducing them on air.

Either before, during, or after the production meeting, the producer, the director, the analyst, and I discuss two areas that are key to the broadcast.

First, based on the additional information we have accumulated from our interviews and tape viewing during the course of the day, the analyst expresses what he thinks are the key match-ups that the truck should be watching on the field. He explains what he thinks is going to happen, including any new wrinkles the coaches have in store. I then go over the stories the analyst and I want to develop, all the sidebar information. The point is to make the producer and director aware of the course the broadcast may take so they will not be surprised. They can then reinforce our stories and ideas with camera shots or graphics on the air.

The other topic we cover is our opening. The analyst and I will give our opinions about what the thread of the broadcast should be. We hope that the points we establish in the opening are the keys that will decide the game, the ones that will make newspaper headlines the next day. The producer agrees or adds his suggestions. He also asks what kind of visuals we might need to support what we say.

After the production meeting, the analyst and I will have a late dinner or go back to our rooms and decide more precisely what we are going to do for our on-camera pre-game analysis. There may be several different points we would like to empha-size. Knowing we have a time constraint, we prioritize them. We handle the opening much like a newspaper writer would develop a story in print, using the pyramid effect. We always lead with our best stuff and progress to the items of lesser im-portance. Almost without exception, we develop more mate-rial than we will be able to say within the timeframe allotted. Therefore, if we have to cut, it will be the lesser material that is cut. It is easier to cut than to scramble to fill.

Our discussion is very informal, very give-and-take. If I were working with Dick Vermeil, our conversation would sound something like, "Here's what I'm going to ask you, Dick . . . What are you going to say?" Dick would then respond, "Well, Gary, basically what I'm going to say is this . . ." The process is similar to creating a new suit. We select the mate-rial, take measurements, design a pattern, even make a rough-cut model we try on to see how it fits. However, the resulting product is not yet ready to go on the air.

As I've mentioned, the last thing I do before turning in the night before a broadcast is go over my boards and notes again. It is the last quiet moment before the storm, the final chance to reinforce memorization.

# *Game-Day Preparation*

$O$n the day of a game, my first priority is to eat a big breakfast, something high in carbohydrates such as waffles. My eating philosophy is similar to many athletes who want to build an energy reserve before they perform. Like any physical effort, doing a live broadcast is very energy draining. You have to prepare your body accordingly. And breakfast is virtually the only time a broadcaster has to eat, since once you reach the ballpark, there is very little time to eat even if you wanted to. (We'll discuss later why you shouldn't eat during a broadcast.)

I like to eat breakfast with the analyst. It gives us a final chance to review our on-camera opening and the sidebar information we plan to develop throughout the game. I also get a sense of how the analyst is feeling toward the game after a night of digesting the input we received the day before. It is the last moment for us to converse in a relaxed environment. Once we get to the stadium, our time and attention will be in constant demand.

Play-by-play announcers are generally scheduled to be at the game site a minimum of two hours before kickoff. I am more comfortable playing it safe, getting there 2½ hours before game time. I've always had a fear of getting caught in traffic and not making a broadcast on time. You've heard of kids having dreams about being locked out of school during an important test. My nightmare is to be locked out of the press box before a broadcast.

When I arrive at the stadium, I check in at the truck, let the producer know I'm there, and see if there have been any changes before heading up to the booth. By arriving early, I have plenty of time to deploy all my materials: to lay out my spotting boards, to make sure my legal notepads are in order, to tape the list of game officials on a monitor or somewhere readily visible. I also have time to become acclimated to my surroundings. I prefer to stand while doing football because you get a better view of the field: a monitor may obstruct your vision if you sit. Therefore, I make sure I can locate all the essentials in the stadium from my standing position: the down and distance, the time clock, and the score on the scoreboard.

Taking note of the scoreboard location seems so basic, but it is a vital step in preparation. Scoreboards are never uniformly placed. If you are not familiar with the peculiarities of each stadium, you leave yourself open to anxious moments on air.

For example, the scoreboards at Sun Devil Stadium in Tempe, Arizona, are directly across from the press box and to your left. During afternoon games, neither is readable because the sun shines directly on them. You have to be aware of that fact because the only other place down, distance, time, and score are shown are on the video replay board to your right. And sometimes that board is showing a replay or commercial message. If they run a replay just as you're about to give the down and distance, the time remaining, or the score, you can stumble on the air.

The shot clock for basketball is usually on the goal standard behind each basket. However, in football, the play clock (giving the amount of time left before the next play has to be run without penalty) is never uniformly placed. In one game I covered between the New England Patriots and the Phoenix Cardinals, Cardinal receiver Roy Greene failed to catch a pass in the end zone and thought the defensive back had interfered. After the play, the official in charge of the play clock set it in motion. Meanwhile Greene argued his case, not realizing the play clock was running. When he finally returned to the huddle he discovered there wasn't enough time for the Cardinals to call a play. To avoid a loss by penalty, they called time. If I hadn't been aware of the location of the play clock and seen it reset, I might have attributed the timeout to confusion in the huddle instead of what really happened.

Basketball has some unique problems for the broadcaster when it comes to clock placement. Many basketball clocks are on a scoreboard hanging high above center court. Since most broadcast positions are at court level, this placement can cause two dangerous problems for the announcer. First, because it takes so long to look up to see the scoreboard overhead, you risk taking your eyes off the action on the floor or off your monitor. Second, because you have to tilt your head back to see the clock, you can accidentally move your headset and end up talking off mike. To keep from bobbing your head up and down all the time, you need to find an alternative. Pick a clock across from you or to either side or use your monitor. Whichever you choose, get in a habit of using the same clock every time when leading to commercial. It would also be a good practice to have an alternate clock in mind, since clocks have been known to malfunction.

Two hours before kickoff, I am scheduled to do voice-overs: adding word accompaniment or introduction to set tape pieces that have been edited together at the network's home base or at the game site. These taped pieces include the opening tease and various informational segments similar to the historical lead-ins CBS ran after commercials during the 1991 Mobil Cotton Bowl Classic, highlighting significant moments in the Cotton Bowl's history. As the producer rolls the tape, I provide a voice-over, reading from a script. I prefer writing the script, but some producers provide the script for you. Often it is a collaboration between the two of us.

After voice-overs, I read the network promotions that I will be doing throughout the course of the game. Each promotion is typed on a 3x5 card that will be handed to me by the stage manager to be read on air at times designated by the producer. Since I have no control over when the promotions will appear, I review them so they will not come as a surprise when it is time for me to read them. If I am unfamiliar with a prime-time program or special or if there is a typo or grammatical error, I can clarify the situation then rather than stumbling over the problem on air in front of the nation.

Sometime before or just after our first on-camera rehearsal, the analyst and I will also review all the graphics and tape pieces put together by the production assistants so we know what might be used during the game. We sit in the booth with our headsets on, watch our monitor, and simply tell the producer when we want to see the next screen.

When the analyst and I do our first rehearsal for the on-camera pre-game analysis, it is a shakedown version. The analyst and I are wired to the truck, are in front of a camera, and are trying to approximate what we will be doing on air, but there is none of the intensity nor emotion that will happen when we go live. We are more interested in content than form. After the previous night's production meeting, we have agreed in general what the opening will contain. The producer has since seen that visuals, both tape and graphic, have been gathered to support our opening comments. Of course, the analyst and I have discussed more than once what we plan to say. I have written out my introduction and leads to the analyst. Many analysts do the same for their responses and, in some cases, such as Dick Vermeil, even commit most of their comments to memory. However, this is the first time all parties bring their efforts together.

During the shakedown rehearsal, we not only iron out the bugs but, most importantly, fit the pre-game analysis into the time frame allotted by the producer. Everyone involved has editorial comment: I give suggestions to the analyst; the analyst makes his observations; the producer adds his input, ensuring what we say supports the visuals or vice versa. Once everything is sorted out, we rehearse once more. The opening has now taken shape: the analyst and I sound professional and have trimmed the opening to its prescribed time frame.

At this point we break. With about an hour and a half before kickoff, I like to take time to go down on the field to get a sense of the atmosphere. I try to track down the head coach, to see how he's feeling. Later you might be able to use your observations on the air by saying something like, "Before the start of the game we were down on the field talking to Lou Holtz and it was interesting how confident he looked." I often watch the special teams practice so I will be able to make comments such as, "I'm surprised how poorly Smith is kicking. Before the game he was really booming those punts." If I know the trainer or the team doctor, I will get a last-minute update on a player's condition. He might inform you that, "When

Lewis went out to practice, he was limping a little bit. We brought him back in, retaped him, and now everything looks okay."

Actually being on the field also gives you first-hand knowledge of the playing conditions. Before one game, I noticed an area of the artificial turf was especially wet. It was particularly strange since the rest of the field was dry, having been protected by a tarp. I asked someone why and found out the tarp had been removed incorrectly, dumping water on that one location, making it slippery. Sure enough, whenever a team was in that area during the game, the quarterback lost his footing. I was able to tell the audience the reason.

I return to the booth approximately 45 minutes before going on air. I give myself plenty of leeway. There have been instances of announcers missing the opening of a broadcast because they were stuck in a crowded elevator.

By the time I return to the booth, the spotter and the statistician have arrived and are arranging their materials. If it is a network broadcast, the spotter and statistician are a part of a crew with which we've worked before, so there is little time needed to pass on last-minute instructions. However, on those occasions when the spotter and the statistician are provided by the home team, you have to allow extra time to sit down and clearly indicate what you expect of each and to see if their systems of operation are compatible with your needs. Waiting until the game starts will be too late.

Thirty to 45 minutes before air, the analyst and I rehearse our on-camera opening again. This is a dress rehearsal. We have our coats on, our ties tied. Our hair is combed and, if needed, we have on makeup. The crew checks the lighting. The stage manager makes sure our hand-mike clips have the network logo facing the camera and our earpieces don't show. The cameraman ensures that we have a proper background. Everyone approaches this rehearsal as though it were for keeps. Our goal is to do the opening so well a tape of it could be used on air.

After the dress rehearsal, I like to clear the broadcast booth of all nonessential personnel so the analyst and I can have a few undisturbed moments to watch the remaining pre-game practice. It is a last chance to visually familiarize ourselves with the players, to note unique physical traits, to evaluate injuries. We often converse. The analyst might observe that so-and-so "is running well. Looks like he's going to be ready to go." Essentially, we use the time to catch our breath and mentally gear up for the onslaught of the broadcast.

The game-day procedure that has just been described is fairly standard for most network broadcasts give or take a few minor variations. However, sometimes things do not happen as you would like. Weather often affects how events transpire, particularly for football. There have been games where the rain or snow was so severe teams shortened their workouts on the field. Some days were so cold you took every opportunity you could to get out of the booth, grab a cup of coffee, and allow yourself a moment of warmth so you could survive the next three hours in the booth. Perhaps more often than we would like, we have to cope with some kind of technical disaster: the mikes don't work, the lighting goes out, the telestrator or one of the monitors is on the fritz. The unforeseen can always alter the procedure.

Sometimes the process changes because of last-minute information. Most SIDs come up to the booth 30–45 minutes before air to answer any questions and wish us luck. This gives us an opportunity to update injury situations and overnight changes in game plans. Occasionally, we are given a usable piece of sidebar information such as the bus driver for the visiting team getting lost on the way to the stadium. And in some instances, we are provided with information so dynamite that it changes our opening.

A good example came before the 1987 Arizona State-Washington football game ABC covered at Husky Stadium in Seattle. After we had concluded our shakedown rehearsal, the Washington SID showed us a copy of the morning *Seattle Times* in which Arizona State's freshman quarterback Paul Justin, who was making his first start, was quoted as saying, "I don't think they [the Huskies] trouble me at all. There ain't nothing we can't do against their defense." We immediately jumped on the story and redid our on-camera opening based on his comment. We even had the truck build the quote graphically. As it turned out, the decision was a good one. On ASU's opening possession, Justin's first pass was intercepted by Bo

Yates who ran 25 yards for a touchdown. From then on it was all downhill for Justin and the Sun Devils. Justin lasted only three series, while Arizona amassed only 20 total yards, all on the ground. The Husky defense was so dominant, the Sun Devils finished the first half with no first downs and 10 total yards (four rushing, six passing). Washington took a 17–0 lead into the locker room and eventually won 27–14.

The final step of preparation happens approximately 10 minutes before going on air. Everyone has taken their pit stop and all are at their broadcast positions. The analyst and I exchange words of encouragement. Last-minute instructions are doled out to the crew. We try to develop a foxhole mentality in which everyone in the booth is a comrade in arms. We want to be on the same emotional level.

We are now ready to give the broadcast our best shot.

# PART III

WORKING IN THE BOOTH

# CHAPTER TEN

# A Typical Broadcast

"We're live."

That simple phrase spoken by the producer in the truck is the starter's gun for a broadcast. You may have been quietly gathering your thoughts, watching the billboards from the network studio on your monitor. But, with those two words, the adrenaline flows. The race is on. It is the moment people in the business live for.

Whether they are calling a Super Bowl, the seventh game of a World Series, the Final Four championship game, or a Game of the Week, play-by-play announcers become emotionally involved with the game they are covering. It is unavoidable, expected. Before the game there is always a heightened sense of anticipation. You always hope for a game-winning play in the final second, a buzzer beater. However, you are just as likely to be working a 30-point rout. In either case, you have a job to do. This chapter describes the details of that job.

The following breaks down the broadcast responsibilities of a play-by-play announcer to their elemental components. Because most of those elements are constantly repeated, the job may sound trivial. Anyone can do it. Right? Juggling in the hands of a competent juggler also looks easy—until you try it.

In a way, play-by-play announcers *are* jugglers. They must develop a rhythm of tossing out descriptions that marshal the event's unfolding action and emotion and, at the same time, juggle the production aspects of the broadcast, working with partners in the booth, on the sidelines, and in the truck who occasionally toss back a scimitar instead of an orange. If this looks routine to the viewing audience, then they have achieved a degree of success. If they can also make the routine seem fresh and new each time they do it, they may be on the road to earning six-figure salaries.

As in the previous section, the illustrations used in this chapter are drawn from television coverage of college or pro football. The production elements are typical of all televised sports coverage regardless of venue. Obviously, the play-by-play requirements differ from sport to sport, particularly from sports like football and baseball which intersperse periods of inactivity with periods of activity sparked by a single action (the center's snap, the pitcher's delivery) to the relative constant action of basketball and hockey. Each sport has its own peculiar rhythm. Those differing venue requirements will be discussed later.

## The Opening

The opening of a sports broadcast should give the viewing audience a reason to watch the upcoming contest. It should set the scene, introduce the participants, establish the keys that will make watching the game interesting and exciting, and should do so in a very concise manner. With the exception of special events such as the Super Bowl or prime-time bowl games on New Year's Day which have the luxury of more time because of higher production values, openings take no longer than five minutes.

A typical opening begins with a tease—a series of brief tape pieces with a prerecorded narration by the play-by-play announcer—that sets the stage for the broadcast. It is similar to the "grabber" in a short story; a first paragraph that is so intriguing you have to read further.

"Championship Tuesday! And now the Grand Finale!" That's how Dick Enberg started the tease for NBC's prime-time Orange Bowl telecast New Year's Day 1991. Though longer (two minutes and twenty seconds) and more elaborate (staged shots of backlit players), it conformed to a common construction for teases, setting the match-up by featuring the strengths of both teams. In his voice-over, Enberg summarized top-rated Colorado's failure to capture a national title the year before when the Buffaloes also entered the game against Notre Dame ranked number one. He then provided a capsule look at Colorado's main offensive threat, Eric Bieniemy. In setting the opposition, Enberg pointed out Notre Dame's past success when facing number one opponents followed by a capsule look at the main threat of the Irish, Raghib "The Rocket" Ismail. This was all dubbed over a production package of clips, including scenes of both locker rooms before the game, moments from the 1990 Orange Bowl, and staged shots and taped highlights of Bieniemy and Ismail. The tease ended, "With his blazing speed, can 'The Rocket' burn another national championship team? And to add to this drama, will this be his final collegiate game?"

The tease is followed by an animation bridge, a set of computer-generated graphics that signals the start of every sports program.

The first shot after the animation bridge is usually a wide shot of the field from the highest point in the stadium or from something above the stadium such as a blimp. Off camera, the play-by-play announcer officially starts the live portion of the broadcast by introducing the setting and the teams playing: "Live from Husky Stadium located off beautiful Union Bay in Seattle, Washington State and Washington meet for the 91st time in their long cross-state rivalry."

Often the introduction of the setting is followed by graphics giving the current weather conditions. In ABC's telecast of the 1990 Peach Bowl, Steve Zabriskie began, "This afternoon, live from Atlanta's Fulton County Stadium, Indiana and Auburn meet in what could be less than the best weather conditions." He then described the rainy and foggy conditions Atlanta had been experiencing all week as a segue to "Today's Weather" graphics that showed game-time playing conditions on the field.

The first on-camera shot for the play-by-play announcer can be either a single-shot or a two-shot at the start of the pregame analysis. If it's a single-shot, the announcer introduces himself—"Hello, I'm Gary Bender"—then makes an observation about the upcoming contest that sets up a lead to or a question for the analyst—"Washington is primarily noted for its running game, but today against the Washington State Cougars the passing game should play an important factor." As the camera pulls back to a two-shot, the announcer introduces the analyst and leads to the analyst's first comment: "With me today is Dick Vermeil, and Dick, I know you talked with the Husky coaching staff about their strategy. What is Washington going to have to do against the tough Cougar defensive front line?" The only difference on a two-shot beginning is that the announcer introduces himself and the analyst: "Hello, I'm Gary Bender along with Dick Vermeil."

To reiterate, the object of the opening's on-camera pre-game analysis is to establish the keys that will decide the game. The opening is comprised of lead questions from the play-by-play announcer which allow the analyst to "analyze" the keys to the game with the help of preselected tape pieces run by the truck to reinforce those points. The analyst rarely has time for more than two or three questions since the time allocated for the pre-game analysis is no more than two minutes. The pre-game analysis by Dick Enberg and Bill Walsh before the 1991 Orange Bowl consisted of five leads and responses and lasted just over two-and-a-half minutes, but that was an example of a prime-time production.

The final segment of the opening is the introduction of the opposing teams as they enter the field. This is the biggest challenge for the play-by-play announcer since the networks have shaky control over when the teams enter the field. Only during big games such as the Super Bowl are team entries orchestrated. Since the play-by-play announcer's introduction of the starting teams may be piped over the stadium PA system simultaneous to its broadcast, the network requires greater control over the timing of the pre-game ceremonies. Any other time, the play-by-play announcer is subject to the vagaries of coaches who are notorious for holding up a team's entry to the field in order to create a psychological moment, or to un-planned occurrences such as scuffles breaking out between two teams that enter from the same tunnel.

When a team does not enter the field at the appointed time, the play-by-play announcer has to fill. Often the fill is planned ahead of time. The truck shows a graphic of a team's record—overall record, bowl record, home record, record in head-to-head match-ups with the opposing team, whatever—and the announcer fills with team history and tradition.

After the teams enter the field, the play-by-play announcer leads to the first commercial, concluding the opening.

A majority of football broadcasts open with the sequence of events just described. There may be minor variations: the introduction of the teams precedes the on-camera pre-game analysis; the field condition graphics or team record graphics are deferred until coming out of the first commercial just before kickoff; the game setting is enhanced with a tape piece showing various campus locations and a pre-recorded voice-over by the play-by-play announcer. However, because of time constraints, there is little room for significant creativity.

With major productions like bowl games, anything goes. For example, NBC's opening for the 1991 Orange Bowl included, in effect, *two* pre-game analyses. The on-camera analysis by Dick Enberg and Bill Walsh was preceded by an in-studio, bowl-day recap, featuring Bob Costas and Will McDonough, that put the outcome of the Orange Bowl into focus in terms of the national title race after the day's results. Costas and McDonough also added some controversial seasoning in pieces about the infamous fifth-down touchdown Colorado scored to avoid defeat against Missouri, plus the NCAA investigation of the University of Minnesota and the potential involvement of Lou Holtz.

ABC's telecast of the 1991 Rose Bowl had a two-part opening with a commercial in between. In the first part, Keith Jackson did a live tease, introducing the setting and its rich tradition over a wide shot of the Rose Bowl. A single-shot followed in which Jackson welcomed the viewing audience. He then led to a field shot of the Iowa marching band playing the national anthem. On the countdown to commercial, the truck ran a tape of the stadium entrances of the Tournament of Roses president, the Grand Marshal (Bob Newhart), and the Rose Queen and her royal court with Jackson providing a live voice-over. The second part of the opening began with a two-shot of Jackson and Bob Griese as they did their pre-game analysis. Jackson then introduced the Washington Huskies and the Iowa Hawkeyes as they made their entrances. All year long, the Iowa squad had made its entrance as a unit, walking hand-in-hand into the stadium. This took time to coordinate, requiring Jackson to fill with the game-time weather conditions, the Hawkeyes' record, an explanation of the delay, and coach Hayden Frye's record.

In all cases, specific responsibilities and associated time limits for the opening are choreographed the day before in the production meeting. Considerable emphasis is placed on the opening since most broadcast crews consider it the most important part of the telecast. If there are no technical glitches, if the play-by-play announcer and the analyst don't stumble over each other's words, if everything goes smoothly and efficiently, then a positive tone is set and the confidence level of the whole broadcast team increases immensely. They are like streak-shooters in basketball: if they hit their first shot, chances are they will have a good game.

## Call of the Game

During the break to commercial after the pre-game analysis, the play-by-play announcer and the analyst switch from hand mikes to headsets and take up their positions to call the game. On return from commercial, they are ready for the kickoff and nearly three hours of intense work.

Describing the action on the field while capturing the emotion of an event is the lifeblood of a play-by-play announcer. Because of the differences in the unique personality and style of each announcer, each broadcast will have a different flavor. However, the broadcast will have no substance unless the announcer heeds the basics of play-by-play.

To illustrate the basics of calling game action, I have included my description for and Lynn Swann's analysis of a four-play series during a 1987 game between Arizona State and Washington covered by ABC. I have identified all the elements of my play-by-play with superscripts that are explained following the illustration. The dialogue has been edited for purposes of clarity and space consideration, but it does represent a typical call of the game.

\* \* \*

**PLAY 1**

**Gary:** First down,[1] the line of scrimmage the 33 yard line of Arizona State.[3] 14–0 Washington.[5] 2:45 to go in the first quarter.[6] [Snap] Here's Weathersby.[8] He cuts it to the 30 and Weathersby will make it to the 28 yard line.[11] Pick up of

5.[4] Good block that time by Pahukoa,[9] No. 58, a freshman out of Marysville, Washington. It's his first start today.[12] It looks like everything Don James did regarding lineup changes and game-plan is working thus far.[13]

**Lynn:** It just seems that he's got this entire team on the same page. They're playing efficient football. They're playing team football. Not one person has to do the whole job by himself.

## PLAY 2

**Gary:** Second[1] and six for the Huskies.[2] Slater split to the near side, Darryl Franklin to the top.[7] Two excellent wide receivers.[12] [Snap] Chandler hands straight ahead to Jenkins.[8] Jenkins breaking one, two tackles[11] to the 15.[3] First down.[1] Nathan Laduke eventually dropped him.[10] You've got to give Jenkins a lot of credit, but, Lynn, Arizona State is not tackling right now.[13]

**Lynn:** [Replay] They're not tackling, but look at Pahukoa. He comes over, gets a piece of the man on the other side, just gives him enough room to go through. And Aaron Jenkins again, not trying to do anything fancy, protecting the ball goes straight ahead and drives for the extra yards.

## PLAY 3

**Gary:** Aaron Jenkins is four for 30 thus far. He had 107 yards earlier this year against Pacific. He was the tailback in that game.[12] First down[1] now from the 15 yard line.[3] [Snap] Weathersby. Weathersby.[8] Kind of picking his way, getting some blocking,[11] advancing four yards[4] to the 11 yard line.[3] Jeff Mahlstede over to make the stop.[10] That play not developing all that quickly, but that's a Weathersby type run.[13]

**Lynn:** It didn't develop because you see one of the drawbacks of this Washington line is that, because it's so big, it's not that fast. He had those blockers out in front of him, ran up their backs, and they had nobody to block. He had to make a decision, moved to the outside, and got tackled. If they were a little faster, he would be right behind them down field, possibly five or ten more yards.

## PLAY 4

**Gary:** It's nice to be big, but you'd like to be fast as well.[13] They're going to give him three yards.[4] Second down[1] and seven now for Washington.[2] [Snap] Hand-off straight ahead,[11] Covington,[8] the other fullback. Tony Covington a junior out of Portland.[12] It was kind of a shovel pass back that time and Covington[11] is very close to a first and goal. They're going to have to measure to see if he got it.[13]

**Lynn:** [Replay] Watch Zandofsky as he makes a block here. They fake the pitch like they've been doing all along, toss it back, and he's blocking on Trace Armstrong right there, stands him up and just moves him away from the point of attack. Great blocking. Great execution.

**Gary:** Zandofsky is the most decorated offensive lineman in the history of Washington. You'll be interested in this, Lynn. He is the first sophomore since Roy Foster to win All-Pac 10. Of course, Roy, an outstanding guard at USC.[12]

**Lynn:** Coaches say about Zandofsky, "He is the kind of blocker who 'buckles' people." Now when you say "buckle" someone, that means you take them straight on, hit them right in the chest, and those knees just give out. Whether you want them to or not, they go.

* * *

The "nuts and bolts" of play-by-play fall into three categories: (a) setting the situation, (b) identification, and (c) commentary.

The play-by-play announcer sets the situation by stating the:

> down,[1]
> distance to first down,[2]

position on the field,[3]
distance a play covered,[4]
score,[5] and
time.[6]

Down and distance to go for a first down should be stated prior to every snap, preferably as the offensive team breaks from huddle. Besides keeping the viewer oriented, constant reference to down and distance builds drama, particularly on a long drive comprised of several third-down situations. Because of their dramatic import, first downs and third downs should be emphasized. First downs should be announced as soon as possible after a play, provided you are certain of the situation.

In fact, all statements of down and distance should be definitive; do not say "It's second and six or seven yards," or "That play covered about 20 yards." Any time there is confusion because of a pileup or a reception or run out of bounds, wait until the ball is placed by the officials before stating distance. On third downs, make sure the distance to first down you say matches the distance shown graphically on the screen. Also, refrain from predicting first downs when a play results in a measurement. In Play 4 of the illustration, I noted that the ball's placement required a measurement, but didn't guess whether it was first down or not. Announcers who repeatedly guess at results risk undermining their credibility with the viewers, especially if they are frequently wrong.

Noting the position on the field before, during, and after a play should occur whenever it helps orient the viewer. Keep in mind that what the viewer sees on the screen is usually not sufficient to tell where the ball is on the field. Unless the truck is showing a wide shot that includes the far sideline, the viewer cannot see the yard markers for point of reference. In addition, you can measure progress up the field by announcing the line of scrimmage before the snap on first-down situations (see Plays 1 and 3 in the illustration).

The two most important dimensions in sports are score and time. The score tells who is winning. Time indicates how long there is to change the outcome. Nothing is more disconcerting to a fan watching on television or listening to the radio than not knowing the score or whether the game is in the first or second half. I was returning from a trip one time and was desperate to know how a particular game was going. I got off the plane, went immediately to my car, turned on the radio, and went crazy when they wouldn't tell me the score. I promised myself I would never allow that to happen to my audience.

Obviously, it is not necessary to state the score and the time remaining in a period prior to every play. So what's a good guideline for stating score and time? I have seen announcers use an egg timer to make sure they had at least said time and score within the last three minutes. Another arbitrary method is to note score and time remaining with every exchange of possession or after every big play. Actually, if you think about it, the character of the game should lead to the moments when score and time are stated without prompting; if something happens that might have a bearing on the outcome of the game, it has a direct bearing on the score. On the completion of a 50-yard pass, the announcer who is into the game will automatically put the play into perspective for the audience: "The Giants are driving for the go-ahead score with 3:23 left in the game."

Whether it's because they are channel switching, are interrupted by the phone, or make a trip to the refrigerator or bathroom, fans are often distracted from the game and need to have the basic parameters reestablished for them. The announcer should give the audience the confidence that they can leave for whatever reason and whatever length of time and, on return, be able to be brought up to date very quickly. You can never say score and time too often.

Whenever pertinent, the announcer should also identify:

> the formation,[7]
> the ball carrier,[8]
> the passer,
> the receiver,
> the blocker,[9]
> the tackler,[10]
> who intercepted the pass,
> who recovered the fumble, or
> who received the penalty.

Though identification is paramount when covering a sport on radio, it is no less so when doing television. The viewer may see what is happening on the screen, may see the numbers of the players, may even be able to read names across the backs of jerseys, but in most cases the play-by-play announcer is in a better position to make identification. How many viewers have memorized the number of every player on the field? How many have a spotting board in front of them or spotter sitting next to them to help? The announcer also has the advantage of being able to see the whole field of action and not just what is on the screen. When the camera is focused on the line of scrimmage, the viewer is unaware the defense has inserted an additional back to protect against the pass unless the announcer states, "The Cowboys have switched to a nickel defense." Also keep in mind, for all the viewers who watch every play intently, an equal number have their eyes focused elsewhere and are listening more than watching.

Finally, the play-by-play announcer comments on the action by

> describing the play,[11]
> describing a player,[12] or
> making a general observation on what has transpired.[13]

A cardinal rule when describing football on television is to lay out before the snap of the ball. That moment of quiet builds tension and allows the viewer a sense of anticipation. Once action commences, the announcer's call is composed of brief statements, almost sounding like shorthand. There isn't time for wordiness. After the play ends, you can summarize in more detail provided you have taken care of the nuts and bolts of down and distance and provided you aren't overstepping the time the analyst has for comment.

Descriptions of players occur before or after a play and are usually succinct ("Two excellent wide receivers," in Play 2). More extended descriptions and general comments are used as a means to stretch until the next play (see Play 3) or until the analyst is ready to take the replay (see Play 2) or make an observation (see Play 1).

Learning to set up your analyst takes practice and team-work. The announcer's lead requires more finesse and timing than just saying, "Take it, Lynn." Both the announcer and the analyst hear from the truck when a replay is coming. At that point, it is up to the announcer to finish whatever thought is being expressed so the analyst can jump in when the producer says, "Replay." The worst thing an announcer can do is to continue talking once the replay is moving, putting the analyst in a catch-up mode. Conversely, analysts must finish their comments soon enough for the announcer to set the situation prior to the next snap.

When the tandem is working smoothly, the announcer and the analyst complement one another. Because Play 4 in the illustration resulted in a measurement, Lynn and I had sufficient time to have a brief dialogue about Mike Zandofsky. While Lynn described Zandofsky's execution during the replay, I was able to consult my notes and followed with information on Zandofsky's being All-Pac 10 as a sophomore. This set up Lynn's relating the coaches' description as the truck isolated on Zandofsky in the huddle.

In order to call a game with fluent rhythm, you must learn to mix the nuts and bolts with relevant commentary without sounding mechanical, repetitive, and unemotional. It requires years of practice to become proficient and even then you probably won't be satisfied. I have never done a game exactly the way I've wanted to and I'm not sure I ever will. I continually work to improve. Every time I return home from a game I hope to be able to say to myself, "Boy, that's about as well as I can do it."

## Handling On-Air Traffic

Besides providing a running account of the action on the field, the play-by-play announcer's other main duty is to be the on-air traffic cop when it comes to introducing various production segments. This includes everything from setting up or commenting on graphics shown on the screen to leading to commercial breaks.

The most common forms of traffic an announcer deals with are game graphics and tape segments.

Graphics are built by production assistants (PAs) using a character generator that is equivalent to an electronic typewriter. It is a very time consuming process. PAs spend all day the day before the game and even right up until game time building preset graphics, including stats and facts that the analyst and the play-by-play announcer have given them.

Tape segments include still stores or mug shots of players, sound bites of players and coaches taped the day before, and film footage from past games. Each tape segment is stored on a cassette that has an assigned identification number. When the producer calls for a still shot of Joe Montana, a PA punches up "1107" and a shot of Joe Montana with built-in graphics of his yearly stats is kicked on air.

Prior to the game, the analyst and the announcer review the graphics and tape segments in the booth so they know what is available to the producer. Though they have been outlined in the production meeting, no one knows for sure when or if any of the graphics or tape pieces will be used. You have ideas on how you would like to use them, but you can't force them into the broadcast. You have to take what the game gives you.

In some instances, there is an attempt to schedule certain preset graphics. For example, it is standard practice to show the starting offensive and defensive lineups for both teams during each team's first offensive series. Typically, lineup introductions are comprised of two or three pages of graphics accompanied by the announcer's live voice-over. During the 1990–91 college football season, ABC used an individual still of the quarterback with graphics of his stats (completions, attempts, yards, touchdowns, and interceptions), followed by a page of offensive backs and receivers (with position and number), followed by another page of offensive linemen (with position, number, and weight). The defensive lineup was also covered in three pages; the first included the defensive line (with position, number, and weight), the second, the linebackers (with position and number), and the third the secondary (with position and number).

Ideally, all pages of the offensive lineup will be shown and introduced prior to the first play from scrimmage and all pages of the defensive lineup will be shown and introduced

prior to the second play. However, there is a factor in this
process that cannot be controlled. The play-by-play announcer
must introduce the lineups (i.e., mention everybody's name
while making appropriate comments such as "Aaron Cox, the
fastest man they have on this team" or "They moved Wiese,
who was the left guard, to the right in a conscious effort to run
more that way") all before the next snap of the ball. Even
under the best conditions, the announcer cannot waste words
when covering a team's complete lineup in the limited time
available. If a team has a short huddle, sets up quickly, and
immediately snaps the ball, the announcer may only have time
to introduce two pages of graphics. In that case, you play
catch-up on the succeeding plays. If the first play from scrimmage results in a touchdown, it will seem as if you are playing
catch-up all afternoon.

Another preset graphic that usually has a predetermined
slot is the list of game officials. Most producers choose to introduce the officials during the brief pause following the first
penalty. Sometimes during a well-played contest the first in-
fraction doesn't occur until as late as the second half. When
this happens, the producer has to be on the ball not to forget to
cue the graphic. Here again, the announcer is constrained by
time. Besides introducing the officials, you have to explain the
penalty, identify the offending player, and set the resulting
down and distance, all before the next snap.

Most of the time, the analyst and the announcer do not
know when or what graphics will be displayed. Consequently,
they have to constantly watch their monitors. If the producer
calls for a closeup shot of a coach or player, the announcer
may have an idea of what graphics the PA has stored, but will
not know for sure until they appear on the screen. At that
point, the announcer can choose to comment or not. Sometimes a graphic is so straightforward it needs no repeating.
Player stats often fall in this category. When a stat appears on
the screen during an isolation on a player, the announcer
rarely comments unless it is significant, such as a rusher leading the nation in yards per carry. At other times, a play-by-play
announcer who has prepared can supplement a graphic. When
I called a Texas-Houston basketball game attended by former
Houston coach Guy V. Lewis, the producer called for a closeup

of Lewis in the stands followed by a still store with graphics showing that Lewis had taken five teams to the Final Four. I supported with a voice-over, stating that three of those appearances were in a row.

Though the producer is the person who gives the instructions to run graphics and tape pieces, the analyst and the play-by-play announcer can trigger their initiation. Since the producer's sensory world is confined to what appears on the many monitors in the truck, the analyst and the announcer often are more in touch with the emotional timbre of the moment. Consequently, the producer occasionally leans on them for direction. Because analysts are wrapped up in the technical aspects of what is happening on the field, especially involving match-ups, their suggestions usually revolve around graphics that accompany isolations on individuals. Play-by-play announcers are more concerned with story lines and the game's overall picture. For example, if I were covering a University of Miami football game in which the Miami quarterback was having a good day, I might suggest to the producer during a commercial that it might be a good time to bring up the tradition of Miami quarterbacks. The producer would say, "Okay," and tell everyone, "On the other side of commercial, let's come back with the package on Miami quarterbacks." The analyst will be listening and may look at some notes. On the return from commercial I will lead to the graphics, and, as they appear, the analyst is ready to make the appropriate comments.

Another form of traffic the play-by-play announcer must contend with is leading to the sidelines announcer. The use of sidelines announcers was once only a special game occurrence. More and more, networks are routinely including sidelines announcers as a part of the broadcast team, especially for football. Their roles vary. Some are used for entertainment and human interest value, doing planned pieces such as showing the boat parties University of Washington fans throw when they attend Husky Stadium on Lake Washington or interviewing nonparticipants such as cheerleaders or parents of players. Others provide ground-level eyes and ears to the broadcast crew. Though they are restricted from interviewing participants, they can overhear sidelines discussions and relate them on camera. By listening to the play-by-play announcer and the analyst, a sidelines announcer can also supplement information. I might say, "Lynn, we haven't seen Mark Wilson during the last two series." A good sidelines announcer would read the cue, investigate the situation, and report back, "Gary, I heard you and Lynn wondering what happened to Mark Wilson. During the last kickoff return, he was accidentally kicked in the helmet and he came off the field dazed. It doesn't appear to be anything serious, but the team doctor wants to keep him on the bench awhile to check him out."

Sometimes field reporting can be squeezed in between plays, but most of the sidelines announcer's segments require time and are generally placed after commercial breaks or during significant lulls in the action. Two examples would be between a score and the succeeding kickoff when the producer elects not to go to commercial or during an injury time-out. After the producer's prompt from the truck, the play-by-play announcers' lead is fairly standard: "It's a nice day to be on the sidelines. Let's go down to Steve Alvarez," or "Let's go down to the sidelines. Here's Cheryl Miller." The sticky part comes on the return from the sidelines. If the sidelines announcer's comments run long or the interview being conducted is a good one, the segment may not end before the next snap. At that point, the producer returns the picture to the action on the field, keeping the sound on the sidelines. The problem comes after the segment finishes. Since at least one play has been run, the play-by-play announcer has to catch up, recap what has happened, and reset the situation often with insufficient time to do so. It is a challenge not to lose your rhythm.

Occasionally, the producer will say to the announcer, "Gary, if the next play is not a big one, get ready to go to New York." After the play, the announcer will summarize the situation and lead to the studio announcer for an update of another game in progress: "It's second down and three. Now let's go to John Saunders in New York for an update of the Michigan-Iowa game." A similar situation may also arise in the first half of a network doubleheader when the producer directs the announcer to lead to the origination site of the second game for a quick promo of the upcoming match-up. In either case, the play-by-play announcer watches the monitor and listens carefully, waiting for the other announcer to throw it back. On return, the play-by-play announcer makes appropriate reaction comments and proceeds with the call of the game. As in the case of cutting to the sidelines announcer, if the other site does not throw it back before the next snap, the announcer must play catch-up.

The most critical traffic handled by play-by-play announcers includes live promotional and commercial considerations and leads to commercial. While graphics and tape pieces can go unused because of time constraints or because the game goes in a different direction than predicted, commercial considerations cannot be ignored. They pay the bills.

There are several types of promotional and commercial considerations, all read live by the announcer:

> **Promos:** These include special graphics that promote the second half of a doubleheader, an upcoming game or event, the network's prime-time lineup that evening, the halftime event, and even other promotional considerations (i.e., "Just a reminder that coming up shortly we will be announcing the Chevrolet Players of the Game.").

> **Disclaimers:** "This broadcast is authorized under the rights granted by the National Football League and is solely for the entertainment of our listening audience . . ." or "The announcers for this game have been okayed by the University of Kansas with the consultation of Creative Sports Management . . ." These are often read without the benefit of graphics.

> **Billboards:** "This ABC Sports exclusive is brought to you by Domino's Pizza because Domino's Pizza delivers. And by Michelob Light. When the sun goes down, light up the night with Michelob Light." Most of the time at the network level, billboards are prerecorded with a voice-over provided by an announcer in the network studio. However, sometimes technical glitches occur, and the play-by-play announcer must accompany the graphics shown on the screen with a live voice-over. The networks are increasingly find-

ing new and creative ways to sell air time. Now the opening kickoff can be sponsored by Budweiser with a Budweiser logo framing the action or the starting lineup might be sponsored by Sears Diehard. These cases also require the announcer to introduce the segment's sponsor by reading a prepared text.

**Sponsored Awards:** At ABC these include the Chevrolet Players of the Game and the Honda Scholar Athlete of the Week.

Live promotional and commercial considerations can run anytime, but, because traffic often gets backed up during the course of the game, they often run in the later part of each half. They are initiated by the producer: "Gary, at the first opportunity, lead me to the Players of the Game." The producer then relies on the announcer's judgment to pick a spot when there will be sufficient time between the completion of one play and the start of another, such as after a long incomplete pass. The truck listens for the announcer's lead, "And our Chevrolet Players of the Game are . . ." and follows with the appropriate graphics. Coordination is all-important. Since part of the sponsor identification is in the graphics, the sponsor may not have to pay for the commercial time if the announcer provides audio without graphic support.

Leading to commercial can be the most challenging form of traffic the announcer has to manage. Commercials can happen any time there is a break in the action. When the break is after a period, at the two-minute warning, or after a score, the announcer knows a commercial is likely to follow. Sometimes after punts or if there is a long delay because of an injury, the producer can call for a break to commercial out of the blue. In either case, play-by-play announcers have to complete their on-air thoughts while the producer is counting down in their ear. The goal is to marry the completion of the announcer's comments with the end of the countdown: run too long and words are lopped off; run too short and there is an awkward silence.

The two ways to lead to commercial depend upon who is airing the commercials: the network or the local station.

Leads to network commercials are very generic. Essentially you can do it any way you want as long as you finish your comments by the producer's count of "one." A typical long lead would be, "Arizona State is a disorganized football team right now in the jaws of the Huskies. Washington has done everything right. The Sun Devils are still looking for their first spark offensively, their first success of the afternoon as they trail Washington 17–0." A short lead might be, "We'll come back to Husky Stadium in a moment with 5:11 to go until half."

Leads to local commercials require more precision in the announcer's words. Saying "We'll return with more of ABC's College Football after this message and a word from our local stations" alerts the local station that the network will be throwing it to them to run commercials for the local market. Saying anything else can cause all sorts of havoc.

## Commercial Breaks and Halftime

When we played tag as kids, there used to be a rule known as "King's X." If you declared "King's X," you were safe from being tagged "it." Commercial breaks and the longer break at halftime are "King's X" for play-by-play announcers and analysts—brief moments of sanctuary from the rat race of the broadcast. In the few minutes off air, you can mentally relax, catch your breath, take a drink of water, and, if necessary, regroup.

However, sometimes the demands of the broadcast intrude on the announcer's safe haven. When problems arise that can't be resolved during on-air time, "King's X" is ignored. During commercials, producers can talk to announcers and analysts who seem to be working different games; announcers can talk to stage managers who aren't handing promo cards to them soon enough or statisticians who are not providing correct information; or the analyst can test the telestrator that hasn't been working. The more critical the problem, the more panicky and stressful the commercial break. This is definitely the case if the communication system breaks down. Television productions use a talk-back system that incorporates a switch—often called a "cough" switch—that allows the announcer or the analyst to talk to the truck without being heard on air. Though the system is checked several times before going on air, there has been more than one occasion when it failed. If the truck can hear the announcer, but the announcer cannot hear the truck, then the announcer is stranded with no sense of direction. It is a situation that must be resolved at the first commercial opportunity.

Frequently, commercial breaks are used to keep one step ahead of the game. When the truck wants to break for commercial, a time-out coordinator on the sidelines signals the fact to the referees, then signals again on the other side of commercial. On the return side, the time-out coordinator has a certain amount of discretion that allows the broadcast team time to be more creative. The producer may want to throw it to the sidelines announcer for a planned piece on a team mascot. The play-by-play announcer and the analyst may want to do a prepared piece on a team's running back tradition, with accompanying tape or graphics. The commercial break allows time to discuss the options and plot a course. Since the announcer is prompted 30 seconds prior to return from commercial, there is time to gather thoughts and prepare for the appropriate lead based on the decision made.

Halftime is an extended version of a regular commercial break. In a perfect world, the play-by-play announcer throws it to the studio in New York for scores, highlights, and other half-time pieces, leaving plenty of time for the announcer and the analyst to make pit stops, comb hair, and adjust ties before their on-camera opening for the second half. Because there is more time, the broadcast team can tackle problems that went unresolved in the limited time during the commercial breaks of the first half. These problems likely have to do with miscommunication between the team members. Halftime allows time for everyone to get back on the same page.

The producer and the team in the booth also use halftime to prepare for the on-camera recap of the first half and opening for the second half done by the play-by-play announcer and the analyst. Highlights are discussed and chosen for replay. Though first half stats shown graphically are fairly standard, you may be able to select the stats you want represented, depending on the technical abilities of the people in the truck.

Here is where a good statistician is invaluable. George Hill, the stats man I worked with most regularly at ABC, was excellent at listening to me and anticipating my needs. I simply had to ask, "What stat just jumps out at you?" George would respond, "Gary, it's incredible how Michigan has held Ohio State to half its average rushing yardage." Based on his input, we might slant the graphics to focus on that fact and reinforce the point, choosing an outstanding defensive play as one of our highlights.

There is insufficient time to rehearse the second half's on-camera opening, so it is done cold. This is not as difficult as it sounds. Since the play-by-play announcer has taken notes on all scoring plays and referred to them more than once during the first half, it is a matter of positioning each replay for the analyst to recap: "It started out disastrously for Arizona State. They started a red-shirt freshman, Paul Justin, and the first pass he attempts is picked off. The game is 43 seconds old and they're down seven to nothing." By the time the announcer's lead is finished, the highlight will have started rolling so all the analyst has to do is walk the audience through the play, redescribing and analyzing as necessary.

After the first-half highlights, there is usually a commercial break. On the return, the first-half stats are summarized just before the second-half kickoff. Again the setup is straightforward. The play-by-play announcer and the analyst will discuss what they want to say in the halftime break so that all the announcer has to do is lead with something like, "Based on what we stated at the top of the show, it looks like USC has really taken UCLA out of its game plan." The analyst will respond, "Terry Donahue told us he wanted to have a balanced attack, but as you can see, the Bruins have thrown the ball successfully only four times in the first half." The on-screen graphics will then support what the analyst says.

Sometimes the play-by-play announcer's "perfect world" crumbles during a simultaneous broadcast of two regional games. Ideally, both games will end the first half at the same time so all the announcer has to do is throw it to the network studio and enjoy a few minutes of peace and quiet. However, most of the time one game will run faster than another. Let's say Keith Jackson and Bob Griese are covering a game that features the University of Miami's extensive passing attack with the inevitable clock stoppages after incomplete passes. Opposite them, Dick Vermeil and I have a game featuring the bruising running game of Ohio State and fewer clock stoppages. Our game would reach halftime much sooner than Keith and Bob's. Consequently, I would have to fill with an additional recap of the first half or with an introduction of the Ohio State band on the field until the Miami game reached halftime and the two broadcast sites could throw it to the network studio at the same time. If the delay is significant, the switch to the studio may be scrapped entirely. The play-by-play announcer would then have to do the entire halftime show on-site, including updating scores elsewhere and leading to the halftime pieces promoted during the first half. When this situation arises, the announcer doesn't get much, if any, "King's X."

## Closing the Game

At the conclusion of a game, the play-by-play announcer has two responsibilities: the wrap-up and the sign-off.

The wrap-up is nothing more than a summary of what has just happened. As the game progresses, I take notes recapping each quarter. Then as the final minutes tick off, I begin to mentally formulate my wrap-up. Because the announcer often doesn't have much time, the wrap-up has to be succinct. The idea is to describe the game's storyline in a way that anticipates the next day's headlines in the paper. In fact, the day after a game, I check the newspaper to see how close my wrap-up came to the actual headlines. The wrap-up will also tie the broadcast together by linking up with the story line introduced in the opening tease and on-air analysis.

The sign-off is a formal way of saying good-bye to the viewers and notifying stations down the line that the broadcast is ending: "For Lynn Swann and Steve Alvarez, this is Gary Bender saying 'So long' from Husky Stadium in Seattle."

There are two ways to end a broadcast: a long close and a panic close.

A long close is used when there is plenty of time to get off the air. The producer will notify the announcer via the talk-back system, "Three minutes until you read the card." Because there is sufficient time, the wrap-up might not only include the announcer's game recap, but also a review of replay highlights by the analyst, a discussion that puts the game into perspective regarding the conference race or national rankings, and a promotion of an upcoming game or program. When the producer says, "One minute until you read the card," final comments are made so the announcer will be ready to read the card at the producer's direction. The card for a long close usually consists of a list of credits—the producer, director, associate producer, executive producer, who sponsored the blimp, etc.—plus a standard sign-off. Since the producer knows how long it takes for the announcer to read the card, the announcer should finish simultaneously with the end of countdown to sign-off.

A panic close is used when you have to get off the air in a hurry. It usually consists of no more than a one- or two-sentence wrap-up, a quick promotion of what program or game is to follow, and a simple good-bye.

When a game is one of two regional broadcasts shown simultaneously or the first half of a doubleheader, the producer may say, "We may be back, so don't sign off." The announcer would then use a generic close such as, "For Lynn Swann, this is Gary Bender, from Husky Stadium where Washington has just defeated Arizona State 27–14." There is no "So long" sign-off so, if the network wants to return to fill for time, it can.

NBC used the following close to conclude the 1991 Orange Bowl telecast: Dick Enberg began the wrap-up, "Led by backup quarterback Charles Johnson, Colorado has defeated Notre Dame, 10–9. Indeed, they *did* get a second chance and they *have* made a first impression." Bill Walsh recapped Johnson's accomplishments. Enberg and Walsh reviewed a replay of the final play of the game, an interception by Colorado's Deon Figures of a Rick Mirer pass. Bob Trumpy interviewed Colorado coach Bill McCartney on the field. Enberg and Walsh reviewed a replay of a critical late punt return by Notre Dame's "Rocket" Ismail that would have given the Irish the lead had it not been called back because of a clip. Enberg announced the players of the game. Finally, Enberg signed off.

Obviously, because of the importance of the prime-time game, the network allowed the broadcast team plenty of time for a long close, including a detailed wrap-up. However, if the network had been strapped for time, the wrap-up could have been nothing more than Enberg's "Led by backup quarterback Charles Johnson, Colorado has defeated Notre Dame. Indeed, they *did* get a second chance and they *have* made a first impression." These two sentences fulfill the requirements of a good wrap-up: They state the story line succinctly in a way that might be providing the next day's headlines; and they tie back to the opening when Enberg noted Colorado's quest for number one after failing the opportunity the year before. The only difference in this wrap-up from the original in the long close is that it does not include the score. Most likely Enberg would have mentioned it as he did in his original sign-off: "For all of us at NBC Sports, thank you for being with us. Happy New Year. Oh my, is it happy in Colorado. The Buffaloes 10—the Irish 9."

## Postmortem

The game is over. You've signed off and are quickly gathering all your material so you can make your escape from the stadium in a race to catch your flight home. The broadcast is history, right?

Not if you're a conscientious professional. Every broadcast team member should want to make the next broadcast better. This means evaluating the broadcast just completed. The military calls the evaluation of a battle a *debriefing*. I call the same appraisal in broadcasting a *postmortem*. Postmortem literally means "after death." It sounds negative, but in the context of analyzing what went wrong with a broadcast, it is really the opposite. To me, postmortem means turning all the negatives into positives.

Often when a problem arises during the telecast, there isn't enough time to be tactful. Voices raise with the emotion of battle, trying to get a point across or resolve the matter in the briefest time available. Though people in the business develop thick hides, people are only human. You can not let something that happens in the booth hurt your relationship with anybody. You have to address the sore points immediately before they fester. The postmortem gives you a chance to open up and say, "Here's what happened. Here's what I did. Now, what would you have been more comfortable with?"

It is especially important not to damage the relationship between the announcer and the analyst, since any friction between the two will eventually be transmitted to the viewers on air. The best time to conduct a postmortem with the analyst is right after the broadcast as you're unwinding, packing your gear, heading off to the airport in the car. You have just spent two to three hours emotionally entwined with your partner in the booth and you are both still attuned to what you liked and didn't like. In other words, the sore spots, if any, are still sore. By being honest, it's easier to resolve any differences then and there.

Sometimes the differences are minor such as clarifying a rule interpretation. Sometimes it's a matter of finding a better way to handle a situation that has never arisen before. Say you are working with an analyst whose only experience is in television. During the broadcast you experience technical difficulties that eliminate the video; the viewers can hear you, but there isn't any picture. The competent announcer would immediately slip into a radio play-by-play that was more descriptive, more wall-to-wall, leaving less time for analysis. Having not worked in radio, the analyst might not know when to say anything or recognize the announcer's leads since there is no replay to analyze. During a postmortem, you can recreate the problem and walk the analyst through better ways of handling it for next time.

When the problem is a bad habit that drives you crazy, you have to resolve it as quickly as possible before it becomes so distracting it destroys your concentration in the booth. Maybe it's *you* who are causing the problem. Maybe you're backing your analyst into a corner. For instance, instead of giving the analyst an open-ended lead which can be accepted or ignored—"That's the third time Anthony Thompson has run over 10 yards on first down. He's having a tremendous game"—you put your analyst on the spot: "He's having a tremendous game, isn't he, Dick?"

A frequent problem, especially when a play-by-play announcer is working with a new analyst who has just left the playing field for the booth, is stomping on each other's lines. The way I've addressed the problem in postmortem is to say, "It sounds to the listeners as if we're fighting for air time when you're saying something the same time I'm saying something. We both have so much enthusiasm. We both have so much information. We have to corral that enthusiasm. Here's what I can do. What would you do?"

When Cotton Fitzsimmons was first used by NBC as a guest analyst during the 1991 NBA play-offs, he was criticized for overdescribing each situation and, therefore, taking too long to develop his point. Executive producer Terry O'Neil made Cotton aware of the situation right away and, by the second half, he showed marked improvement. This illustrates two points about a postmortem whenever it might occur: You have to be aware of a problem before you can solve it; and the sooner you address a problem, the less likely it will become ingrained.

Coaches often say they can't tell how well their team played until they've had an opportunity to view the game film. Sometimes it's the same for the broadcast team. You have a sense that something went wrong but you can't pinpoint it. You air the feeling in a postmortem immediately after the game, but the actual resolution might happen days later. When I worked with Dick Vermeil, we would go home after a game, review a taped copy of the broadcast on Monday, taking notes, then talk to each other on the phone. "Dick, I watched the tape. Here are three or four things I'm not comfortable with. I need your input on them." Dick has improved on the efficiency of this process by purchasing a Sony Watchman. He is now able to watch a dubbed copy of the game on his flight home so he can get an immediate handle on what he's done.

Some people are their own worst critics. But, even though it is sometimes painful, all announcers should watch tapes of their performances if for no other reason than to weed out overused words and phrases.

Often during the course of a conversation, your mind needs a moment to formulate its next thought. In the interim, your mouth is stuck with stalling. This tactic results in the use of what I call "crutch" words or phrases. Everyone has seen young athletes who pepper their interviews with "uh" and "you know" as they mentally construct what they want to say. Broadcast professionals have the same problem on occasions, but handle it in a more sophisticated way. For instance, an announcer grasping for the next thought might stall by stating the score.

Any use of crutch words and phrases is okay until they become repetitive. The audience can get very irritated hearing the same phrase over and over and over. A writer once jumped on my case for saying "young freshman" every time I referred to Michael Jordan his first year at North Carolina. Not only was the phrase redundant—all freshmen are young—but the same description became monotonous: so much so that it was the only thing the writer remembered about the broadcast.

Reviewing your own tapes can help you identify crutch words or phrases that have crept into your play-by-play, allowing you to eliminate them or at least to substitute new ones so they don't become repetitive.

Clichés are another story. One man's cliché is another man's clear understanding of what has happened. The best advice regarding clichés is to try to avoid them, because they usually slip into a broadcast when you've lost your concentration. Single out the times you repeat a cliché and you'll note situations to watch out for in the future when you're most vulnerable to saying something off-hand.

The postmortem is not limited to just the on-air talent. It can involve anyone in the booth and the truck. On one occasion, I was continually giving a down and distance different from the graphics shown by the truck. It was particularly noticeable on third downs. I would say "third and seven" and the truck would show "third and eight." We resolved the discrepancy in a postmortem. The best way to keep me on the same page as the truck was for the statistician to write the down and distance on a piece of paper for me to see after supplying the truck with the same information to show on the screen.

The first time Curt Gowdy, Jr., produced one of my games, he spoke to me in a postmortem about talking too much during the broadcast. We agreed to review the tape of the game and get back to each other. A few days later, Curt called and admitted his first impression had been incorrect. Working with a new crew, he had been distracted by the confusion and emotion in the truck and had not viewed my performance objectively until he saw the tape.

The last story was included to illustrate a point: a post-mortem cannot achieve positive results unless the participants listen. Though I was not aware I was saying any more than usual, I still listened to Curt's opinion. Not everybody is right. But you still need to listen.

# CHAPTER ELEVEN

# *Working with the Analyst*

*T*here was a time when sports broadcasts did not have analysts or color men. In their day, such legends as Ted Husing, Lindsey Nelson, and Bill Stern worked alone.

But the broadcast world was simpler then. The media, especially television, have evolved to become more sophisticated both technologically and as forms of entertainment. Now we have the ability to cover any sporting event more comprehensively and more precisely than ever before. Because of these advancements, a broadcast has become too complex to be handled effectively by only one individual.

Probably the single most important innovation that led to the creation of the analyst position was the introduction of instant replay. Before Tony Verna first used the replay in a 1963 Army-Navy game, all play-by-play announcers needed to do was describe the action on the field as best their eyes and memory could capture it. Instant replay eliminated the guesswork. Every action was all there in front of you to dissect and analyze over and over again—provided you had the expertise to do so. Thus, the need for the color analyst was born.

Today, virtually all network and major-market sports broadcasts have an on-air twosome in the booth.

The play-by-play announcer's role is to lead the broadcast. Like a good point guard in basketball, he initiates the game plan, feeding the analyst for the score.

The analyst is the expert. Good analysts know the ins and outs of the sports they cover: They keep the audience apprised of all the whys of what has taken place while, at the same time, alerting it to all that might happen.

Good analysts are not only measured by the knowledge they impart, but also by the manner in which they impart it. Personality is key. A lot of people are enthralled by the likes of Dick Vitale and John Madden, and viewers will turn in to one of their broadcasts regardless of the game's interest. Consequently, many analysts act as bait to lure the sportsviewing public to the tube.

The analyst as headliner has become the rule rather than the exception at the network level. Can you imagine a play-by-play announcer trying to dominate a Vitale or a Madden? That's why announcers such as Al Michaels, Dick Enberg, and Pat Summerall are so good. They give their color analysts room to do their thing. If Al wanted to dominate a broadcast, there would be no way he could work on "Monday Night Football." The play-by-play announcer must be first and foremost a traffic cop and Al is one of the best. One of his strengths is his ability to weave not one, but *two* analysts in and out of the broadcast.

The rule is sometimes reversed, however, when announcing teams are associated with a single team. As analyst for the Phoenix Suns, Cotton Fitzsimmons rarely has an opportunity to contribute more than brief sentences when working in and out of the broadcast. This isn't because Cotton does not have the capability to do more. It's just that Al McCoy is the voice of the Suns. Cotton's role is to reinforce Al.

In any case, the play-by-play announcer and the analyst are the point men on the broadcast team. They are the ones dodging the live bullets, the ones who are in front of the viewing audience. They both must recognize and respect each other's role. They must understand they have to work in tandem for either to survive, and this cannot happen in a vacuum. To succeed, the two must communicate.

Some time back, Vin Scully and Hank Stram, two of the most talented people in the business, were teamed to cover the NFL on CBS. During their first broadcast together, one would say something, then a few minutes later, the other would repeat the same thought, using different words. This continued until the third quarter when the producer finally came on their headsets during a commercial and said, "Mr. Scully, would you turn to your right and introduce yourself to Mr. Stram. Mr. Stram, would you turn to your left and introduce yourself to Mr. Scully." What was obvious to everyone but Scully and Stram was that neither was listening to what the other was saying. The most basic interaction between the two was not happening.

Communication with your partner in the booth should not be limited to verbal exchanges. When you watch golfers walking up a fairway after their tee shots, the way they walk will give you an indication as to how well they are playing. Similarly, being sensitive to the body language of your analysts— their posture, gestures, voice inflection—can provide vital information when something is wrong.

John Madden and I once worked a Detroit Lions football game in the Silverdome for CBS in which everything had gone smoothly during rehearsal. Then, shortly after the broadcast began, John's mike on his headset went out and they gave him a stick mike to use. Immediately, John's entire demeanor changed. He was obviously uncomfortable. More importantly, he didn't say much and what he did say lacked any enthusiasm.

During our first commercial break, I turned to him and said, "John, what in the world is wrong with you? You've got to fight through these technical problems. You can't let them take you out of the ball game."

John still had a puzzled look on his face when we returned to the game and his participation was again below par. At the next commercial, I was really feeling exasperated and told him, "John, come on. You're tougher than this. You've got to work through this trouble. You're just not helping me at all."

Still no improvement occurred during the next segment of the telecast. But, just before going to our next commercial, I caught the look in John's eyes as the light of realization turned on. In commercial, he said, "I know what's wrong. I can't talk with anything in my hand."

John Madden is as good an analyst as has ever worked in the booth. Part of the reason he's so good is the emotion, the energy, the excitement he brings to the broadcast. Anyone who has seen one of his commercials or seen him speak in person, knows how animated John is when he talks, arms flying every which way. In fact, later that year when we were working a Kansas City Chiefs game, he got so excited, windmilling his arms about, he hit the side of my head, knocking my glasses off, sending them out the front of the booth and into the stands. Though it was a temporary inconvenience to me, it was well worth it. When John Madden is on a roll, the whole broadcast gets on a roll. Putting a mike in John's hand is the equivalent of securing him in a straightjacket. By simply exchanging headsets and giving me the hand mike, John Madden finally got in the groove and the rest of the broadcast went well.

Because they are increasingly being chosen for their knowledge and their drawing power as a personality, few analysts today come from a broadcast journalism background. They are drawn from the arena in which they played, managed, or coached and are frequently thrown into the breach with minimal training. Some have innate talent and are able to learn quickly, make the transition, and blossom into the Tim McCarvers, the Dick Vitales, or the John Maddens of sports broadcasting. More often they are unable to adjust to the new environment and wilt under the pressure of having every statement placed under the microscope of attention by a national audience. The unfortunate slip from view after a year or two.

Many of the adjustments ex-players or ex-coaches must make when they enter the booth have to do with the technical aspects of broadcasting. They have to learn to continue talking on-air even while someone is giving them instructions over their headset. They have to take direction, a new experience for many ex-coaches. Most importantly, they must adjust to an environment in which timing is everything.

The analyst's moment in the spotlight is a "ten-second world." The actual time limit varies from situation to situation and from sport to sport, but regardless the circumstance, analysts must be concise. Nothing aggravates a play-by-play announcer more than to have the analyst continue talking during the snap of the football, while a critical free throw goes through the net, or at the crack of the bat on a deep drive to center.

A number of would-be analysts from the sports world have been stymied by the demands of the ten-second time frame in which they have to work in the booth. One particular example was the outstanding former coach at Michigan State, Duffy Daugherty. Duffy may have been the finest after-dinner speaker I've ever heard. He could keep a banquet audience rolling in the aisles with his stories. He was truly a hilarious man. However, his personality as a humorist never translated to television. Why? Duffy could not be funny in short shots. He did not have a bag of one-liners like Henny Youngman. His stories were long and detailed. Under the time constraints of the booth, there was never enough time for Duffy to be Duffy.

Since today's analysts do not come from a broadcast background, they are particularly reliant on the play-by-play announcer when it comes to the technical aspects of the broadcast. The first time I worked with Doug Collins was an NBA game in Salt Lake City for CBS. During halftime, my earpiece went out so I was unable to hear anything the truck said. Fortunately, I saw the stage manager point to me to go, knew the tape piece we were planning to run next, and led to it blind. Coming out of the tape piece, the stage manager signaled again and I led to commercial.

During the commercial, I told the truck, "Hey! I'm not hearing a thing."

The truck replied through the stage manager, "You took the countdowns perfectly. How could you not be hearing us?"

I reiterated, "I heard none of the countdowns. I was just guessing and it happened to work."

They tried feverishly to get my earpiece to work, but the break was shorter than expected. Since I couldn't hear the truck and the stage manager was preoccupied with my earpiece, the truck screamed at Doug whose earpiece *was* working. "Take it, Doug. Gary can't hear. You've got to take it and lead us to the next commercial."

Doug is a polished broadcaster now, but at the time he was just starting in the business and the moment overwhelmed him. He reached over, pulled on my coat sleeve, and said, "Please, Gary. Take it. You can't hear them, but, please take it." Unfortunately, he forgot that we were live and on camera.

When he got home that night, Doug's daughter Kelly greeted him at the door with, "Daddy, Daddy, did you know that you were on the air trying to tell Mr. Bender to say something?"

Doug and I laugh at the story now, but when it happened, it was a desperate situation for both of us. It points out how dependent the analyst is on the play-by-play announcer. The analyst must feel confident that, like the captain of a ship, the announcer will be the last to go down when problems arise. Consequently, the more the play-by-play announcer can relieve the analyst from worries about the technical aspects of the broadcast, the freer the analyst will be to concentrate on the game.

How many times have you heard a coach say, "You know, we really had the talent on this team to win it all, but we just didn't have the right chemistry." Chemistry is equally important to a broadcast team and no more so than in the relationship between the play-by-play announcer and the analyst. An audience can tell if there is friction between the partners in the booth or if the personalities do not mix simply by the subtle nuances conveyed in the interaction of the two. On the other hand, if the relationship is strong, the chances are the broadcast will also be strong because the partners respect each other, know each other's strengths and limitations, and are willing to support each other under duress.

It is difficult to predict whether a match will have the proper chemistry beforehand. Sometimes you simply get lucky.

When I was selected to be the lead college basketball announcer for CBS in 1982, I had never worked with Billy Packer. We met for the first time during a promo shoot, standing in front of the New Orleans Superdome where the Final Four would be played. We had flown in from opposite ends of the country and had no time to talk to each other. The producer did not give us a script, but told us to wing it. "We just want your personalities to come through."

We ad-libbed the promo and got it on one take. Afterwards, Billy turned to me and said, "Man, I feel like I've worked with you forever."

The friendship that Billy Packer and I later developed when we worked together at CBS was so strong we would have done anything for each other. On one occasion when we were following the crazy NCAA Tournament trail, we covered a game in Kansas City then flew the same night to Knoxville to do the Louisville-Kentucky game the next afternoon. We arrived at our Holiday Inn so late we simply went straight to bed to get what sleep we could. The next morning we got up, ate breakfast, and drove to the game site.

As we were about to enter the old University of Tennessee field house, a security guard grabbed me and pulled me back. "Where are you going?"

I told the guard we were there to do the game for CBS.

"Not without credentials," he said.

"Wait a minute," I said. "I arrived late last night, got only four hours of sleep, and haven't had a chance to get my credentials yet. I'll go in and get whatever credentials you need. You can see I have my CBS blazer on. Who in the world do you think we are?"

"I don't care who you are," he said.

Tired and frustrated, I ignored him and tried to walk by. As I did, he grabbed me and began wrestling me around. Immediately, Billy jumped the guard and threw him off me. Fortunately, someone saw what was happening, came over, explained who we were, and said, "For heaven's sake, let them in."

Billy later told me he was outraged that the guy had grabbed me and acted instinctively when he came to my rescue. As far as he was concerned, "if you attack my partner, you're attacking me." That kind of relationship is a direct by-product of fighting together on the front line in the booth.

When Brent Musburger moved from the studio to courtside and I lost Billy Packer as a partner, CBS gave me a couple of names to choose from for my analyst. At the network level, choices like that are not offered every day. Usually you accept an assignment and hope the chemistry works. In this case, I jumped at the opportunity and made my decision instantly. "Unequivocally, I'd like to work with Doug Collins."

At the time, Doug was at a crossroads in his career. His playing days were behind him and he was torn between coaching and trying broadcasting. While working as an assistant coach at Arizona State, he had done a one- or two-game audition for CBS. The network was high on his potential.

The reasons I opted for Doug were threefold. First, I was familiar with his playing background and his reputation for being a coach's player—someone who was continually study-ing the game. That is exactly the type of knowledgeable indi-vidual you want sitting next to you at courtside. Second, I had met Doug on a couple of occasions and sensed our chemistry was right for each other. Third, both of us lived in the Phoenix area. In all my years at the network level, I had never flown with anyone with whom I worked and it seemed like an excellent arrangement for game preparation.

As it turned out, I could not have made a better choice. Doug began to call me "Chief"—after Hall-of-Fame pitcher Chief Bender—and looked to me for guidance. He was as stu-dious about the broadcasting business as he was about the game of basketball. It was great being able to prepare together flying to a game, then after the game, debriefing each other on the flight home. We played golf together. Our families became close. It was the perfect environment for a working relation-ship to flourish.

And it showed on our broadcasts. A poll in a Denver news-paper rated us the #1 college basketball announcer/analyst team on television. Other papers were saying the same thing. Then CBS Executive Producer Ted Shaker, in all his wisdom, decided to break us up. Why? Because we sounded too much alike. For the 1985 NBA play-offs, Doug was paired with Jim Nantz and I was teamed with Hubie Brown.

My pairing with Billy Packer had worked like a dream from the outset. My teaming with Doug Collins was calculated to be a good match and became one. But, on paper, there seemed no way that the Hubie Brown-Gary Bender marriage would ever work. Talk about "The Odd Couple." How could a streetwise guy from the East ever have anything in common with a Midwestern farm boy? My perception of Hubie Brown was how I saw him as a coach—foul-mouthed, screaming at his players, at the officials, at everyone, almost always in a rage. When we first met, I'm sure we looked at each other as though saying, "Who is this guy?"

Our relationship started on shaky ground. At the first practice we attended, we kept each other at arm's length, with Hubie continually challenging me. The whole preparation process went the same way. There seemed to be nothing but bad chemistry.

However, as soon as we got into the broadcast, everything changed. Hubie realized that I was knowledgeable about the game and was willing to give him the space he needed to work. I learned that, rather than being a crude individual, Hubie was, in many ways, a poet laureate of basketball with a unique way of describing action. We ended up having a terrific time together.

My last game for CBS was with Hubie Brown. After the game, Hubie turned to me and said, "I'll never forget how much you've done for me." That's how far our relationship had evolved.

It takes a mutual effort to make any relationship work. In sportscasting, this can only happen if you invest time with your partner outside the booth. When I first worked with Boston Celtic legend Bill Russell for CBS covering the NBA, I was very intimidated by him and subconsciously kept my distance. One time after making a comment about him, he immediately responded, "You don't know me well enough to say that." Of course, he was right. I had not spent enough time with him to get to know him. I made an extra effort to rectify the problem and, as time passed, Bill began to trust me to the point that I could joke with him about things I hadn't been able to before.

Often the time you invest in getting to know your partner pays dividends beyond the work environment, developing long-lasting friendships. I've never learned more about the game of football than I have from watching tapes and talking with Dick Vermeil. I'm sure he feels the same way about me regarding the broadcasting business. The many hours we've spent together off the air have led to an understanding of each other's likes and dislikes. Moreover, it has spawned a mutual respect for one another that makes our pairing in the booth like a good marriage. We trust each other implicitly.

But sometimes the chemistry just isn't there no matter what effort you make. The combination of Bill Russell, Rick Barry, and Gary Bender was one such marriage that was doomed for the rocks. The year the team covered the NBA was a difficult one at best. Rick and Bill simply didn't get along very well. It got to the point where the two would not spend time together off the air. I would spend time with each individually, but we were never a trio until broadcast time.

The situation reached a head during the 1981 NBA Championship series between the Boston Celtics and the Houston Rockets. It was Larry Bird's first NBA championship, and it was obvious early on that the Celtics would win. It was just a matter of how long it would take. We went into Game Five in Boston, knowing a blowout was a distinct possibility. Our producer, Bob Stenner—one of the best—had prepared for the likelihood by putting together a set of black-and-white photos of Russell and Celtic assistant coach K.C. Jones when they played on the 1956 gold medal Olympic team that competed in Melbourne, Australia.

Late in the game, with the Celtics comfortably in front, Stenner told us in commercial, "We're going to show the Olympic pictures of Bill and K.C. on the other side." None of us had seen the pictures before. They were not of the best quality, showing the two holding what looked like bottles of beer and smiling. When they came on air, Rick saw them first and said, "Look at these pictures. Who are these guys with the watermelon grins?"

I did not hear his comment because I was listening to Stenner, telling me where we were going next. But I was sitting next to Bill and noticed his body language change. He stiffened up, shut down, and quit broadcasting. I tried to get Bill to help us make the difficult blowout interesting, but his participation was minimal.

Afterwards as were walking to the car that would take us back to the hotel, Bill came up to me and said, "Do you know what happened tonight?"

I said, "No. Why did you quit on us?"

"Did you hear what Rick said?"

When I said I hadn't he told me about Rick's watermelon-grin comment. "That's the most racist thing I have ever heard in my life," Bill said. "I refuse to work with Rick again."

The ride back to the hotel was very quiet. When we got there, I pulled Rick aside and asked him why he had made the statement about the watermelon grins.

"What do you mean?" he said.

"Well, it's really upset Bill. He says he won't work with you anymore."

Rick was genuinely surprised and said, "Wait a minute. I didn't mean it as a racial remark. That's a description we used in New Jersey regardless of whether a person was black or white."

"Bill didn't understand it that way," I said and suggested the two should talk to clear the air.

To show how poor their relationship was, instead of sitting down to talk eyeball to eyeball, Rick called Bill and discussed the situation over the house phone. Ten minutes later, Rick tracked me down and said, "It's okay. Everything's taken care of. Don't worry about it. It was just overblown."

The next day before leaving for Houston for Game Six, I went jogging. When I returned to the hotel, a writer stopped me in the lobby and asked, "What do you think of this story?" He held up a paper with a headline suggesting that Rick's watermelon-grin comment had been a racial slur.

Of course, when the papers picked it up, the whole situation became serious for the network. I got calls from CBS executives, wanting to know what really happened. It became so critical that Stenner and I were asked to a meeting with the network brass to decide whether something drastic should be done. Stenner convinced them to defer any decision until after the production meeting before Game Six. Based on how that meeting went, it would be determined whether the team was to be left alone, or whether Bill or Rick would be dropped.

Everything was tense before the production meeting. No one knew what to expect. Then, Bill walked in very animated, not appearing at all to be upset. Rick was equally friendly. There was no evidence that anything out of the ordinary had ever happened. Bob Stenner gave me the high sign and everything proceeded as normal.

However, after the completion of Game Six, when the Celtics took the series four games to two, the Russell-Barry-Bender team never worked together again. The bottom line was, had the chemistry between Bill and Rick been good, had they been able to communicate with one another better, the whole situation would not have occurred.

The previous story also illustrates how difficult it is to work with two analysts. Instead of factoring all the potential problems by two, you now factor them by three. The play-by-play announcer's role becomes more critical as a traffic cop because you have to balance working both individuals into the broadcast. You also have to deal with a three-way chemistry.

On paper, the Russell-Barry team looked like it couldn't miss, but it did. ABC went through a number of combinations to get the right one for the "Monday Night Football" crew. To get the proper mix, it seems you have to pick analysts who are diametrically opposed to one another so their roles don't clash. Look at some of the ones that worked: Billy Packer-Al McGuire; Howard Cosell-Don Meredith; Dan Dierdorff-Frank Gifford. Each pair is almost as north-south as you can get.

Though the chances of success are limited, when the networks put together a team of three that does work, it has a lasting impression on the viewing audience. The really good trios—Al Michaels-Jim Palmer-Tim McCarver, Dick Enberg-Billy Packer-Al McGuire, or the best of the "Monday Night Football" crews—seem to bring more to the broadcast. However, for all the three-man teams that have worked, there is a trail of bodies of those that didn't. You can find my body among them.

My one other experience working as part of a threesome was even worse than the Russell-Barry-Bender troika. Unlike with Bill and Rick where I had a whole season to work to improve the situation, there was no time to rectify the problems facing the team I worked with for the 1988 American League Championship Series. The combination was thrown together as an afterthought. Throughout the summer, the trio of Michaels, Palmer, and McCarver had worked as the #1 baseball team for ABC. Joe Morgan and I were the #2 team. However, when Michaels, Palmer, and McCarver were assigned to do the NLCS, someone thought the announcing team for the other championship series should have equal numbers to achieve proper balance. Enter Reggie Jackson.

When Reggie was teamed with Joe and me, it created an impossible situation that was unfair to all involved. Because he was added at the last moment, Reggie could not be worked in slowly. Where Joe and I had had a summer to develop as a team, Reggie had to charge out of the batter's box.

Reggie is one of the strongest personalities I've ever met. He epitomizes the big-name athlete who has become a great player, in part because of his ego, but who does not have the sensitivity to let go of that ego when working with others. Consequently, Reggie demanded things he hadn't earned the right to demand. He wanted more attention. He insisted we adjust our way of doing things for him. He even made demands of the producer and director.

The whole week went badly. Finally, during the production meeting before the final game of a four-game sweep by the Oakland Athletics over the Boston Red Sox, Reggie confronted me in front of the whole broadcast crew, saying, "I just can't be comfortable with you."

I was floored. I asked him, "What do you mean?"

"Well, anytime I turn to talk to you, you break my concentration."

I said, "I'm sorry. What can I do to change?"

He didn't have an answer.

We continued with the meeting until the point where we started preparing for the opening. We tried an informal walk-through where I turned to Joe, told him how I would lead to him, and he described how he would respond. Then I turned to Reggie to do the same. Reggie froze just as he had been doing during the three previous broadcasts. He couldn't get anything out.

I said, "Am I making you uncomfortable right now?" He didn't say anything, but everybody realized at that moment that he was blaming me because he couldn't pull the trigger.

Whatever working relationship we did have fractured irrevocably during the final game of the ALCS. I was into the wrap-up at the end of an inning, just before going to commercial when Reggie signaled that he had something to add. The countdown was already down to seven or six and he knew I couldn't throw it to him. But he furiously waved his arms for me to do so. As soon as we got to commercial, Reggie ripped his headset off, slammed it down, turned his back on me, and stomped out of the booth.

Joe Morgan talked to me after the series. "I want you to know you did all you could do," he said. "If it's possible, I want to continue to work with you. Bringing Reggie in was the worst decision they ever made. I fought it. I want you to know I thought it was bad going in. It was even worse than I thought."

Working that ALCS was one of the hardest times in my broadcasting career. It is a painful memory because I've always believed I could make everything work, that no situation could not be resolved. However, it did illustrate a maxim I've always believed in: It's all right to have an ego as long as you don't become one. Reggie Jackson's ego is huge and has been detrimental to his career in broadcasting.

In the era of the-analyst-as-headliner, the good play-by-play announcer has to be particularly aware of ego. Announcers have to suppress the desire to be center stage, while setting their partners up for all the good lines. Announcers have to be like game officials: The only officials who are remembered are those who are embroiled in controversy; the good ones are conspicuous by their absence.

# CHAPTER TWELVE

# *Working with the Broadcast Crew*

*I*n the broadcasting business, the play-by-play announcer and the analyst are commonly referred to as "the talent." Since they are the only ones visible to the public, they often reap the glory or weather the criticism for a sportscast. However, it takes more than on-air talent to broadcast a sporting event. It takes an invisible team of professionals who are rarely recognized other than when the credits roll at the end of a game.

A televised sportscast originates from a box-like truck generally located on the outskirts of a stadium, far from the action. Linked by tentacles of wire to all the on-site sensory equipment that capture the sights and sounds of an event, the truck is a broadcast brain that screens input, chooses the best pictures and sounds, then passes them along the airwaves to the viewing audience. To the outsider, the activity in the truck during a broadcast may seem like the site of a train wreck with yelling, screaming, and apparent mass confusion. To the professional, it is the language of the instant communication necessary to capture instantaneous moments for the viewer.

The broadcast runs like a superbly conditioned machine only when all the body parts work in coordination with each other. Consequently, the play-by-play announcer must understand the function of the other broadcast team members and how to interact with each.

## The Producer

At the network level, the overall boss for a broadcast is the producer. Producers are responsible for planning all the elements of a broadcast and seeing that every detail of the plan is implemented. Since they control every segment of the telecast—what replays are run, when time-outs are taken, when promos are run—they have to be coordinators deluxe with almost omniscient awareness. When any issue arises before or during the broadcast, producers have the final say.

Producers give the sportscast its viewpoint, its flavor. The best producers are master painters, Picassos or Rembrandts: The mechanics of their profession—the hows and whens to use different brush strokes—are second nature to them so they are able to rise to another level, combining the individual strokes to create a masterpiece that interprets the world in a unique way. The best producers have the mechanics of the broadcast down cold so they are free to develop a storyline, using the talents of the broadcast crew as their brushes.

Good producers have three common characteristics: (1) they are organized; (2) they are cool under pressure; and (3) they respect and support the broadcast team working with them.

One of the best producers I worked with at CBS was Bob Stenner. Stenner was the most organized person I have ever been around. Even his briefcase had the Good Housekeeping Seal. He was always on top of everything. He had the ability to make you feel like the astronauts must feel just before lift off—everything that should have been done, has been done. Just before air time, you felt the greatest confidence in the world that every "t" had been crossed and every "i" dotted, and you were ready to pounce on the broadcast.

The fact that Stenner was so well-prepared was probably why he never lost his cool under pressure. In fact, I can't remember many crisis situations arising where he even had the opportunity to lose his cool. Everything ran smoothly when he was in charge.

But sometimes events don't always go as planned. Ned Simon had every right to lose his cool while covering the speed-skating venue for ABC at the Calgary Olympics in 1988. With the rapidly unfolding ordeal of Dan Jansen and the death of his sister, the remarkable efforts of Bonnie Blair, and the controversies surrounding the East Germans, it seemed every time you turned around there was a new story breaking. When you spend three or four weeks together at the same venue, you get to know a person's strengths and weaknesses. I found Ned to be one of the most stable and pleasant people I've ever worked with. Regardless of the next surprise, Ned was flexible enough to change directions when the circumstances required without having a nervous breakdown.

Of all the characteristics a good producer should have, respect and support of the broadcast team has to rank as the most important. One of the reasons Bob Stenner was so tremendously popular with everybody was that he knew everyone on a first-name basis. The on-air talent especially appreciated that he was interested enough in the issues surrounding a game to sit in on our tape sessions and our interviews with the players and coaches. There wasn't anyone who didn't respect him.

One of the ways a producer can help support the rest of the broadcast team is by acting as an additional set of eyes and ears for everybody during the telecast. In the truck, the producer helps the director by reviewing and selecting the replays to be aired and suggesting shots the director might miss by being engrossed elsewhere. After a touchdown by the halfback on an off-tackle run, the producer might suggest something like, "Let's run this sequence: run tape X (of halfback scoring from the end-zone camera), then tape Y (of the isolation on the offensive tackle blocking), followed by a closeup of the coach from [camera] 5." The director will then implement the sequence.

Good producers help the play-by-play announcer by acting as a Jiminy Cricket, offering helpful ideas in your ear. On a sidelines shot of the coach, the producer might say, "Don't forget to mention he took his wife fishing after the game last week," or "Remember, if they win today, this will be his 100th victory."

Also like Jiminy Cricket, producers act as a conscience for the on-air talent. If someone inadvertently says "Don" Landry rather than "Tom" Landry, the producer will say in the talent's ear, "I think you just said 'Don' Landry," thus allowing the

announcer or the analyst the opportunity to correct themselves on the air. Though the writers tend to disagree, it is the
feeling of those in the business that an errant call is not a
mistake if you go back and correct it on air.

Some producers communicate over the talk-back system
more than others. Some even interrupt the announcer in the
middle of expressing a thought on air. Announcers have to
learn to fight through the distraction and recognize they can't
react to all the suggestions made. They have to use their own
judgment regarding what should or should not be aired.

For the announcer, the most aggravating producers are the
ones who are doing a different game than the one you are calling. While you are in the middle of developing a particular
story, they may all of a sudden want you to read a promo on air
or cut to a replay that has nothing to do with what you're saying, thus destroying your rhythm. This situation often stems
from the fact the producer does not know the emotion of the
moment.

I once worked with a producer who had never done
football before. Every time a replay was run, it was never from
an angle that best showed what had happened. There were six
monitors in the truck, four hooked for replay. It turned out that
when the video tapes were reracked to be previewed on the
four replay monitors, the producer was unable to orient himself regarding the four angles shown. He simply could not figure out what he was seeing. It was so bad, the director had to
take over, essentially becoming both producer and director.

When shots appear on the monitor that don't correspond
to what you are saying or when the coordination of the broadcast begins to break down, the announcer and the analyst can
only look at each other and shake their heads. They know the
producer probably doesn't know beans about the sport or is
new to producing. In such cases, you almost expect the worst.
You have to discipline yourself to remain focused, to keep from
being dragged down emotionally by the negative atmosphere.

Producers who admit up front that they haven't worked a
sport are a different story. I worked with a producer who told
me early in the week before the broadcast, "I really don't know
basketball that well." Because of his candidness, I knocked
myself out to make it easier for him, letting him lean on me for

guidance throughout the game. During commercial he would ask, "Gary, what do you think we should do?"

"Well, the big factor in the game right now is that Kentucky isn't hitting from outside. They're only four of 14 from three-point range. Let's come out with a graphic on it."

When the crew openly recognizes each other's strengths and weaknesses, an atmosphere of cooperation is established that leads to the best broadcast possible.

When they *do* know the sport they are covering, producers can lead *you*, really get your wheels moving. I particularly appreciated working with Kenny Wolfe, the lead producer for college basketball at ABC. Since he played basketball in college at Harvard, he knows the game and loves the sport as much as any fan. Consequently, you respect the ideas he expresses during production meetings and the suggestions he makes during the game. He is a low-key individual who doesn't say much, but when he does speak, you listen. He knows how to make a basketball game come alive.

Good producers like Kenny are on the same wavelength as the talent in the booth. They know the story lines you plan to develop, even do much of the same preparation you do. They listen to what is being said on air and try to reinforce it with visuals or graphics. They anticipate situations and challenge you, raising your play-by-play commentary to another level. They know the proper time to suggest, "Hey, Gary. Wouldn't this be a good time to talk about Bobby Knight's chair-tossing incident?"

Sometimes there is a fine line between helpful suggestions and overproduction. The line is violated when producers force their ideas instead of complementing the efforts of the broadcast team. As in all walks of life, the broadcasting business has team players and individuals who think their way is the only way.

On the Thursday before the opening broadcast of the college football season, the producer I was teamed with that year sat down with me one-on-one and asked me to change my style: "I want you to say things with more impact, be more dramatic, say less."

This producer was one of the most creative people I've been around—but you paid a price to be a part of his creations.

He was very emotional, a noted screamer. Working with him drained you.

I don't know why—maybe I was trying to avoid the inevitable emotional confrontation—but I agreed to try his idea. During the broadcast, I said very little and, when I did say something, I said it with a solid, gutsy delivery. The producer thought I was great. I came out of the game feeling uncomfortable and thoroughly confused. I didn't like how I sounded. I talked to friends who had seen the broadcast and they had wondered what was wrong with me.

The change in style turned out to be a one-game experiment. I realized the producer's suggestion was equivalent to Pat Riley telling Patrick Ewing to change his shooting style just before the NBA play-offs. My style was a product of years of development and had served me well. Any attempt to modify it at this stage was not going to be beneficial.

At some point in their careers, all play-by-play announcers will have to contend with a strong-willed producer. Be aware of the danger signs when strong personalities are involved. Trust your own instincts. Believe in yourself.

We've talked about the things the producer does that affect the play-by-play announcer. What about vice versa?

If you want to get a producer down on you in a hurry try missing a countdown to commercial, leading to the wrong sound bite, or leading to the wrong replay during the halftime highlights.

Some years back, CBS used to do what they called a "whip around" where they went from game site to game site in order to set the stage for each of the NFL games they were covering that day. When the whip around reached one location, the producer cued the play-by-play announcer. The announcer looked into the camera, but didn't say anything. The producer cued him again. Again, the announcer remained frozen. Afterwards, the irate producer said, "That guy just put the whole world on hold."

Though you may be absolutely riveting in your call of the game, fail producers with any frequency and their trust level in you disintegrates. It's like borrowing a friend's new car and returning it with the front end smashed in. Would your friend ever loan you his car again? And remember the producer is the person in authority on site. At the network level, all the producers return to New York after a broadcast, meet with senior producers and the executive producer, and debrief each other regarding the problems that occurred that week. Normally, the loyalty of the broadcast team extends to these meetings. But give a producer a reason to lose confidence in you and it can be detrimental to your career.

## The Director

While the producer gives the broadcast its overall view, it is the director who implements the view mechanically. Directors are responsible for positioning the camera crew and calling the shots: "(Camera) 1, give me the coach. Take 1." What ultimately makes the air is the decision of the director.

During the telecast, the director is the second in command. However, depending on their working relationship, the director may have a stronger hand in the story-development process than the producer. In fact, it used to be in some cases that the director was above the producer in the network pecking order.

When I first came to CBS, there were two or three directors who ran the show. One was the most powerful director I've worked with—Tony Verna, the man who initiated instant replay. Tony was a legend in his own time. He was a big-timer, a large, suave, sophisticated guy who impressed everyone and knew it. Tony may have had a big ego, but he also knew his job. He received so much press regarding his broadcasts, he could get away with almost anything. He developed so much clout at the network that when a game was running long and he had a plane to catch, he would simply say, "I'm leaving for the airport. See you next week." Bob Stenner would then have to step in and produce and direct the final three or four minutes of a game.

Since the buttoned-down Stenner was the buffer for the team in the booth, working with Tony was fun. He was always telling stories and kidding around with us. I once worked a game with Pistol Pete Maravich in Oakland between the Golden State Warriors and the Los Angeles Lakers that turned into a blowout early. The Lakers weren't very good because they had traded practically their whole franchise to Milwaukee to get Kareem Abdul-Jabbar. During commercial, Tony would say, "What a rotten game. Come on, you guys. Make this sound interesting. I'm getting bored. I'm about to go to sleep here in the truck."

Today the interaction with the director is significantly less. Most directors are very low key and too busy to talk. If they talk with the talent, it is to ask a question during commercial break. A majority of the communication from the truck comes from the producer.

Though producers are more likely to place their stamp on a broadcast in their development of story line, directors can also leave their signature. Some directors are identifiable by their use of extreme closeups, frequent crowd reaction shots, or a set replay sequence after a touchdown or a home run. Their style becomes a trademark.

Knowing a sport is a key for the director. The best directors can slide in and out of the different sports, adjusting to the unique rhythm of each, with no discernible degradation in the televised product. The hardest sport to master is baseball. Though there are many more moments of inactivity, when things *do* start happening, there is no way to capture the action with just one camera. Take a line shot to the gap in right center with the bases loaded. The director has to catch the swing, the fielder chasing the ball, the runners circling the bases, the fielder's throw, the runner rounding third, the relay, and the play at the plate. Everything is bang, bang, bang. Some directors can't measure up to the murderous instant decision-making required. That's why those who are good at baseball, like the great Harry Coyle of NBC, tend to stick with it exclusively.

One of the best directors in the business is Bob Fishman at CBS. Besides being knowledgeable about the sports he covers, Bob is also extremely quick. He not only has the ability to cram more production techniques (replays, still frames, crowd shots, etc.) in a space of time than anyone else, but it all makes perfect sense when viewed. I have no idea how he does it.

When Lorenzo Charles made "the shot heard around the world" in North Carolina State's upset of Houston in the 1983 NCAA championship game, Fishman captured all the excitement on camera. He cut from shots of Wolfpack players hugging each other, to the dismayed Houston players pounding the floor, to Jim Valvano running through the mass of people on the court, trying to find somebody to hug. With each new picture on the monitor, he would tell me "Isn't this unbelievable. Isn't this unbelievable." The smartest thing I could do was to lay out and let his shot selection tell the story.

Good directors like Bob Fishman are so skilled at their job they develop a rhythm, a pace when cutting from one camera to another. When the play-by-play announcer's call of the game is synchronized to the director's rhythm, everything runs like clockwork. The problem comes when the two fall out of sync.

The most disconcerting thing a director can do to the on-air talent is to continually throw pictures onto the monitor that have nothing to do with what is happening on the field. Say the fullback takes the hand-off and barrels up the middle for 25 yards, dragging tacklers all the way. It's a spectacular effort and you're all geared up to talk about the player who accomplished it. However, as you begin talking, the picture suddenly cuts to the quarterback. The announcer or the analyst is stuck with either talking about someone who is not on camera—a no-no in many schools of tv sportscasting—or delivering a non sequitur that makes them look like they didn't recognize the significance of what just happened.

Detroit Tiger announcer Rick Rizzs once worked with a director who liked to follow a batter all the way back to the dugout after making an out. Rick said it was really frustrating. "Here you are ready to talk about the man who's coming to bat, the guy who has the potential to decide the game, and the camera is still on the guy who has just failed. He's done. He's not going to win it for you."

The best way to prevent problems between the on-air talent and the director is through communication. When the play-by-play announcer and the analyst make the director aware of the material they have developed on certain players or coaches or of the key match-ups that are liable to take place, the director has a chance to look for shots that support the call of the game rather than shooting from the hip.

When I worked with Bob Fishman, I would occasionally hear him say in my headset, "Gary, look at this." Then he'd cut to a picture, challenging me to put a caption to it. I wasn't surprised, however. He knew the material I had prepared, found a shot that was right for it, and let me take it from there. Nothing more needed to be said.

There is little opportunity for the pictures to be in sync with the words if the director isn't listening. While some can do their job just by watching the monitors, the good directors will listen to what's being said in the booth.

Of course, if the director hears "I sure hope the guys in the truck got that" or "we should have that on replay in a moment," then all bets are off.

When John Madden was first starting in the business, he had a habit of innocently saying something like, "Boy, what a great play! I can't wait to see the replay."

Then on one occasion, someone came back on the headset and said, "John, we don't have that."

John learned quickly that the talent in the booth does not produce or direct on air. As soon as you do, you not only create the potential for embarrassing yourself, but also the people in the truck. And if you want to maintain a good working relationship with the broadcast crew, you don't embarrass the people in the truck.

## The Support Crew in the Booth

In football, there are three people who provide direct support to the play-by-play announcer and the analyst in the booth: the spotter, the statistician, and the stage manager. With the exception of the stage manager who is located directly behind the on-air talent, the arrangement of people in the booth varies. In most situations, the statistician is to the left of the announcer and the analyst to the right. The wild card is the spotter. When the analyst needs help in spotting, the spotter sits offset between the announcer and the analyst so their view of each other isn't blocked. If analysts prefer to do their own spotting, the spotter sits to the immediate left of the announcer with the statistician to the far left.

Since baseball, basketball, hockey, soccer, and tennis have few people in action at any given time, the play-by-play announcer and the analyst don't need help identifying players.

In up-tempo sports such as basketball and hockey, the statistician may act as a spotter on occasions when there is a close call, such as identifying who made a tip-in or committed a foul. Even then, the announcer may hold the call in reserve until seeing the replay. Only golf and football require spotters. Why? Golfers don't wear numbers and during every football play there are 22 people in action at once. In fact, spotters are so essential to football, sometimes two are used (especially for college games), one for each team.

The spotter's function is very basic: make identifications of players involved in the action and pass on the information to the on-air talent. Spotters have to convey confidence and decisiveness in their communications, without being distracting. This is not as easy as it seems.

To begin with, a good spotter has to have a sense of the game. You cannot take the average individual off the street and make him or her a spotter. It takes more than reading numbers through binoculars. Spotters must know the sport well enough to anticipate what might happen. For example, good spotters would not identify the tackler as the first man off the top of the pile. They would follow the play and know who was at the bottom of the pile, the man who made the initial contact.

Second, spotters have to know the players as well if not better than the play-by-play announcer and the analyst. Some spotters develop their own additional spotting boards. One spotter I worked with designed a set of boards for each special-teams unit, so that during a kickoff he was able to slap down a card and point immediately to the returner.

Since I know my spotting boards so well and rely on them, I prefer the spotters I work with to be as familiar with player placement on them as I am. There isn't enough time to make recognition of a player on the field, hunt for the player on the boards, then point him out to me. The process is even more critical on plays requiring several spotting identifications. Consequently, spotters frequently take my boards, copy them, then study them the night before the game. They know the day of the game is too late.

In order for spotters to communicate their information to the on-air talent in a timely and unobtrusive manner, a system of hand signals has to be devised. The actual signals used differ from broadcast team to broadcast team. For example, a doubled fist might mean a good block, hunching forward as if hugging an invisible ball might mean a fumble recovery, or walking your fingers away from a player on the spotting board might indicate who blitzed. Some spotters even bring a towel with them and toss it in the air when a flag is thrown.

After spotters make their identifications, they must also communicate them in the proper sequence. If spotters hear the play-by-play announcer mention the ball carrier, they must automatically move down a priority list established beforehand, noting who made the tackle, who made the block, or someone who wasn't directly involved in the tackle, but made a good play.

Though it is a requirement of the spotter's job to provide the needed identification quickly, the play-by-play announcer has to be careful about adding to that pressure. If the announcer says, "Metcalf carries for four yards. Tackle by . . ." then frantically points at the spotting board for the answer, the spotter is placed in a do-or-die situation. Continue applying pressure like that and you will likely affect your spotter's performance. Instead, learn to talk around the missing information until the spotter has it.

At the network level, announcing teams usually work with the same spotters throughout the season. Before the first game, play-by-play announcers must define their signals and state their expectations. Refinements might be made during the first few games, but they are rarely necessary as the season progresses. However, in the cases where announcers work with different spotters every game, sufficient time should be set aside before the game to go through everything. Once the broadcast starts, there will be no time for voice communication other than during commercial breaks.

The most important requirement of a spotter is to be accurate. A good spotter is like a good referee: call a controversy-free game and nobody notices you; make a mistake and everyone jumps on your back. All spotters have to do to shake an announcer's confidence in them is to identify a player on a long run or a long pass and, thirty yards later, change the identification. If an announcer begins distrusting or second-guessing the spotter, it's all over. Consequently, spotters must have the courage of their convictions.

In 1969, I had the opportunity to work as the spotter for Jim Simpson and Al Derogattis during NBC's coverage of the Orange Bowl. The contest is still remembered for its ending. With the game on the line, Penn State tried a two-point conversion and failed. However, Kansas was penalized for having 12 men on the field. With a second chance, Penn State scored and won the game.

What few people know is that Kansas got away with having 12 men on the field five snaps earlier. I had covered the Jayhawks all year and knew the team inside out. I immediately knew there was something wrong because there were two players who played the same position standing in the same area. I assumed there had to be an extra man on the field.

However, I didn't say anything. Why? First, I was intimidated by the network people, Simpson, in particular. Second, spotting was something I didn't do all the time, and I doubted my ability. Finally, I didn't think they would even listen to me since they didn't know me well enough to take a chance on my being right. When the game ended as it did with the same thing happening again, I kicked myself for my silence. What an insight I could have given the broadcast if I had had the courage of my convictions.

I've had spotters who were terrific for two quarters; then, because the game went south, they got tired, or the cold got to them, their concentration would lapse. They wouldn't be as sharp, wouldn't get information to me fast enough. When spotters start dropping things, knocking binoculars to the floor, or forgetting to flip spotting boards to the right team, you can tell they're struggling. In such instances, you have to be both encouraging and forcefully direct to the person about what is happening and what needs to happen. Again, you only have commercial breaks to remedy any unsatisfactory situation.

If I were to grade the spotters I have worked with in the past, they would typically rate either A or D. There are no average spotters. This makes sense when you think about it. If spotters are slow or inaccurate, the announcer is almost better off ignoring their input rather than risking making a mistake on air. Their usefulness is negligible. However, if spotters do their job, they are an invaluable extra set of eyes.

The information a statistician provides can be equally invaluable. In fact, I am so bad at math, a good statistician is a necessity for me. During a football game, I am constantly relying on the stats person to tell me how far a play covered, because I have trouble making the calculation mentally if the play went for a lengthy distance.

Good stats people must be accurate in their gathering of information, be capable of analyzing that information and picking out facts that are significant, and have the type of personality to be cool under fire. It's easy to keep score at home. It's a different matter when the information you're tracking is needed by others at a moment's notice. Basketball is particularly murderous. The pace of the action is often so frenetic, there literally isn't enough time to catch your breath. And once statisticians start missing things, it snowballs. Sooner or later they will give the play-by-play announcer or the people in the truck who build graphics inaccurate data.

To be useful to the on-air talent, good stats people also have to listen to what is being said. By doing so, they will be in a position to supply the talent with information that enhances their comments. When Dick Vitale says, "I can't believe how poorly the Tar Heels are shooting" and the statistician immediately slips him a piece of paper with "34%" on it, the stats person makes Vitale look like he's on top of the game.

Because statisticians serve two masters, they have to guard against distraction. I've had stats people so involved with talking to production assistants responsible for graphics, I've had to tug on their sleeves or write notes to ask for things that should have been anticipated.

I've also experienced stats people who inundate you with information. All the notes flying at you can be disconcerting. In such cases, you have to make editorial judgments regarding what to use.

This leads to a major issue—what is the difference between a good stat and a bad one? In today's world of computers, any type of statistic you can imagine can be produced in the blink of an eye. In fact, at the professional and collegiate levels, the amount of statistical information at the announcer's disposal is, at times, so overwhelming, you can easily end up using stats for stats' sake. As soon as that happens, you're in trouble because you've forgotten what's important to the fan—the game.

Like good play-by-play announcers, good stats people have to keep an overall perspective to the game. The conclusions derived from their record keeping should help tell the story. They should be significant, substantiating trends the viewer sees in the action.

The best illustration of a good stat I can think of occurred in CBS' coverage of the 1991 NCAA basketball championship game. It was a ragged contest because both teams were obviously fatigued from their semifinal victories—for Kansas an unexpected win over North Carolina and for Duke an incredible upset of number one UNLV. Throughout the contest, both coaches substituted freely, especially Duke's Mike Krzyzewski when it came to resting the Blue Devil's key big man, Christian Laettner. Then, during a free throw in the final ten minutes, Billy Packer said, "Mike Swanson, our outstanding stat man, just pointed out something that looks like the theory Mike Krzyzewski is using. He's taking Laettner out a minute and ten seconds before he thinks the next tv time-out's coming, so he can use that minute plus the tv minute to really get a long blow for Laettner." That single stat captured how important fatigue was to Krzyzewski's game plan. Duke won 72–65.

A few seconds after airing Swanson's observation, Billy chuckled and said, "Mike must have a computer in his head over there." I agree. Mike Swanson, who has worked the Final Four for many years, is the best stats man I've ever had. He has the ability to weed out the mundane in search of the enlightening jewel. If it comes from Mike, there is no question it should be used on the air.

The weakest link in network television is the stage manager. Some producers and directors have the same stage manager week after week, but in most cases, stage managers seldom travel and are hired on site. They are often friends of someone and do not cost very much. The attitude toward filling the position seems to be "You want a job? Nobody's doing stage managing. How about that?"

A stage manager has four basic responsibilities: (1) cater to the needs of the booth personnel whether it be water or heat; (2) keep unauthorized personnel out of the booth; (3) act as a liaison between the talent and the technicians when resolving problems that occur during a broadcast; and (4) hand the appropriate promotional cards to the play-by-play announcer when they are to be read on air.

Good stage managers are out to protect the booth personnel and are efficient in doing so. If the announcer or the analyst likes Evian water or Diet Coke, they see to it that there is an ample supply on hand. They have runners to get sandwiches or other needs. On cold days, they make sure there are enough heaters. When the telestrator goes on the fritz during the broadcast, they coordinate with the technicians to get the problem fixed as quickly as possible.

On the surface it would seem that the stage manager is little more than a gofer. However, there are four or five times during the broadcast when a stage manager can mean all the difference to the announcer.

Let's say the producer determines that the next commercial break will be a local station break. He tells the associate producer and the associate producer tells the stage manager, "At the next break, hand Gary the local station break ID card." Unfortunately the stage manager gets confused, for whatever reason, and doesn't hand me the card. On the countdown to break, I ad-lib a generic lead instead. All those station engineers from Toledo to Boise are waiting to run their local commercial tapes, but don't get the proper cue to do so. The result can be dead air and irate calls at the network from station managers across the country.

Similar scenarios to the one just described have happened to every announcer in the business. It's even happened to the Enbergs, the Michaels, and the Summeralls. No wonder play-by-play announcers often look at the stage manager with a paranoid glare as if to say, "Are you sure?"

If there were more time to work with stage managers beforehand, to establish trust, to help them develop confidence in handling their job, then a lot of the problems would be eliminated. Unfortunately, the way the networks operate now, what you see is what you get.

On the other hand, not every stage manager is an accident waiting to happen. One stage manager researched all our likes beforehand, knew our drink preferences and where we wanted our headsets. She even found out I like M&Ms. When I got to the booth, there was a cupful of M&Ms at my position. That kind of attention to detail instills trust.

## The Support Crew in the Truck

There are some support personnel the play-by-play announcer never interacts with. In fact, they may not even be wired to the announcer:

*Video replay engineers* are the advance men for the producer. They monitor the replay equipment, watching for moments that should be aired. If Ric LaCivita is producing a baseball game, the video replay engineer might say, "Hey, Ric! I've got something for you on X." When they roll the tape on X, they see an emery board sticking out of the pitcher's back pocket. Ric would say, "Oh, my gosh! That's great!" then tell the talent in the booth, "Okay, guys. At the first opportunity, we've got something you won't believe."

The *video engineer* is responsible for making sure the pictures transmitted have the correct shading and color—a difficult task when you're covering a game in the late afternoon and the stadium's shadow begins to wash across the otherwise sunlit field.

The *switcher* is the director's right-hand man. On the director's command, the switcher physically throws the levers that switch the picture from camera to camera, overlays the graphics to the picture, or creates dissolves and other visual special effects.

*Chyron operators* run the graphics generator. They work under the direct supervision of production assistants, keying in information PAs want displayed graphically on air.

The rest of the support crew in the truck interact with the play-by-play announcer in varying degrees:

The *associate producer*—the producer's alter ego—fills in the cracks, covering the areas the producer can't attend to. Associate producers are in constant contact with central control in the network studio, advising the producer what the network wants. They make sure commercials are racked in the proper order and ready to roll. As mentioned before, they are wired to the stage manager and trigger the handing of promo cards to the play-by-play announcer.

The announcer works with the associate producer mostly before game day. Since associate producers usually want to become producers one day, they try to learn as much as possible, taking all the initiative they can in the planning and organization of the telecast. Many times in the preparation process, it is the associate producer not the producer who works with the talent. Most frequently, this involves supplying information that needs support from tape. Associate producers are the ones responsible for putting together the tape packages.

*Production assistants* are the entry level positions of the sportscasting business. They are truly glorified gofers—but with a lot of responsibility. They do everything from picking up everyone at the airport on their arrival and making sure everyone's escape route after the game is well planned, to paying the people who were hired locally to assist in the broadcast.

PAs are energetic and eager to please. Once, after a Friday night production meeting before a Saturday game at Husky Stadium in Seattle, I handed a sealed envelope with a name on it to a new PA and told him, "Please leave these tickets at Will Call."

Though he looked at me kind of puzzled, he said, "Sure," and took off.

As Dick Vermeil and I were leaving the stadium to go back to the hotel, the PA furiously waved his arms for us to stop the car. I rolled down the window to see what was the problem. He said, "Is that 'Mr.' or 'Mrs.' Will Call?"

The reason PAs are so eager to please is that they want to be future producers or directors. They welcome any help the play-by-play announcer can give them. As mentioned earlier, this usually occurs in the form of providing them information that can be represented graphically.

*Audio technicians* are very important to the play-by-play announcer. The sound technician sits alone behind glass in the truck, not only providing the mix the viewer hears on air, but also the mix the talent hears in their headsets. Sometimes the mix can include so much crowd noise, you cannot hear yourself or the analyst. On the other hand, not having any mix at all is equally disconcerting, because, without it, you lose touch with the emotion surrounding the game.

Invariably, no matter how many times you check out your headset beforehand, some adjustment is required once the game starts. Billy Packer has a theory why this happens. He showed me one time by taking three sugar packets and lining them in a row on the table. "Now, the sound people know the three packets have to be in line for everything to work right," said Billy. "So they move this middle one just a little out of kilter. Everybody starts yelling and screaming for their help and expertise. Since they already know how to fix the situation, they do it quickly. They're heroes. They just want you to know they're around."

The fact is there is no way to approximate the crowd's sound level before the game. The sound from an empty Michigan Stadium is considerably different from when it's filled with 100,000 screaming fans. And those fans aren't screaming all the time. The noise level is measurably lower when the Wolverines trail Ohio State by 21 points than when they score a touchdown to take the lead.

One of the best sound people I've worked with is Bob Siderman at CBS. At the first commercial, he would always come in my ear checking, "Hey, Gary. How's the sound out there? You okay?" I might tell him that I could barely hear Bob Stenner, our producer. He would respond, "Let me try this." Siderman epitomized what you value from the support crew: someone who gives instant attention to problems so the broadcast runs as smoothly as possible.

## The Camera Crew

The unsung heroes of any televised sportscast are the people who operate the cameras. If they don't capture the pictures, you might as well be doing radio.

There used to be a cameraman at CBS who was so skilled he developed a reputation for being able to follow a punted football in closeup. Others have reputations for following field action, still others for being good with the hand-held camera. Producers and directors fight for people with these skills. At the network level, producers bid for the camera operators they want the week before a game. They want the best because it makes their job so much easier.

The simplest way to illustrate the importance of the camera operator is in the example of capturing an appeal on a checked swing in baseball. If the camera operator waits for the director's cue to swing to the umpire, two things can happen: the director calls for the camera and gets a whip pan as the camera sweeps across the field; or the director gets a great picture of the umpire with his hands already back in his pocket after his signal. Unless the camera operator is on top of the game and reacts automatically to catch a moment, that moment is gone.

This is where the play-by-play announcer can really help. The camera crew isn't wired to the announcer, but you are wired to them. If they're good, they listen to everything you say. A simple "It's a checked swing" or "Did he go around?" can alert them to take instantaneous action. It's all a part of the teamwork required to broadcast sports.

# CHAPTER THIRTEEN

# *Radio Versus TV*

$U$p to this point, everything we've talked about has been directed at doing play-by-play on television. So how is calling the game different for radio? The answer should be obvious.

In television, the picture tells the story. If a fullback powers 20 yards for the winning touchdown in the final seconds of play after nearly being downed three times and dragging tacklers with him over the goal line, anything the announcer says to try to describe the moment will be superfluous. The viewers see with their own eyes the incredible effort that is required to accomplish the feat. They hear the explosion of noise as they watch the crowd respond. All the play-by-play announcer can do is make sure the audience was aware of the game situation beforehand, help identify the participants during and after the play, and possibly underscore the magnitude of the run afterwards, putting it into perspective.

In radio, the picture that listeners "see" in their imagination totally depends on the verbal imagery painted by the play-by-play announcer. Without the announcer's words, the listener is blind.

Consequently, radio play-by-play announcers can hold considerable power over their audiences. But, in order to wield that power, they have to fulfill certain obligations.

The cardinal rule for radio announcers is take nothing for granted. If television viewers lose their sound, they can still watch a game and tell what's going on with reasonable accuracy. Graphics provide score, player identification, the down and distance, balls and strikes, outs, the number of fouls, you name it. Even without graphics, knowledgeable viewers can make their own player identification, track all the game's measurements, and keep on top of what is happening by simply watching the screen. But the radio listener knows nothing unless the announcer says it.

Given this maxim, setting the situation becomes paramount for radio play-by-play. A tv announcer can conceivably forget to give the down and distance or the count on occasion because graphics on the screen will orient the viewer accordingly. On radio, the announcer has to set the situation before each play or risk confusing the audience. Remember, many people listen to radio while doing something else; washing the car, ironing, jogging, driving to the airport. Usually their concentration on the game is secondary to the activity they're engaged in. As their concentration fades in and out, they lose track of what's happening.

One of the easiest ways to reorient the radio audience is to mention the score. Like a number of announcers, I used to bring an egg timer with me to the booth to ensure mentioning the score at least once every three minutes. There is no set standard for how often to state the score, however. If there is a rule of thumb, it is err on the side of too much rather than not enough since the score can never be mentioned too often.

Setting the situation is also important in developing the audience's sense of anticipation. Television viewers set their own sense of anticipation by simply watching. When they see Roger Clemens start his windup or Ken Griffey, Jr., cock his bat or Joe Montana set up under center or Kevin Johnson drive the baseline, the viewer is prepared for something to happen. If radio announcers can create that same sense of anticipation in their call of the game, the audience will hang on every word. It can be as simple as Harry Carey's "Here's the windup . . . the pitch" to Vin Scully's eloquent word pictures: "Sandy backs off . . . mops his forehead . . . runs his left index finger along his forehead . . . dries it off on his left pants leg." Each readies the audience for action.

Since the play-by-play announcer is the radio listener's eyes, everything said over the air should be as descriptive as possible. Any announcer can say, "Kevin Johnson brings the

I began my network career with CBS in 1975, covering the NFL.

One of my early assignments at KWBW radio was covering Hutchinson Community Junior College basketball games. The Blue Dragons' head coach (to my right) was NJCAA Basketball Hall-of-Famer Sam Butterfield and his assistant Gene Keady, later head coach at Purdue University.

I was John Madden's first full-time partner with CBS. With his effervescent personality and knowledge of the game, it was readily apparent that he could become one of the best football analysts in broadcasting.

From 1987 to 1992, I worked for ABC covering college football and basketball, major league baseball, the 1988 Olympics, and numerous "Wide World of Sports" events.

Tension anyone: Rick Barry, Bill Russell and myself during CBS's coverage of the 1981 NBA finals.

I worked my second Final Four for CBS in 1983. Here I am at courtside prior to the Houston-North Carolina State championship game, featuring Lorenzo Charles's "shot heard around the world."

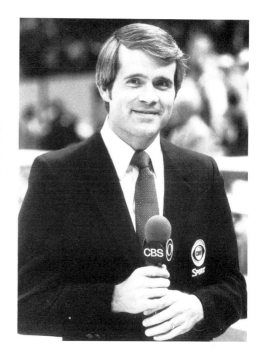

In my first year at the network level, it was a real honor to work with Johnny Unitas, a football legend, covering the 1975 "Hail Mary" play-off game between the Dallas Cowboys and the Minnesota Vikings at Metropolitan Stadium, in Bloomington, Minnesota.

The NFL announcers for my first year at CBS included (left to right, top to bottom): Sonny Jurgensen, Johnny Unitas, Johnny Morris, yours truly, Alex Hawkins, Lindsey Nelson, Al Michaels, Paul Hornung, and Hank Stram.

I was enjoying myself along the sidelines during Super Bowl X between the Dallas Cowboys and the Pittsburgh Steelers when I learned I would conduct the post-game interview from the loser's locker room.

In the mid-1980s I was teamed with Hall of Fame quarterback Sonny Jurgenson, now a radio analyst for the Washington Redskins.

In 1985 I had the unique opportunity to choose Doug Collins (far left next to then Michigan coach Bill Frieder and University of Alabama-Birmingham coach Gene Bartow) as my broadcasting partner for CBS's college basketball coverage. He has since become one of the game's best color analysts and I was fortunate to be teamed with him again at TNT.

A reunion of five former voices of the Kansas University Jayhawks who later climbed the ladder of broadcasting success: (left to right) Tom Hedrick (Kansas City Chiefs, Cincinnati Reds, and the Texas Rangers); myself, Monte Moore (Kansas City/Oakland A's), Merle Harmon (Kansas City A's, Milwaukee Brewers, and Texas Rangers), and Bill Grigsby (Kansas City A's and Kansas City Chiefs).

Before a 1979 pre-season game in the Astrodome, I interviewed Philadelphia Eagle head coach Dick Vermeil (middle) and his assistant Marian Campbell. Dick led the Eagles to the Super Bowl that year and eight years later would become my partner in the booth at ABC.

After retiring as a player with the Los Angeles Rams, Fred Dryer worked one year as a color analyst for CBS. During the year we were teamed together, Fred spent much of his off-hours taking acting lessons from actress Nina Foch. The next year he jumped to NBC to star in his own detective series, "Hunter."

Later my partner at TNT covering the NFL, Pat Haden was first teamed with me at CBS in the early '80s, covering college football.

The 1982 CBS college football crew: (from left to right, top to bottom) Charley Neal, Verne Lundquist, Scott Hunter, Frank Herzog, CBS Sports President Neal Pilson, Steve Grote, Jack Snow, Steve Davis, Ara Parsegian, Pat Haden, myself, and Lindsey Nelson.

Former Kansas City Chief coach Hank Stram was my broadcasting partner two different times, including my last year at CBS. Hank now does analysis for "Monday Night Football" on CBS radio.

It is always a thrill to interview a legend. In this case, it was John Wooden during the 1990 McDonald's All-American game broadcast for ABC.

When I moved to Turner Broadcasting in 1992, I was teamed with analyst Pat Haden, producer Peter Lasser, and director Lonnie Dale to cover the NFL for TNT.

Former All-Pro wide receiver Lynn Swann was my first and last college football broadcast partner for ABC.

I covered three Final Fours with Billy Packer, recognized as the best college basketball analyst today.

Three of the most enjoyable years I've spent as a sportscaster were the three years I was teamed with Dick Vermeil at ABC, covering college football.

In my younger years, my father Herb
worked a farm to supplement his income
as a coach at Pratt High School.

I grew up on a farm located near Macksville,
Kansas, 30 miles from Pratt.

At five years old, I was ready to see the world
as a sailor.

In the seventh grade, I tried to emulate one of my baseball heroes—Mickey Mantle.

In the eighth grade, I was a starting forward (#70) for the Ulysses Junior High basketball team. Sam Fuller (#40), my best friend, is now the president of a bank in Ulysses.

A tailback for Ulysses High School, I was named All-State my senior year. Another All-State selection that year later achieved considerably more success in the sport than I did—John Hadl.

I continued my football career at Wichita State University where, in my sophomore year, I purchased my first car, a '54 Chevy.

As a graduate student at Kansas University, I worked on several television projects. Here I'm with fellow grad assistant Terry Shockley whom I would later work with when I moved to Madison, Wisconsin.

The booth at Bud Detter Field in Hutchinson, Kansas, where the local American Legion baseball team played, was old and rickety, and I broadcasted the games for free. Yet, I enjoyed myself there as much as anywhere else I've worked.

This picture was taken on my first trip home from college. Between my mother and father are my three brothers, Dell, Kelly, and Blaine.

My brother Dell (to my right) is now a child counselor in Fayetteville, Arkansas. Kelly (to my immediate left) is pastor of the First United Methodist Church in Wichita. Blaine runs a natural gas plant back in our old hometown of Ulysses.

At our home in Phoenix, my wife Linda and I are flanked by our sons Brett and Trey and our dog Chamois. Brett and Trey have followed in my footsteps: Brett is director of media relations for Phoenix Arena Sports, and Trey is a sports broadcaster with KGME radio in Phoenix and voice of the Arizona Rattlers arena football team.

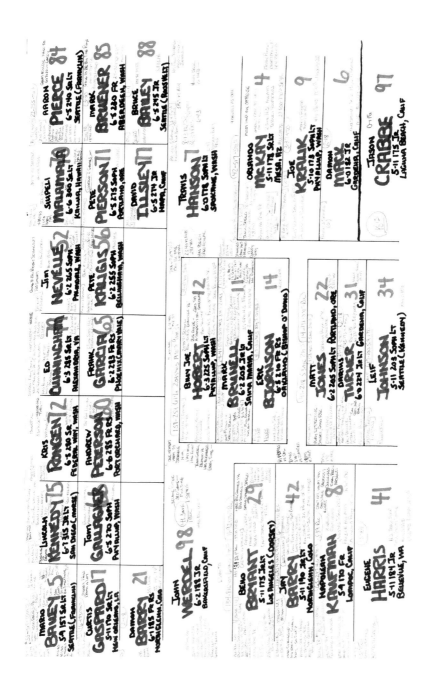

My offensive spotting boards for football include any information I think will be of interest to my audience. The arrangement of the information probably only makes sense to me, but it does include the top two players at each offensive line position and a three-deep representation of the skill positions (backs and receivers).

My defensive spotting boards are typically only two deep at each position. Occasionally, I add a third spot when a team has exceptional depth at a position.

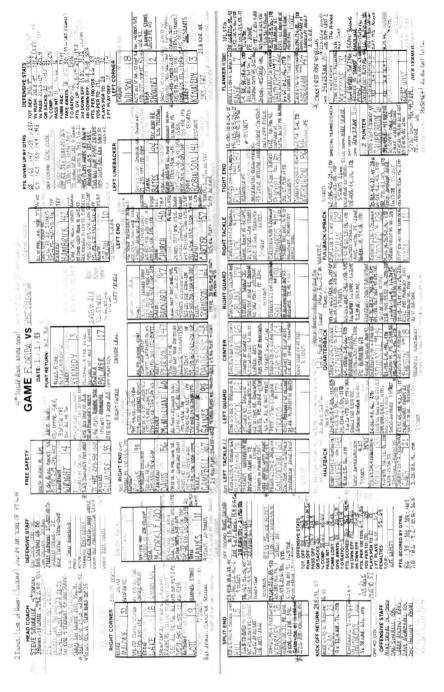

Spotting boards are highly personal. Dick Vermeil has developed his own spotting board form that is a work of art when filled out. He uses multi-colored pens with each color having a different significance, allowing instant visual recognition. The written notes are so cryptic only Dick can interpret them.

_____ Defense W__ L__ T__

Defensive Coordinator _____
Offensive Coordinator _____

| | | |
|---|---|---|
| Total Defense | _____ Yds. | |
| Rush Average | _____ Yds. | |
| Pass Average | _____ Yds | |
| Score Average | _____ Points | |

Interceptions _____ Sacks _____
Fumble Recoveries _____
Giveaways ___ Takeaways ___
Average _____

| No. | Name | Pos. | Notes |
|---|---|---|---|
| | | | |
| | | | |
| | | | |
| | | | |
| | | | |
| | | | |
| | | | |
| | | | |
| | | | |
| | | | |
| | | | |
| | | | |
| | | | |
| | | | |
| | | | |
| | | | |
| | | | |
| | | | |
| | | | |
| | | | |
| | | | |
| | | | |
| | | | |
| | | | |
| | | | |
| | | | |
| | | | |
| | | | |
| | | | |
| | | | |
| | | | |
| | | | |

Not all spotting board systems are as graphic as mine or Dick Vermeil's. This form allows the announcer to list the players (in this case, on the defensive side) in numerical order with room for appropriate notes.

ball up the court . . . passes to Barkley . . . back to Johnson . . .
he shoots . . . he scores." The better announcer says, "Kevin
Johnson brings the ball into the offensive end of the floor, look-
ing to get it deep in the paint to Miller. They're fronting Miller.
Instead, Johnson kicks it off to the left wing to Barkley. Sir
Charles fakes a drive to the baseline, pivots, dishes back to
Johnson all alone at the top of the key beyond the three-point
line. K.J. lets it go. It swishes for three!"

Because they have to be more descriptive, radio announcers often say things never mentioned on television. For example, only on the rarest occasions would you say a player's
jersey number on tv. You might note that a player had switched
to a different number or that he wears the same number as a
great player from the past, but you would not use the number
as a means of identification during a play. Saying a number
rather than a name indicates a lack of preparation or a faulty
memory on the play-by-play announcer's part. However, on
radio, giving the player's number sometimes adds to the vivid
word picture that will create just the right mental image for the
listener: "It's a long fly to deep center. Griffey turns with his
No. 24 to the infield. He's almost to the wall . . . and he makes
a terrific catch over his shoulder! He made that look easy."

One of the ways to make your call of the game on radio
more descriptive is to constantly provide the location of the
action so listeners can add dimension to their mental imagery.
In football this means paying particular attention to the yard
lines, whether the run is to the left or the right, whether the
offense is moving from left to right, whether the wide receiver
is split to the far side or near side. In basketball, action takes
place just beyond the time line, at the top of the circle, at the
foul line extended left or right, at a 45 degree angle 18 feet
from the basket, in the left-hand corner, on the baseline just
right of the lane, in the paint. In baseball, the pitch isn't just
fouled off. It's fouled straight back, fouled wickedly on a line
to the left three rows above the Yankee dugout, fouled deep in
the second deck just outside the right field foul pole.

Where mentioning offensive or defensive formations are
optional on television because the viewers can see for themselves, the radio announcer should not only identify the formations when possible, but also who is positioned where: "for

the first time in the game, the Cardinals are in their trips formation with Green, Proehl, and Smith all split to the wide side of the field toward the far sideline"; "Duke has switched to a 1–3–1 with Hurley at the point, Thomas Hill and Koubek at the wings, Laettner at center, and Grant Hill on the baseline"; "the Royals have put on the O'Brien shift with Stillwell, Shumpert, and Brett positioned on the right field side of second base, leaving Seitzer all alone on the left side."

Radio announcers also have to be careful in their choice of words when describing situations. A listener once told me he felt uncomfortable every time I said a pass was "caught" when calling a football game. The word always raised a question mark in his mind because it could mean that either the offense or defense had hauled in the pass. A more precise choice of words would be to say "completed" when the offense catches the pass and "intercepted" when the defense does.

Which leads to the subject of accuracy. Television announcers must always be accurate because, if they're not, the picture on the screen will point out their falsehood. On radio, there is no built-in conscience. The radio announcer has omniscient control over the listener's mental vision of a game and can say almost anything as long as the details match the box score in the newspaper the next day. That's why for many years, radio stations chose the more economical method of re-creating a team's away games.

When I was working for WTMJ in Milwaukee, covering a Wisconsin-Nebraska football game in Lincoln, the producer sent us away for a series of commercials and we missed the kickoff. Normally, we would have apologized to the listeners on return and simply updated what had happened. But, Wisconsin ran the kickoff 80 yards for a touchdown. It was the biggest play of the day for the Badgers. So, on return from commercial, I called the play as though it were live, using the actual crowd reaction we had taped. No one ever caught it.

Sometimes the radio announcer will be tempted to stretch the truth as a means of expediency: you misidentify the ball carrier; you lose track of the count; you can only mention two passes when three were actually made in rapid succession. Everyone does it at some time when the pace of the game or the action happens faster than you are able to describe. But if you make a habit of taking a shortcut in your description, you will be flirting with danger. In effect, you will be cheating your audience. And unless the game you are broadcasting is an away game that is beyond the radio station's signal and is not being televised, there will always be someone listening who is also watching and will know the difference.

Using a color analyst on radio broadcasts poses a unique problem for the play-by-play announcer. Television is so structured that the analyst takes over at natural points, the most common being replays. When the producer calls for a replay, announcers know to finish their comments as soon as possible so the analyst can pick it up when the replay starts rather than in midstream.

There are no replays in radio. And because the play-by-play announcer has to keep a steady stream of description going to apprise the listening audience of what is happening, there are no clearly defined times when the analyst should talk. Consequently, radio announcers have to learn how to include the analyst in the broadcast. For sports with continuous action like basketball and hockey, this problem is magnified by the fact that there are no natural breaks in the game. The only time the action stops is when the whistle blows. Even sports like football and baseball, which have moments of inactivity spaced between the action, cause a problem because there is no visual cue to suggest that it is the analyst's turn to speak.

How do you include the analyst in a radio broadcast and avoid stomping on each other's lines? If the game is also being televised, the simplest way is to use a monitor. When the monitor shows a replay, that can be the cue for the analyst to respond just as if it were a tv broadcast. However, most of the time, working with a partner in the radio booth has to be an instinctive proposition. The analyst has to become familiar with the announcer's play-by-play rhythm to know when it's okay to break in for comment without disrupting the flow. The announcer has to watch for visual clues that the analyst has something to add—maybe the analyst leans forward slightly, looks directly at the announcer, raises a hand or finger, or squeezes the announcer's arm—and the announcer has to use open-ended leads and pregnant pauses to signal the analyst to come in. If a team works together for any length of time, this all becomes intuitive.

My first game for CBS was between the Green Bay Packers and the Detroit Lions. Just the week before, I had been the voice of the Packers, doing their preseason games on radio. During that first network game, I continually reminded myself, "This is television. This is television." Anyone who has shifted between radio and television probably has had to do the same because the pace of each medium is so different. Radio discipline instills a constant fear of dead air, forcing the play-by-play announcer to be verbose, to fill every minute with description. In television, the opposite is the rule; less is more. If you ever watch a simulcast game on tv where the announcer provides the play-by-play for radio and television at the same time, you will know it immediately. Your reaction will be, "Why is the announcer talking so much?"

Most play-by-play announcers agree it is far more difficult to go from radio to television than to go from television to radio. It's easier to add than to subtract.

When to lay out during a television broadcast, letting the picture tell the story, is one of the hardest things for any play-by-play announcer to learn. Just think how difficult it is when coming from a medium in which silence is anathema.

On Bob Costas' NBC late night program "Later," Vin Scully said, "I have learned a long time ago that there is no way that my words can adequately describe the emotion better than sitting back and listening to the crowd roar."

Scully credits Jack Benny for being a strong influence in the importance of being quiet. On his old radio program, Benny once did a skit in which a robber accosted Benny with a gun, stating, "Your money or your life." There was a long pause. Then Benny said, "I'm thinking. I'm thinking." That pause led to what many consider the longest laugh in radio history.

When Hank Aaron hit the home run that broke Babe Ruth's career mark, "I'll bet you no one has ever let the crowd roar as long as I did," said Scully. "I got up, put the microphone down, went back, poured a cup of coffee and some cream and sugar because I had nothing else to say. That was *the* home run. And everyone in this world knew it broke

Ruth's record. And the crowd was screaming and rockets were going off. What am I going to say: 'The crowd's excited?' I said nothing."

If you ask play-by-play announcers whether they would rather call a game on radio or television, they'll probably hedge their answer. From a career standpoint, they'll most likely choose television because the medium is more lucrative. But if they answer based on the medium that gives them the most enjoyment, a vast majority will say radio. Why? Because from the opening kickoff, the starting tip, or the first pitch, announcers get to paint the whole picture for their audience, using words they choose themselves. It is a challenging job that has almost limitless possibilities and freedom.

Television, however, imposes restrictions on play-by-play. No longer are the announcer's words the driving force of the medium. Those words must now team up with pictures. And the announcer has no control over what the audience sees. The producer or director has the responsibility to select shots that create the atmosphere of the ball game. The play-by-play announcer and the analyst still have to describe and inform the audience as in radio, but now they have to fit what they say to the pictures shown on air.

We have already mentioned the relationship between the on-air talent and the people in the truck who control what the viewing audience sees. The situation is not unlike a finely choreographed dance between two partners who both want to lead. Under the best circumstances, who leads is compromised. Sometimes it's the announcer saying, "There's activity down in the bullpen," which leads the director to show Dennis Eckersley warming up. At other times, it's the producer telling the on-air talent, "Look at this," over the talk-back system, leading the announcer or analyst to comment on a picture of Eckersley running to the bullpen mound. For this relationship to work effectively, two things have to happen: The people in the truck have to listen to what is said by the on-air talent; and the on-air talent has to watch what the truck is showing on camera.

The first thing a play-by-play announcer must learn when moving from radio to television is how to work with a monitor in the booth. When you watch the monitor depends on the sport. However, the rule of thumb is, once action begins, concentrate on the field of play, not the monitor. Think of it this way. How accurate would your call of the game be if your sole view of what was happening came from what you saw on your television set? If you were calling a tennis or Ping-Pong match where a wide shot could take in the players and the whole field of play at once without losing perspective, you might do very well. But the only shot that might capture the entire field of play in baseball would probably be from a blimp, a perspective too far away to do accurate play-by-play.

Even with sports in which most of the action can be caught on screen, it is better to call the game live than from the monitor simply because of the pace of the game. Basketball and hockey are the prime examples. Quite frankly, for these sports, I never look at the monitor unless there is a stop in action. Since there is a continuous flow of movement in these sports, I find the naked eye is able to capture more than the camera—especially with hockey. It's hard enough to see the movement of that small whizzing piece of rubber when it's live, let alone pick it up on the tv screen.

Because of the spaced breaks between moments of action, it is probably easier to integrate the use of the monitor when doing football than any other sport. I use the following routine when calling a televised football game: from the moment of the snap, I watch the play live; after the play ends, I watch the monitor until the replay starts; while the analyst comments on the replay, I return to the field to note substitutions; I return to the monitor as the analyst finishes to see if I can add something and to watch where the director takes the camera; then just before the next snap, I return to the field of play.

Baseball is unique when it comes to using the monitor. First, because there is so much inactivity between pitches, there is time for the camera to go almost anywhere. Whether the camera supports what the announcer and analyst are saying or whether the announcer and the analyst support what the camera is showing, the play-by-play announcer has to be aware what is on the monitor. Second, it is sometimes easier to call location and type of pitch from the monitor than it is from your vantage point in the booth, especially if the shot is from center field. This has to be done with extreme care, however.

Once the ball is hit, you have to be watching the action live or risk losing sight of the ball and having no idea where it went.

Regardless of the sport, television play-by-play announcers should get used to noticing changes in the picture on the monitor out of the corner of their eye. This can be facilitated by the exact placement of the monitor in the booth. As has already been mentioned, before a game starts, announcers should check to see that the monitor is situated so that it does not block their line of sight to the action on the field and at the same time is positioned in a way that reduces the amount of head turning to a minimum.

The odds are very good that you will start out in radio since it is the proving ground for most play-by-play. If your goal is to reach the network level or become the voice of a professional team, at some time you will also want to work in television. Hopefully, you will have the opportunity to do both. But, in any case, having the ability to excel in either medium and to effortlessly shift back and forth between the two only increases your value in the marketplace.

# CHAPTER FOURTEEN

# *Other Venues*

*T*he goal of previous chapters has been to illustrate the basics of preparing for and calling a game using football as an example. Though there are similar elements to all play-by-play regardless of venue, each sport has its own rhythm, its own unique requirements.

This chapter is devoted to other sports and the special challenges they pose for the play-by-play announcer. We will first examine the two other major sports covered by the networks (basketball and baseball), then develop guidelines for doing play-by-play when you're assigned to a venue that is new to you.

## Basketball

Just as when covering football, announcers have to address the basics of play-by-play when calling basketball; they still have to set the situation, identify the participants, and comment on the action. Only the specific elements of each differ because of the sport. For example, to set the situation in basketball, the play-by-play announcer must keep the viewer informed of the game score, individual scoring, the time left in the period, the time left on the shot clock, the number of individual fouls, and the number of team fouls (which notes any bonus free throw situation).

What makes this challenging is, since basketball is a game of continuous action with a running clock, there are no regular breaks in which to reset the situation for the viewer. Announcers have to work them into their play-by-play when the moment allows. This means mentioning the time remaining during dead-ball situations, stating a player's foul predicament or scoring total while free throws are being shot, or updating the game score after a basket.

The rhythm of basketball also influences the announcer's identification of players. When preparing for a football game, the play-by-play announcer's goal is to etch into memory the link between a player's number and a player's name so that, when watching action on the field, the eye will pick up the number and the brain will automatically translate it into the correct name. Because of the speed of the game and the frequent inability to pick up numbers immediately, basketball announcers have to find a shortcut. Consequently, when preparing for basketball, the announcer's goal should be to associate names with physical appearances.

Instant recognition based on physical appearance is possible in basketball because of two reasons: (1) there are fewer participants to memorize; and (2) most announcing positions are at courtside, placing the play-by-play announcer near the action. By watching game films or practices, the fully-prepared announcer should have little problem calling the game without referring to numbers.

However, there are two instances when resorting to numbers for identification may be required. First, when the announcing position is far away from the court, the announcer may be forced to resort to using numbers for identification because the distance makes it impossible to note subtle differences in physical appearance that are readily noticeable at courtside. Second, when you do a series of games in a short period of time, such as covering a tournament, the total number of participants will be too great to trust your memory.

Though it may be necessary to fall back on associating names with numbers, the announcer's goal should still be to try to identify the players physically, starting the game identifying players by number, then learning each player's physical appearance as the game progresses. When your broadcast position is high above the arena floor and one team's uniforms are light blue with white numerals or white with gold numerals, you will understand why it is so important to look for knee braces, elbow wraps, wrist bands, distinct haircuts, any physical characteristic to distinguish one player from another.

Because of basketball's constant back-and-forth, up-and-down nature, play-by-play announcers also have to guard against repeating the way they describe things. This is particularly true when it comes to updating the game score. Saying "the Bulls lead 45–40 . . . the Bulls lead 45–42 . . . the Bulls lead 47–42 . . ." gets monotonous. You have to vary the way you update the score: "the Bulls lead 45–40 . . . the Lakers cut it to 45–42 . . . 47–42 Bulls . . ." In fact, since there is so much scoring in basketball, stating the exact score is less important than stating the difference in score. By also paying attention to scoring trends, you can really vary your call: "Bulls lead 45–40 . . . Los Angeles down by three . . . Chicago ties its largest lead at five . . ."

Even if you vary the way you update the score, it has more impact on the viewer or listener if you also include the time remaining. As with all sports that are played with fixed time limits, stating the amount of time left in the contest adds to the drama of the situation. This is particularly so for basketball. Since points are scored so frequently, just saying "the Bulls lead by seven" is meaningless. When time is added to the call, it provides the audience with a ruler to measure the progress of the game much like down and distance does on the football field. When you mention "the Bulls lead by seven with 4:15 left in the first period" then say "the Bulls are up 15 at the 2:15 mark of the first quarter" two minutes later, the audience has a way of gauging how the game is going. Of course, adding the time towards the end of periods and at the end of the game also adds to the drama. Saying "the Lakers are down five to the Bulls with 1:15 remaining in the game" causes internal tension for both Los Angeles fans who see time slipping away and Chicago fans who want time to evaporate.

Finding new ways to be descriptive is even more important for radio announcers than for tv announcers. Former Oakland Athletics announcer Monte Moore, who worked all three major sports at one time or another on both tv and radio, says calling basketball on the radio is probably the easiest to do "because there's so much going on all the time. If you're good at memorizing numbers and names . . . and talk pretty quickly, [you] can do basketball." This doesn't mean saying "Pippen shoots . . . he scores . . ." is good enough to land you a job as the voice of the Chicago Bulls. A lot of people can call basketball, but not a lot of them can call it well. According to Moore, "The guy who does basketball well on radio is the guy who doesn't just tell you names and numbers, [but also] describes how things happen." For example, if Scottie Pippen takes the shot, the good announcer tells how he got open—off a screen by Cartwright, off a good fake and drive to the baseline, or off a court-length pass from Armstrong.

Few announcers who work for a network or who are the voice of a professional team are required to keep stats because a statistician is provided. But there are many times when play-by-play announcers *are* required to keep their own stats, especially starting out. Because of the speed of basketball, handling the dual tasks of calling the game and keeping score can be extremely challenging.

For example, say a team scores a basket. As you note over the air who scored, you look down at your score book to enter the same information. As you're looking down, a full-court press forces a turnover on the inbounds pass and immediately results in another basket. Since your head was down, you missed it all. If noting who scored can cause such a problem, what about keeping shots taken, rebounds, assists, and turnovers?

There are announcers who keep all their own stats without missing a beat in their call of the game. They keep everything. This ability didn't happen overnight. They spent years learning to juggle the two tasks. They learned shortcuts such as putting their pencil next to the scorer's name and waiting until the ball has been brought safely up court before entering a score in the book. Necessity has been the mother of invention.

If you are starting out in broadcasting and have to do your own basketball stats, you should stick to the basics first—know who scored, how many points they've scored, and how many fouls they have. You can wait for the official stats at halftime or after the game to determine turnovers and shooting percentages. More sophisticated stats should only be added when scorekeeping has become second nature and not a distraction to your play-by-play.

One final issue for play-by-play announcers covering basketball—location of the broadcast position. It has already been mentioned how distance from the court affects the announcer's identification of players. Distance will also affect the announcer's call of the game. The further you are away from the floor, the more you are subject to missing who fouled or not hearing a referee's explanation of a call. You also lose some of the game's emotion. At courtside, you can see every elbow thrown and hear the grunts of exertion. At the top of an arena, those distinctions are lost. The difference is comparable to a reporter covering the Persian Gulf War from the behind the lines in Saudi Arabia and one alongside the troops entering Kuwait City.

How do you compensate if you're stuck in a broadcast position high above the court in the Los Angeles Forum or at Madison Square Garden? You can do very little. It's just a different game up there. If you are doing television, you at least can fall back to relying on the monitor more. But if you're doing radio, you will end up describing a little less because you can't see the hand checking going on, you didn't understand the discussion that went on at the scorer's table, you didn't hear what the coach yelled at his players. You simply have to persevere and do the most professional job you can.

## Baseball

If there is anything 180 degrees from the rhythm of basketball play-by-play, it's calling baseball. It's been said many times that doing baseball is hours of boredom interspersed with moments of panic. The challenge for baseball announcers is not describing the bang-bang moments in a game, however. It's filling the long gaps of inactivity in between.

What can an announcer say between the over 200-some pitches thrown in a baseball game? Almost anything. Because of the rhythm of the game, baseball announcers can take more liberties, cut a greater swath than any other sport. You can discuss how the pitcher is throwing. You can analyze what changes the team needs to make to move into the first division. You can talk numbers. You can give the scores of other games. You can talk weather. There are 25 players per team not counting coaches and managers. Pick out any one of them and you should be able to tell a story. There is always something to talk about in the game of baseball. And when your words dry up, you can always lay out and let the crowd noise fill the void.

As in calling any sport, baseball play-by-play has some basics that must be tended to. When setting the situation, the announcer has to mention the score, the count, the number of outs, the inning, the number and position of the runners, what the pitcher has done, and what the batter has done. The emphasis of each will vary with the situation. A three-two count with two out in the bottom of the second in a five-run game has less drama associated with it than a three-two count with two out and the bases loaded in the bottom of the ninth of a one-run game. The good announcer knows how and when to build the audience's sense of anticipation accordingly.

There is another aspect to setting the situation that is unique to baseball. Because of the game's slower rhythm, there is plenty of time to talk strategy if you're knowledgeable enough to do so. And the intricacies of baseball allow for almost any level of strategic discussion. You can talk about how the outfield is shading a batter to the right and why. You can speculate whether and when a runner might try to steal second. You can analyze how a reliever just in from the bullpen will pitch to the clean-up hitter with the game on the line. You can guess whether the manager will call for the sacrifice bunt or the hit-and-run. The beauty of baseball is that there is something for everyone to enjoy whether it be the fan who's sitting back munching popcorn, hoping for a foul ball and is just glad to be there, or the die-hard who keeps track of every pitch thrown and every ball hit. As long as you take care of the basics for the casual fan, you can take the game to as cerebral a level as you want.

Even after setting the stage, baseball announcers still have plenty of time to fill. They do this with commentary that generally falls into two distinct categories—stories or stats. How to balance the two opens a real debate for the professionals who cover the game.

When advising young people just entering the baseball broadcasting business, Seattle Mariner announcer Dave Niehaus suggests, "Don't become mathematics nuts. Don't number people to death. A lot of announcers try to do that because it's such an easy crutch. You have so much time between pitches to bring up home runs, RBIs, what [a player] did at two o'clock, what he did when the sun is just off the horizon, what he did against this pitcher and that pitcher, [all of] which probably isn't relevant to that particular moment.

"Certainly home runs and RBIs and doubles and triples and singles and earned run average are very important, but I think you can become too much a slave to [them]. I think you have to know anecdotes. I think you have to know the personalities of ball players. I think the people who are really good in this business can tell good baseball stories. They know good baseball history."

Because of the sophisticated graphics capabilities provided by the truck, this is particularly true for television announcers. Monte Moore says, "I think stats are less important all the time. They're so available on the screen for every batter." To prove the point, Moore and his Oakland Athletics broadcast partner Ray Fosse once tried a one-game experiment in which they refrained from stating stats. Instead, they concentrated solely on telling personal stories about the players or simply talking about the game itself.

However, completely ignoring stats means ignoring an aspect of the sport that has great appeal to the fan. No other sport is so driven by statistics as baseball. The desire for more and more sophisticated stats—made possible because of computer data bases—has even created a small, lucrative industry for such organizations as the Elias Sports Bureau, Howe SportsData International, and SportsSource, Inc.

Rick Rizzs, Niehaus' former broadcasting partner in Seattle, agrees that it's not good to inundate the fan with numbers, but also thinks "you do have to have some stats." The challenge, particularly at the major league level, is which stats to use. "You could come to the ballpark," says Rizzs, "pick up information along press row, and sit for three hours looking at it if you wanted to."

Consequently, the announcer has to become a sieve, sorting out the stats that will have relevance to the fan. When he prepares for a game, Rizzs chooses potential story lines that answer the question "What are the most important things the fans should know about this game?" He then looks for stats that support or refute each story line.

For example, in any game in which Randy Johnson is to start for the M's, a definite key would be Johnson's control. "If Randy Johnson walks people, continues to get in trouble," explains Rizzs, "the Mariners are going to have a tough time. If he's out there throwing strikes, the Mariners are going to win." Rizzs looks for stats such as Johnson's leading the league in walks per nine innings or the fact that he has won every game in which he gave up five or less walks. "If you can paint that picture by using a few stats like that, then the fans understand what you're talking about. Then, you're informing. Then, you're educating."

Whether announcers use stories or stats to fill the empty moments of a broadcast, it takes time to prepare. Don't think that because baseball is more relaxed, an announcer can show up just before game time and do a good broadcast. The truth is, because baseball is a sport played virtually every day, announcers have to manage their time to ensure that they are fully prepared. In fact, many baseball announcers often show up at the ballpark long before the teams arrive in order to sort through the mass of information available to them. And on road-trip flights, most use the air time to peruse press guides and newspapers to catch up on the next opponent.

The fact that baseball is an everyday sport does have its advantages, however. No other sport affords the broadcaster a daily opportunity to get close to its subject. Between the hours spent traveling with a team and talking to the players, coaches, and managers before games, a good announcer can pick up story after story that will educate, amuse, or entertain the fan. The key is getting to know the people in the sport.

During a conversation before a game between Oakland and Seattle in the Kingdome, former Mariner coach Ron Clark told Monte Moore that, in his 30 years in baseball, he had never seen a curveball as good as Erik Hanson's. "You don't get that kind of stuff unless you know the people in the sport," says Moore.

"The most important job you have when you come to the ballpark is to establish rapport with players, the coaches, the managers, and the umpires so you can feel comfortable going up to them and talking to them," says Moore. "If you're one of these guys who gets a job in the big leagues and you're intimidated by all these guys and you stand around the batting cage—you're out there every day but you don't talk to anybody—then you're not learning anything except what you overhear someone else saying. And if they don't say it to me, I figure it's not to be said on the air."

A story source that is unique to baseball is the announcing crew for the opposing team. Though baseball announcers may broadcast other sports during the year, baseball is their first love. As a result, the fraternity of baseball announcers is very close. They pass information back and forth freely, including stories they can't use themselves because friends and families of players might be listening.

Another issue that is unique for the baseball announcer is keeping score. Most announcers who cover other sports such as basketball and football would prefer that a statistician keep track instead. Baseball is the only sport in which announcers prefer to keep their own score book. There are a few announcing teams who alternate keeping score for the innings they work. But, on the whole, it's almost a requirement that each announcer keep score, if for no other reason than no two people keep score the same way.

Keeping score for baseball is a very personal endeavor. I've seen a score book in which dots represented RBIs and another in which they meant pitches thrown. I've seen some announcers document a single by charting its distance and direction in the outfield while others simply enter "1B." All announcers have specific needs that only their system can address. Your system will be equally personal.

One final issue for the baseball announcer—working with a partner. Baseball is the least structured sport regarding bringing in the analyst. In many cases, your teammate isn't even an analyst but a second announcer who shares play-by-play duty with you. How you work together will depend as much on your relationship with one another as any prescribed delineation of responsibilities. Through time you learn when your partner is into a rhythm and you should lay out and when to break in with an observation.

Monte Moore's practice for working with a partner is that both microphones are open at all times because baseball is a conversational sport. "A guy by himself at a ballpark does not have as much fun as he does with somebody with him," says Moore. "I've always told my color guy, 'We're representing the fans at the ballpark. We're two guys sitting, talking about the game.' "

There are so many nuances to the game of baseball, so many things can happen on the field at one time with so much time to talk about them, there is plenty of room for two sets of eyes and two sets of opinions on the air.

One additional comment: When you talk to baseball announcers, they almost unanimously prefer doing the game on radio versus tv. As Dave Niehaus puts it, "I think baseball is a mind game more than a video game. I enjoy listening to a game on radio much more than watching it on television. If you have any command of the English language at all, you can be creative in describing weather conditions, where the wind is blowing, the shades of the green of the outfield and infield grass, and the shadows."

Niehaus grew up listening to Harry Carey on KMOX in St. Louis and remembers being disappointed when he saw his first major league game. "Because I put these guys on a pedestal in my mind, I expected more than I got when I went there. You conjure up these ideas of these super heroes and really all they are are human beings who are a little more gifted than the normal person."

That shows the power of the baseball radio announcer. Because they are in your home three-and-a-half hours at a time, for nearly six months of the year, baseball announcers can become part of the family. You become so comfortable with their style, they are like old shoes you put on to relax in at home. Just think of the announcers whose names have become eternally linked with a team: Mel Allen and the New York Yankees; Red Barber and the Brooklyn Dodgers; Vin Scully and the Los Angeles Dodgers; Ernie Harwell and the Detroit Tigers; Bob Prince and the Pittsburgh Pirates. The announcer who can excel at baseball play-by-play on the radio can become your friend for life.

## Developing Play-By-Play Systems for Other Sports

When I first started in broadcasting at KWBW radio in Hutch-inson, Kansas, the local YMCA built a beautiful Olympic-sized swimming pool, one of the nicest in the state at the time. In order to draw attention to it, the organization sponsored one of the largest swim meets ever held in south central Kansas. To further gain publicity, they convinced me that the radio station should consider covering the event.

I was eager to try anything in order to call a sporting event on the air. I sold the station on the idea, secured sponsors for the program all over the city, wrote and taped all the commercials, and worked with the Y to hype the meet. I also prepared for my call by getting as much pre-race information as I could, even interviewing some of the participants.

By the day of the meet, I knew every lane assignment and had background information on every swimmer. As the swimmers lined up at the end of the pool for the first event, I was confident, pumped, and ready.

Then the starter's gun went off and the swimmers dived into the pool.

Have you ever heard a swimming event broadcast on radio? I hadn't.

Have you ever thought about how you might call such a race? The thought had never crossed my mind.

I had gotten so engrossed in selling the program and preparing for it, it never occurred to me what might happen once the swimmers were in the water and they all suddenly looked alike. It was as though they had jumped off the face of the earth. On television, you can see each racer's stroke, can see and hear the emotion on the sidelines. But how do you describe that to your listeners on the radio? Also, I knew everything about the participants: I knew they were 16 or 17 or 18 years old; I knew they represented Hutchinson High School, Trinity High School, or Nickerson High school; I knew if they'd been class president or played the trumpet in the school band; and I knew if they were the favorite in the race. What I didn't know was a method of working that knowledge into the broadcast of that race.

The first event was two laps. It took one lap for me to recover from shock enough to speak. Needless to say, the rest of the day was a real learning experience.

Most young people who enter sportscasting want to work in one or more of the big three sports—football, baseball, and basketball. Since they are the most popular sports, everyone wants to do them. But even if you are fortunate enough to create a career path that immediately leads to the sport or sports of your choosing, odds are you will at one time or another be asked to call a sport you have little affinity with or know nothing about. If your goal is to reach the network level, it's almost guaranteed.

In my broadcasting career, I've done play-by-play for 29 different sports, 27 at the network level. They have ranged from the common to the uncommon.

---

Sports I have called at the network level:

| | |
|---|---|
| Football (Pro & College) | Volleyball |
| Basketball (Pro & College) | Indoor Soccer |
| Baseball (Pro & College) | Full-Contact Karate |
| Track and Field | Rodeo |
| Marathon | Wrist Wrestling |
| Gymnastics | Log Rolling |
| Swimming | Roller Skating (the same |
| Diving | kind of competition as |
| Bowling | ice skating except on |
| Weight Lifting | roller skates) |
| Boxing | Acrobatics (a contest |
| Golf | in which teams did |
| Tennis | pyramid building) |
| Ice Skating | Battle of the NFL |
| Speedskating | Cheerleaders |
| Snow Skiing | Shark Tagging |
| Horse Racing | |

Other sports I have called:

Hockey (College)
Wrestling (College)

---

Knowing how to do football, basketball, and baseball came almost naturally because I grew up with them, having played or followed them from childhood. But how do you call shark tagging or the Battle of the NFL Cheerleaders when the event has been created for television and has never been conducted before?

To begin with, doing play-by-play for a sport you know little about requires considerable additional preparation time because you not only have to learn about the participants, but you also have to learn about the sport itself. Say you were called upon to cover the World Series. You've probably played baseball in Little League, collected baseball cards, or participated in a fantasy league. You may need to check out certain details, but on the whole, because you've followed baseball for so many years, you have a solid historical background. You know the players, the teams, and the language of the sport. Now, say you are asked to cover the World Swimming and Diving Championships. Not only have you never been to a swim meet, you don't even know how to swim. You don't know the different strokes, let alone who are the defending world champions. Suddenly, you have to become a quick study about competitive swimming.

The first step in learning about a new venue is to get an overview of the sport, a historical perspective. This requires reading whatever you can get your hands on about the sport. For first-time events such as shark tagging, this will be impossible. But most lesser known sports have some sort of trade magazine or newsletter that fans of the sport subscribe to. When I covered full-contact karate for CBS, Joe Corley, who publishes a magazine devoted to the sport, sent me a copy of every edition. They were immensely helpful in learning the ins and outs of a sport I knew nothing about.

Second, somehow you have to understand the emotion of a sport, what makes people want to participate or watch it. I understand the emotion of football and basketball because I've played them. However, I've never competed in gymnastics. How can I capture and reflect the emotion of that sport for the viewing audience?

The key is eliminating your ignorance of the sport and finding out why others appreciate it. You have to be an outsider who wants to become an insider. To do this, you need to talk to the people within the sport. Sometime before the event, you have to sit down with the organizers of the event, the officials of the sport, your analyst (who is usually a former participant in the sport), anybody who is even remotely connected with the sport, lock the doors and keep them there until you've asked every question you can think of. The questions might sound stupid to them, but there are never stupid questions when you're trying to learn the details, the nomenclature, the emotion of a sport.

During the course of the briefing, you also have to make sure you direct your line of questions to two areas. First, you have to learn the pitfalls for announcers. For example, you might ask, "What tips people off that you don't know this sport?" or "What kind of word usages or descriptions would make people say, 'Hey, this announcer doesn't know what he's talking about'?" Second, you should ask, "If you were in my position, how would you like to have your sport described?" People who are involved in sports that do not get a lot of media coverage will bend over backward to help you. Since it will draw attention to their sport, they have a vested interest in making sure the broadcast goes well.

The production team should also do the same type of questioning: "What camera angles best show your sport?" "What camera angles are worthless?" "Where should we put the broadcast position?" If they don't, problems may ensue.

In the spring of 1989, ABC broadcast a swim meet between the East Germans and the United States in Charlotte, North Carolina. Because the network didn't want to spend a great amount of money to cover a limited number of races, no one went down ahead of time to determine the best broadcast location. When Donna DeVarona, John Nabor, and I arrived to call the meet, they located us poolside in the corner with the swimmers coming towards us. We had no pre-race rehearsal. The first time we saw the racers in the pool, we were live.

Unfortunately, our location was at such an angle that we were unable to tell who was winning. To us it appeared everybody was running neck and neck. The camera angles on our monitor didn't help either. Donna and John looked at me desperately while I stalled, calling lanes. We knew we were in trouble. At the end of the first race, I guessed the winner and hit it right. It was pure luck. During commercial break, we told the truck about our dilemma. By shifting the cameras, they were able to improve the situation some, but it was still a difficult afternoon.

Even learning everything you can about a sport does not eliminate problems. Some sports get so little attention, the people in the sport are not used to being around television and do not know television's requirements.

I once did a bout featuring Bill "Super Foot" Wallace, who was the Muhammad Ali of full-contact karate (sometimes referred to as "kick boxing"). The fight was broadcast live in Wallace's hometown of Indianapolis, Indiana, as a segment of "CBS Sports Spectacular." Since CBS bounced from one segment to another, the Wallace fight was held up until the network was ready. On New York's cue, the plan was for us to take it, do a tease, go to commercial, then immediately start the fight on return.

The event had been put together as a syndicated package and the gentleman who had sold it to CBS was eager to help in any way possible. Consequently, our producer gave the packager the responsibility of starting the fight. When the packager got the cue from the stage manager, he would signal the people in the ring by lowering his raised arm.

When CBS threw it to us, we did our tease, setting the scene, building up Wallace, the greatest full-contact karate fighter of all time, who could throw his leg at a devastating 60 miles an hour. We then cut to commercial.

Everyone ringside—the referee, the aides, the officials, and the boxers—waited for the signal. Unfortunately, the packager forgot himself for a moment and lowered his arm. The fighters immediately went at each other. Pandemonium ensued as everybody screamed at each other trying to stop the action. The fight went 10 or 15 seconds before they could get the boxers back to their corners.

Luckily, there was sufficient time to get everything settled down. Everyone acted as if nothing had happened, the commercial ended, the packager signaled the start, and the nation never knew how close to embarrassment we had been.

Of course, when you cover an event that has never been staged before, anything can happen and there is little you can do to prepare for it. The oddest sport I've ever announced was a shark tagging contest held in the Virgin Islands. It was literally a made-up sport. They invited four professional divers to compete by tagging sharks with bang sticks that released a dart into the hide of the shark with a flag at the end. The winner would be the diver who tagged the most sharks in a specified period of time.

Because of its beautiful location, the event not only attracted the attention of CBS, but also *Sports Illustrated.* When we went out to tape the show on our luxury yacht, we were accompanied by a flotilla of fishing boats. There were hundreds of interested spectators.

The problem was—we couldn't find any sharks. Day after day, we would go out and come back empty-handed. After a while, pressure began to build. In fact, we even hired a farmer to kill some goats so we could drain their blood in the water to attract the sharks. Nothing worked. Finally, interest waned to the point we were down to the basics—myself, a shark expert, the diving teams, and the crew of cameramen.

After several days of seemingly waiting forever, all of a sudden sharks appeared and things happened bang, bang, bang. But, nothing worked as we had planned. First, the oxygen tank of one of the divers exploded and he came shooting to the surface. We thought he had been bitten by a shark. Second, though there were plenty of sharks, few were tagged. The event obviously wasn't what everyone had expected.

When we came back to New York to put the tape piece together we found we had even less than we thought. The cameras we used under water had never been used before. They were built inside special watertight containers so the cameramen could go down with the divers. Unfortunately, it had been too dark for them to pick up much. That and the fact that few sharks were tagged left us with very little usable footage.

We slaved for four long days and nights editing bits and pieces, with me providing voice-over commentary. We even reshot interviews with a shark expert in a desperate effort to make something out of nothing. The event aired, but it's the last time the network has considered covering shark tagging.

All the preparation in the world would not have saved our shark tagging coverage. However, any time you cover a sport that has had little if any media attention, you need to sit down with the people involved and learn every nuance of the sport, every problem that might arise. Don't think they won't be able to help just because the sport has never been televised. They will. They've lived for the day their sport gets a television audience. They've thought about how they want to be represented and are so emotionally immersed in their sport, they will do anything to make sure the broadcast comes off well.

Once you've learned as much as you can about a new venue and the people participating in it, the next step is to figure out a way to disseminate that information in your play-by-play since each sport has its own rhythm.

First of all, you need to develop a system that organizes your material and presents it in a manner that can be used for memorization or quick reference; in other words, you have to design spotting boards that apply to that sport.

Just before covering the speedskating venue at the 1988 Olympics in Calgary, I sat down with my analyst, Olympic great Eric Heiden, and our researcher, Leah Mueller, also a former World and Olympic speedskating champion, and asked them first what information they thought the average viewer wanted to know, then what information the knowledgeable speedskater wanted to hear. My goal was to address both segments of our audience.

We then asked Leah, who had worked the speedskating venue with Keith Jackson at the 1984 Olympics, how they had done it in the past. What we came up with was a two-part form with the top and bottom halves corresponding to the skaters as they lined up on the ice for each heat. Prominent space was allocated in each half for basic info such as name, height, weight, age, home town and country, and best time in the event. There were also blanks to write down splits for that particular race. The rest of the space in each half was relegated to other information about the skater—pertinent quotes, past successes, hobbies, etc.—with the facts arranged from left to right in order of importance. We used a word processor to update the information daily and to print out "spotting boards" based on the lane and heat assignments for the day. I would get the printout early enough to work on memorization, then used the form for reference during each race.

But, as the story about my YMCA swim meet experience points out, having the information available and knowing when to use it are two different things when doing play-by-play. About two days before the opening of the speedskating venue, producer Ned Simon took us to a nearby studio, ran video from previous Olympics, and told Eric and me, "Now, call it." We were awful. We didn't have anything to say. I realized I couldn't call a race cold without any information about the skaters. And, without the practice, Eric and I didn't know the proper times to talk.

Eric and I later determined we would dole out our call of each race in much the same way that track and field meets are called. Before each event, I would introduce the skaters and set the scene. Eric would follow with a comment about how he thought the race would be run. When the gun fired, I would take the call to the first turn. On the backstretch, Eric would provide commentary on how the skaters were doing. Then, I would take it down the stretch. Afterwards, Eric would analyze what had happened, using replay if available.

We also decided on the information each would provide to the viewer. Eric would describe strategy and evaluate the skaters based on splits to that point in the race and how they were skating. I would provide pertinent tidbits of background on each skater.

Once the speedskating venue started, it didn't take long for us to become a well-oiled machine. Depending upon the length of the race, I knew exactly when it was my turn to lay out and Eric's turn to take it. Leah played an integral part, much as a football statistician does in the broadcast booth. As the splits were shown on the screen after each lap, Leah signaled thumb up, if the skater was above world record pace, or thumb down if under. She also listened to what Eric and I were saying and occasionally pointed out things we should mention.

Spotting boards similar to the ones we used at the 1988 Olympics can be developed for most other racing sports such as track and swimming with the exception that they will have more lanes than just the two used in speedskating. The pattern of exchange between the announcer and the analyst will also be similar. The only major difference occurs in short sprints such as the 100-meter dash and the 50-meter freestyle. Since these events are over in seconds, there isn't sufficient time for any interjection by the analyst.

If I had called a 100-meter dash with Marty Liquori, it might have gone something like this:

**Gary:** The lanes to watch are Lewis in lane 4, Burrell in lane 5. Burrell is the world record holder at 9.90, which broke the three-year-old record Lewis held at 9.92.

**Marty:** The thing to watch in this race is the start. Lewis is known for not getting out of the blocks quickly. On the other hand, Burrell explodes out of the blocks.

[The gun fires.]

**Gary:** Lewis in lane 4. Burrell in lane 5. Burrell with the early lead. Lewis slow off the start. It's still Burrell and Lewis. Lewis closing the gap. Here comes Lewis. And he wins! Burrell second, Marsh third.

**Marty:** As I said at the beginning of the race, Lewis is noted for his slow starts, but still has the power to overhaul the competition. As you see here in the replay, Burrell was out of the blocks first, Lewis last. At the 50-meter mark, Lewis started his move then, with his long strides, blew past Burrell just before the tape.

Sometimes if you have a system that has worked for you in the past in another sport, you can bring it across the street and, with some modifications, use it when you work a new venue. At other times, the new sport's rhythm and how it is broadcast is so radically different, you simply have to start from scratch. If that's the case, you had better lean on the experts in that sport, let them tell you what has been done in the past, and adjust accordingly.

Of course, when you work with analysts who come from a sport that has had little media coverage in the past, there is an excellent chance that they, too, will have had little exposure to television. Therefore, you have to be prepared to help them as well.

Knowing when to burden your analysts with the technical aspects of a broadcast and when to just leave them alone to describe their sport as best they know how while you adapt to them varies depending on the strengths of each analyst. You'll find some people have natural abilities which are immediately transferable to television; others simply can't do it at all.

I once did a taped show with an analyst who had never worked in television. Each time it was his turn to provide description in postproduction, he stumbled over his words. The more times we had to do a segment over, the more upset and frustrated he became. It was obvious we would be there until the turn of the century unless something was done.

Instead of being critical, I talked with him about what was happening and found out he knew exactly what he wanted to say, but just couldn't pull the trigger when it was his turn at the mike. So, just before each segment, we would walk through what he wanted to say and I would write it down. Then when it was his turn to provide commentary, all he had to do was read it. Having his thoughts in front of him relieved him of the pressure he felt when it was his turn to speak.

Doing postproduction on a taped show is one thing. Covering an event live with someone who has never done it before is something else. And rehearsals don't always clue you in to whether or not an analyst can handle the job.

Based on our pre-Olympic practice session in the studio, I'm sure Ned Simon thought there was no way Eric Heiden would be able to perform what was required, especially knowing there were millions of people watching. What he didn't know was that Eric is a laid-back guy or, in sports vernacular, a gamer. Gamers may walk through practice, but when it's game time, they crank it into high gear. When it came time to do our first broadcast, Eric was ready and performed as well as anyone who ever did color for the first time.

I've also experienced the reverse situation.

The first time I was assigned to cover boxing was the World Light Heavyweight Championship between England's John Conteh and Yacqui Lopez, a popular boxer from California. My partner was former light heavyweight champ Bob

Foster who was also doing his first boxing broadcast. The fight took place in Copenhagen, Denmark, and on the flight over, I pumped Foster and his trainer, Billy Williams, for as much as I could about the sport. It was a long flight so I had plenty of opportunity to get to know Bob. He was articulate and had a terrific personality. I told myself, "This is really going to be great."

When we got to Copenhagen, Bob and I rehearsed and rehearsed. We had our problems, but considering it was a new experience for both of us, I felt we were ready to go.

The fight was scheduled late at night, Copenhagen time, so it would air live mid-afternoon in New York. We had an elaborate opening that included all sorts of aerial shots of the city while Perry Como's "Wonderful, Wonderful Copenhagen" played in the background. Then I took it: "Hi, everybody. This is Gary Bender with Bob Foster in the Sportz-Hallen in Copenhagen, Denmark, as today we bring you the Light Heavyweight Championship of the World between John Conteh and Yacqui Lopez."

Then I turned to Bob to introduce him and do my first lead. I immediately noticed his eyes were glazed. In fact, it appeared he was almost in a state of shock. When I asked him a question I had asked him at least six times in rehearsal, he didn't answer. I answered for him. I asked a second question, again one we'd rehearsed. Again, Bob was silent.

By this time, the producer was in my ear asking, "What's going on out there? What's wrong? Just wrap it up. We'll go to the fight." So I led them to commercial.

While in commercial, Bob grabbed me in almost a death grip and apologized, "I don't know what happened to me. I just really couldn't seem to think."

"That's all right, Bob," I said. "We'll be okay."

But, we weren't. Before our return from the break, they started the fight. When our stage manager saw what was happening, he jumped up to try to get them to stop, forgot he still had his headset on, and was yanked back down. He ripped of the headset and ran over to the timekeeper to try to stop the fight. However, this was a world championship in boxing, not full-contact karate. They weren't about to stop the fight and start over.

Fortunately, the people in our New York studios who were receiving the satellite feed noticed the fight begin, dumped the commercial, and returned it to us. I took it and played catch-up. Foster said very little.

As the fight progressed, I repeatedly asked Bob, "Who's winning?" He'd reply something succinct like "I don't know. It's just a close fight" and nothing more. To make matters worse, the fight went the distance—15 rounds. It was one of the hardest telecasts I've ever gone through in my life. I've never done boxing since and I don't care if I ever do it again. I'm sure Bob Foster is also much happier being a sheriff in Albuquerque, New Mexico.

# PART IV

## DEVELOPING A PLAY-BY-PLAY PHILOSOPHY

*I*t may surprise most listeners and viewers, but sportscasters do have a philosophy, a reason for doing what they do. The guiding light of a play-by-play announcer may differ from that of a color analyst or a studio host. One announcer's beacon may even differ from another's though they're covering the same sport. But regardless of the position, the assignment, or the individual, competent sportscasters have spent time thinking about what they want to accomplish on the air before ever entering the booth. And that personal goal-setting doesn't just happen at the beginning of a career. It's a constant process. With each new experience, broadcasters often alter their objectives as they grow in the business.

The next section examines the basic role of the play-by-play announcer, the various issues most announcers must address at some point in their careers, and some suggestions that will help the young broadcaster avoid philosophical crises.

# CHAPTER FIFTEEN

# The Role of a Play-by-Play Announcer

## Bridging the Mechanical Gap

A friend once described seeing the psychedelic rock band Jefferson Airplane at a concert in Fargo, North Dakota, just before the group reached the height of its popularity in the late 60s. Fargo was not and has never been associated with being a hip place, part of the mainstream, and it was obvious the band felt this way. Though the large audience was more than receptive to the Airplane's different sound, the group appeared to play only for itself to the point that band members even turned their backs to the crowd and gave knowing nods to each other.

My friend said the sound was great, but the experience was disappointing. "It was as though an invisible curtain separated us from them. They seemed unwilling to let us share the emotion of their music."

One of the first things young broadcasters must learn is that their reason for existence is the audience that sees and/or hears them. Without someone to listen to or watch a sportscast, there is no reason for broadcasting the event. However, it is one thing to relate to an audience that is live and visible before you and another to do so when your only connection with the audience is a microphone and a camera.

Bridging the mechanical gap between you and the audience can be a supreme challenge. Just think of a late-night disk jockey. He's all alone at the station. Everyone is at home and very likely in bed asleep. In fact, it's so late, he's not even sure *anyone* is out there listening. For all he knows, it's just him, the turntable, his records and tapes, the board—and the microphone. If he's not careful, he might forget himself and start talking to and playing things that only appeal to him. He may be entertained, but it's unlikely anybody else is who's listening. Because he is unable to personify anyone on the other side of the microphone and equipment, he risks losing what little audience he does have.

A professor once told me the best way to overcome the distance between the microphone and the living room of your audience is to mentally picture a family at home—a father, a mother, a teenage daughter and son—and try to communicate to each one individually. It's a solid idea I used as a boy on a tractor long before I was aware of what I was doing.

The concept of visualization is nothing new. Athletes use it all the time. Walter Payton, the great Chicago Bear running back, once told me he would go out onto the field prior to every game with a football in the crook of his arm and walk the entire length and width of the field to determine where the footing was good and bad, all the time mentally envisioning the moves he would later make in the game when running on that part of the turf. Al DelGreco, a former place-kicker for the Phoenix Cardinals, always went onto the field before everyone else and took practice kicks, without using a football or a holder. He went through the motion of kicking the ball, looked up after making imaginary contact, and mentally pictured the ball sailing through the uprights.

At times during a game, announcers might address comments and ask questions of their teammates in the booth, using their partners as substitutes for the audience. But, if they carry it too far, they end up simply entertaining each other. As a play-by-play announcer, you must constantly keep in mind who is on the other side of the microphone and camera and try your best to keep them interested in the game.

Whenever I run into someone who is deeply concerned about the outcome of the game I'm covering that week, I often tuck that individual away in my mental filing cabinet. Then on game day, I picture him or her as a living, breathing person in my audience who is hanging onto each word I say. If I'm interviewing a coach live, my attention may be directed at the coach, but the questions I ask are based on what I think that viewer might want to know.

## Being a Reporter Versus Being a Fan

The prime objective of a play-by-play announcer is to accurately report what is happening in an event. This includes capturing the event's emotion. But it is one thing to reflect the excitement on the field and another to get wrapped up in it.

My son and I were riding in the car listening to a Kansas City Royals game in the late innings of a very close contest when an opposing player hit a slow roller to the first base side of the infield. Royals announcer Denny Matthews described the play this way: "It's going to be a tough play. No one's covering. No one's covering . . . He's out!"

I looked at Trey and he looked at me as if to say, "What?"

What had happened was Matthews had gotten so engrossed in wanting someone to cover the bag, he forgot to tell his audience that Jeff Montgomery, the Royal reliever, had gotten a late break off the mound and was racing to cover first, reaching it just in time.

It is sometimes difficult not to be affected by the high emotions of a dramatic moment even when you don't have a vested interest in the outcome of an event. I've already cited the example of Billy Packer vacating his broadcast position after "the shot heard around the world," giving North Carolina State the upset victory over Houston for the NCAA Championship in 1983. Who can forget the emotion in Al Michaels' voice as he said "Do you believe in miracles?" when the U.S. hockey team upset the Soviets in the 1980 Olympics. Or the emotion evoked from the usually laid-back Jack Buck as he called Kirk Gibson's game-winning homer in the bottom of the ninth in Game One of the 1988 World Series for CBS radio, ending with the classic statement, "I don't believe what I just saw!" The emotion doesn't even have to be joyous. There was no way Dick Enberg could disguise the obvious shock and pain he felt after Go For Wand broke down during her neck-and-neck stretch run with Bayakoa at the 1990 Breeder's Cup. The point is play-by-play announcers are human, too.

However, maintaining a reporter's objectivity in the face of emotional situations has to be a goal of all play-by-play announcers.

As Red Barber put it in his book *The Broadcasters,* "The listener wants to know, deeper inside himself than he consciously thinks, what is going on. He does not want to know what the announcer wants to see happen, but what he actually sees. He wants to know a line drive is a line drive, no matter who hit it. The listener needs the constant assurance that he is getting an accurate report of the event.

"To care, to root, to anguish, to rejoice—these are the rights of the fan. They are not the rights of the professional announcer, any more than they are of the umpire who rules safe or out . . . ball or strike."

Vin Scully, a protégé of Barber, told Bob Costas on his NBC program "Later" about the origin of his professionalism: "I think that goes back to the training from Red, the attitude, if you will, that you're not going to the ball park to enjoy the game. You're not going to the ball park to holler and scream and root. You're going to the ball park to work and to work as best as you possibly can whether it's the World Series or a very quiet afternoon in the great indoors of Houston.

"I'm not a fan . . . Sure, I am paid by the Dodgers. I am an employee. I am insured by them . . . and I would like to see them win. I really would. But when we're on the air, I try as hard as I can not to root. I learned a long time ago that I did not want to see things as a fan. A fan sees what he wants to see. So, in the ninth inning, if a hitter comes up, down by a run, and he hits a fly ball, the fan wants a home run. He goes crazy. But it's only a fly ball. He has seen it with his heart. I can't afford that. I have to see it with my eyes."

## Being a Reporter Versus Being an Authority

Some play-by-play announcers are often too quick to lend authority: stating their opinion on a given situation, they forget their first responsibility to take care of the nuts and bolts, the down and distance, the time, the score. It's an easy trap to fall into because, in fact, announcers often are experts simply from the amount of preparation they do.

The telltale sign of an announcer crossing the fine line between being a reporter and being an authority is the use of what I call I-isms: "I don't think they should have run on third and ten. They should have passed" or "I think this . . ." or "I think that . . ."

A way to avoid sounding like a know-it-all yet give credence to what you're saying is to refer to others who *are* authorities such as players and coaches. For example, instead of saying "I think the Bears are playing with extreme confidence right now," it would be better to say "When I talked with Bill Cowher on the field before the game today, he seemed very confident. The way the Bears are playing right now, they share that same confidence." By referring to the true expert, you validate your statement. You also show the audience you went the extra mile to provide them with important inside information.

However, there are a couple of cautions to linking yourself with authorities from the field of play.

First, if you say "I really enjoyed our golf game with Bill Cowher yesterday," you sound self-serving, as though you are trying to impress the audience with the people you know. When mentioning your association with players and coaches, you must be sure you are passing on information the audience wants to know: "When we played golf with Bill Cowher yesterday he played very well, as though he didn't have a care in the world. The Bears are playing with that same confidence on the field today."

Second, if you refer to having talked with someone, be sure you really had the conversation. Putting words in people's mouths will catch up with you and probably get you fired.

When I cover an event, I don't believe the audience cares what Gary Bender thinks. They only want to see that I have done my homework, that I am knowledgeable, that, if I had an opinion, I could substantiate it. The play-by-play announcer is a recorder of events not a molder of public opinion.

## Being the Voice of a Team Versus Being a Network Announcer

Play-by-play announcers at the network level must always be neutral in their call of the game, showing no bias for either team. An announcer who is not impartial will hear about it. (You may hear about it anyway. After calling a televised Kansas-Kansas State basketball game as a neutral announcer, I received six letters of criticism. Three said I favored the Jayhawks and three said I was for the Wildcats. I must have done something right to receive a split vote.)

If you were to talk to Red Barber, he would say this same objective view should also apply to an announcer who is the voice of a team. As he put it in his book *The Broadcasters,* "A sportscaster has an obligation to see a contest as it happens and not as he would like to see it happen."

However, another school of thought says the voice of a team can take certain liberties regarding emotionally pulling for their team. This doesn't mean you have to be a cheerleader, blatantly using the word "we": "We've got to score this run if we want to get back in the game." Instead, your emotions come through in your vocal inflections. Anyone who hears Baseball Hall of Fame announcer Harry Carey say "Cubs win!" after a Chicago victory has no doubt which side he is emotionally tied to. Judging from the fact that he is an institution in Chicago, Cub fans wouldn't have it any other way. They want their announcer to reflect their feelings.

If you were to poll team announcers, most would share Barber's ideal. Yet, after traveling with the players and coaches, seeing them day in and day out, the game takes on a different importance. It's hard to separate being "for" and being "fair."

Seattle Mariner announcer Dave Niehaus takes pride in not being a "homer." He believes he is being complimented by people who say they can't tell whether the Mariners are winning or losing when they turn on the radio in the middle of a game he is calling. Still, "you *do* live with these guys. You live and die with them." Therefore, Niehaus admits, "I'm as objective as my subjectivity will allow me."

Because getting too close to your subjects can compromise objectivity, Barber lived by this rule of thumb: "To be fair to all the players, to be able to report them for what they do, I always felt I should be on good, friendly working terms with them, speak to them all, be interested in them and their work, but no more interested in one of them than in another." Barber said he never socialized with ballplayers, never asked them favors, and even had his wife sit with her own friends or alone, not with the players' wives.

Niehaus also follows similar guidelines. "I don't go out to movies with (players). I don't shop with them . . . I can't. After their career is over, I'll be happy to be buddy, buddy with them." To do his job, Niehaus says he has to be objective, not only pointing out the heroic efforts, but also the errors, mistakes, and bonehead plays. "I have had ballplayers who were not my biggest fans because I *do* tell it like it is. I can't worry about (how they react). My audience is not the baseball players, their wives, and relatives. My audience is the fans."

Impartiality at the network level means not only being emotionally neutral, but giving equal time to both teams. Network announcers and producers prepare for each game with this thought in mind and frequently review past tapes to check whether their coverage of a game might have been slanted because of the amount of information given about one team compared to the other.

An announcer's preparation as the voice of a team may differ in that the information used on the air will have a slant toward the team represented simply because that's where the audience's interest lies. As the radio voice for the Phoenix Cardinals, I had to know every detail about each Cardinal player because the fans wanted to know anything and everything about their team. They were far less interested in the details about the third-string punt returner for the San Francisco 49ers who was unlikely to play.

This doesn't mean you don't thoroughly research the opponent. In order to paint a clear portrait of how Phoenix is doing, I often talked about the opposition's strengths and weaknesses, why they had or had not been successful, and why they might present problems to the Cardinals.

In fact, when it comes to preparing spotting boards or score books, announcers will probably spend more time on the opposing team than on their own. For example, since a team faces a single opponent no more than twice during a season (not counting preseason), the voice of a professional football team has to spend time virtually every week preparing spotting boards for the opposition while the spotting boards for the team they are covering needs to be prepared once then simply updated weekly.

Regardless of whether you are a network announcer or do play-by-play for a team, your first concern should be your audience. As Detroit Tiger announcer Rick Rizzs puts it, "The people who really sign your checks are the fans because, if they don't like you, they can write in thousands and thousands of letters and you can be on the street looking for another job.

"I broadcast to the fans. They're my employer. When they tune in, they want to find out the facts. Sometimes the numbers are real good. Sometimes the numbers are not real good. But the fans need to know those numbers good and bad. It's fun when you're winning eight games in a row. It's not so much fun when you're losing eight games in a row. You can't hide the facts. The fans are smart. They know exactly what's going on."

## Being an Informer Versus Being an Entertainer

For years, a debate has raged among sportscasters: Are play-by-play announcers informers or entertainers?

According to *Webster's*, to entertain means "to hold the attention of pleasantly or agreeably; to divert; to amuse." Though to many of its participants it is a business, to the viewing public sports are a diversion from the hard realities of life. And, because sportscasters attempt to make any sporting event they broadcast as pleasant and agreeable an experience as possible, play-by-play announcers would have to be considered, in the broader sense, a part of the entertainment industry.

However, when the specific function of the announcer in the booth is examined, the role seems to be more informer than entertainer. If you liken a football broadcast to another diversion—reading—the play-by-play announcer is equivalent to a talking bookmark. Using chapters and pages as yardsticks, the bookmark (announcer) reliably measures the reader's progress through a book, guiding the reader with occasional synopses of what has transpired. The book provides the entertainment, not the bookmark.

But if bookmarks (announcers) do their job in a way that enhances the reader's reading, which helps keep the readers' attention, aren't they adding to the entertainment value of the experience?

Are play-by-play announcers informers or entertainers? The truth is they're probably a little of both. Within the context of their job in the booth, announcers are primarily informers whose information aids in the entertainment of the audience.

The confusion about the issue comes because some announcers interpret "to entertain" as the third part of *Webster's* definition—"to amuse." As one play-by-play announcer put it, "What we're doing here isn't brain surgery. It's got to be entertaining and it should be fun."

But "fun" does not necessarily mean "funny." How many play-by-play announcers have you heard who are noted for their one-liners? For speaking engagements, I can relate amusing stories that draw laughter from the audience. In the booth, I can tell a piece of sidebar information that will be humorous to the viewers. But I am not inherently funny. I am not a wit. If my job depended on that facility, I would not have lasted in the business.

People also have fun when they go to a movie. But not all movies are comedies. There are many movie genres, each evoking some level of human emotion, and all are considered forms of entertainment. By the same token, if an announcer can capture for the audience the various emotions that human competition evokes—"the thrill of victory, the agony of defeat"— doesn't the announcer have entertainment value?

If a comedian is in the booth it is more likely to be the color analyst. In fact, the announcer is often Bud Abbott to the analyst's Lou Costello, acting as a straight man. When a humorous story should be told during the broadcast, it is usually the analyst who tells it prompted by the announcer's lead.

However, problems arise when the team in the booth tries to interject humor on a planned basis. A Saturday college football game is not the same environment as a taping of "Seinfeld." The actors for a sitcom have a script they rehearse to get the proper comic timing; they control the situation. A football game has no set script. Therefore, the broadcast team has no control over what might happen. Unless humor is inter-jected as a spontaneous reaction to something occurring on the field, it has a good chance of falling flat.

Also, humor is sometimes inappropriate. No announcer would dream of cracking a joke with two outs in the bottom of the ninth when the bases are loaded in a one-run game or when a no-hitter is on the line.

The point is, the event is the entertainment. Play-by-play announcers are secondary to the event and can only augment the experience for the viewer or listener. They can't force a game into a direction it's not going. They have to take what the game gives them.

Because they spend so much time in research, watching films, visiting with coaches, digging up information about play-ers, learning the issues, sportscasters often develop expectations about how a game will play out. If they carry those expectations into the booth, preparing for only one course of events and no other, their lack of flexibility will come back to haunt them.

Pat Haden and I once covered an Air Force-New Mexico football game in Colorado Springs, a rarity for the Air Force Academy. They were so excited about being on national tele-vision they proposed an elaborate opening to the telecast: the Academy's parachute team, the Wings of Blue, would para-chute the game ball into the stadium just before the kickoff while our cameras captured the event live. Our production team agreed with the idea, thinking it would be a unique way to start the broadcast.

As planned, the show began with a taped tease Pat and I had done ahead of time followed by our on-camera pre-game analysis. Then, on cue, I turned to the field behind me and said, "Now, ladies and gentlemen. Today we have a special presentation of the game ball—the Wings of Blue!"

However, when I looked there was nothing. Absolutely nothing. Not a dot in the sky. The prevailing winds had blown the parachutists off course behind us out of range of our cameras.

Immediately, the producer screamed at the cameramen to "please find the parachutists" and, at the same time, yelled at me to "fill, fill, fill." Eventually, one of the parachutists did enter the stadium. But it was the wrong one, not the one with the game ball. I struggled to find something to say for another few minutes before the right parachutist finally landed on the field.

After the shaky beginning—which went out live and uninterrupted across the country—we went to commercial and tried to catch our bearings. But as soon as we returned, New Mexico returned the opening kickoff 95 yards for a touchdown. Then, after the Lobos kicked off, Air Force threw an 80-yard touchdown pass on its first play from scrimmage. The game went that way the entire afternoon. Pat and I never did catch up, never got into any rhythm.

This story doubly illustrates what can happen if you try to force a sporting event into preconceived parameters instead of showing flexibility, reacting to and reporting the event as it unfolds.

First, we had this grandiose idea, this unusual production, that we thought would knock the socks off our viewing audience. But when the production didn't come off as planned, everything else went down with it. When the parachutists didn't appear, the producer should have had me say, "We've had a delay. We'll be back after this commercial." Then, we should have taped the parachutist bringing in the game ball and used it to pad on the other side of commercial.

Second, from our preparation, Pat and I came into the game not expecting it to be a high-scoring contest. When the bombs started falling we were caught off guard, becoming almost like little kids—"Wow! Look at this! This is unbelievable!"— building the game into something it wasn't, possibly trying to make up for the fiasco beginning. The truth was it was a poorly played game with incredible breakdowns in defense which we should have brought to the attention of the viewers.

At least Pat and I didn't give up on the game. Announcers have a duty to stay emotionally into every game from beginning to end. They may not remain emotionally involved in the outcome when the game has long been decided, but they must remain emotionally committed to making it the best broadcast possible. The minute you quit on a game, the audience will quit on you.

Hotly contested games that go down to the wire with big play after big play will carry any announcer. But there are times when announcers realize giving the audience the time, down and distance, and score will not hold the audience's interest anymore because the outcome of the event is no longer in doubt. When this happens, announcers have to give the audience something that persuades them to stay with the broadcast—they have to become entertaining.

The way most play-by-play announcers keep audience interest during blowouts is to be informative. Blowout material is really nothing more than an extension of the material you ordinarily prepare for a game. It is often historical information that looks at past players, traditions, or highlights of the teams playing, something that takes time to develop. Frequently, as you and the analyst are doing your on-site preparation, a piece of sidebar information catches your attention. One or the other will say, "That's interesting. We ought to get into that if we have time." "Time" often implies "in the case of a blowout."

Even though the game has reached the point where fans are losing interest, blowout material has to relate to the participants in some way. If I were calling a blowout between the University of Washington and UCLA in early October, I would not ask my analyst about the World Series. I would lead to blowout material we have developed about the two schools—Washington's quarterback tradition or the running back tradition at UCLA—or about the Pac-10 race or the national rankings and how this game affects the overall picture of both.

It's very difficult to predict blowouts. Announcers become so involved with the coaches on both sides, they often come away thinking both teams have the capability to win. The more I am in this business, the more I'm surprised that one team gets hammered by another. But, even when there is an apparent mismatch, you can be surprised. Billy Packer and I prepared pages of blowout material for the 1983 NCAA Championship Game between Houston and North Carolina State because we both anticipated a lopsided win by Houston. In fact, we believed it would be the worst final of all time. There was even a point early in the second half during commercial when I turned to Billy and said, "We better get our blowout material ready." Then Houston started missing free throws, allowing the Wolfpack back in the game. The rest is history. We never did get to use to our blowout material.

When the time is appropriate for going to blowout material, it is a challenge for announcers to work it into the broadcast without belittling or completely ignoring what is happening on the field. The announcer and the analyst have to learn to interweave their stories while still providing the basics—the down, distance, time, and score. This is easier to do on radio than television because you are not constantly tied to what the camera is showing the audience. It is also easier to do when covering baseball, because the sport's rhythm allows significant time between pitches to develop material.

Whether the game is a blowout or is decided on the last play, whether the announcer is viewed as an informer or an entertainer, the audience should be of primary concern. The announcer's goal should be to create such a sense of anticipation that viewers or listeners will believe they might miss something if they turn away.

# CHAPTER SIXTEEN

# *Handling Weather and Other Difficulties*

*I*'ve done games in a driving snowstorm where it was hard enough just to spot the players let alone the yard markers. I've experienced rainstorms that not only destroyed my spotting boards, but also knocked out our TV cameras. I've endured canceled flights, car problems, nights without sleep, and bad head colds. All announcers can relate similar experiences that have affected their ability to do their job in the booth. But the fact that these difficulties affect the announcer is of no interest to the viewers. They don't want to know about you. They want to know about the game on the field.

If the conditions affect play on the field, that's a different matter. The last annual game between the college all-stars and the defending NFL champs was eventually called because it was raining so hard at Soldier Field it not only knocked out cameras, but made play on the field extremely hazardous. There was no way the ABC broadcasters could sit there and ignore the situation.

Announcers are also obligated to speak out when the audience is also a victim of the weather. CBS covered a play-off game between Philadelphia and Chicago at Soldier Field that got so foggy, no one could see the field. Because they had to put the camera at field level where there was no perspective, the announcer had to tell the audience, "Hey, folks. We're just like you. We can't see a thing."

Still, broadcasters have to be careful how they relate the conditions to the audience. Announcers can talk about how it's 30 below, making it hard to catch the football or making the footing on the frozen field precarious, but they shouldn't move the weather into their arena—the booth—unless it's to illustrate the conditions. It's okay to show a thermometer registering 30 below then cut to the announcer and the analyst in the booth all bundled up in parkas, but it is not all right to say, "Ladies and gentlemen, we're having a tough time talking today because it's so cold our teeth are chattering."

Why? When an announcer says something like "This is the most miserable situation I've ever been in," there will be thousands of people in the audience saying to themselves, "You so-and-so. You're telling me *you* have a tough life. How would you like to be working on an assembly line for eight hours, then hold down a second job just to make ends meet? I'd love just to afford to go to a game. *You've* got problems? I don't want to hear about them."

This caveat also applies to mentioning technical difficulties. The audience will want an explanation when audio or visual difficulties affect their viewing, but it could care less if the broadcast team's talk-back system has failed.

Weather conditions are beyond the announcer's control. Generally, so are technical difficulties. But broadcasters do have a degree of control over health problems if they practice preventive medicine. And the one thing they have to be most protective of is their voice.

The voice is an announcer's livelihood. It shouldn't be abused. But many novice announcers abuse their voice through bad breath control, poor physical conditioning, and bad environment.

The proper use of the voice requires an understanding of the physiology of singing. My background in singing taught me that by using my diaphragm, I could better control my breathing, therefore extending the length of time I could use my voice.

Pitchers talk about getting into a zone or a groove where their fastball goes exactly where they want it with no stress on the arm. Likewise, announcers have to find a vocal range that represents a groove to them where they can talk indefinitely and be able to walk away from the booth without being hoarse. When you find it, you'll know it.

When I first started out, I had a tendency to push my voice—the equivalent of trying to make yourself heard in a crowded room. I didn't relax my throat or vocal cords. Consequently, there were a couple of times I nearly lost my voice late in a game.

A lot of young announcers get into the same rut. They force their voice to show excitement or to be resonant or to do something that is not natural, taking it out of its normal groove. You can still communicate excitement and vitality without pushing your voice beyond its normal range. It simply requires learning voice projection and how to use proper enunciation in which stressing various words and syllables communicates emotion with no strain on the voice.

When you are in poor physical shape, it directly affects your voice. It will become especially noticeable when you call a three-hour football game. Consequently, it is advisable to work out on a regular basis in order to build stamina and develop a healthy body.

However, everyone will eventually fall victim to a virus. The common cold is public enemy number one to any broadcaster.

One of the first major assignments I had at KWBW at the beginning of my career was the endurance test known as the Juco Tournament—a five-day, 26-game event held annually in Hutchinson with each game broadcast on the radio. Just before the tournament, I caught a miserable cold almost overnight. I made it through the tournament's first day and part of the second. Then, something happened to me that had never happened before. I had no voice. None.

I first went to a doctor who prescribed something that must have been some kind of an upper because I felt I was ten feet off the ground, flying around. If I had gone on the air that way, it would have been a disaster. My wife Linda doctored me at home with all sorts of cold remedies and a humidifier. I was able to make it back into the booth for the final two days of the tournament, but the whole incident really scared me.

Since then, I have learned to recognize the difference between a stuffy nose due to allergy and a cold virus. At the first signs of a cold, I jump on it immediately. It may sound like hypochondria, but if I start getting a sore throat, I don't mess around with it. I instantly go to the doctor.

As my experience in Hutchinson showed me, you have to be careful what you take before entering the booth. The first thing I tell a doctor is I can't take anything that will cloud my mind. Some cough syrups almost make you sound like a drunk. Lindsey Nelson once took some cough medicine for a bad cold just before doing a nationally televised game and it affected him so badly his partner Paul Hornung had to take over.

You also have to be careful of medicines that dry you up. Some medicines, like antihistamines, dry up everything—the runny nose, the itchy eyes. But they also dry up moisture in your throat. You end up with a very thin, raspy voice. Your doctor has to find something that will prevent coughing and lubricate the throat. I've learned to keep lozenges and nose sprays around the booth that help me to breathe freely, allow sinus drainage to occur, while at the same time keep my mind clear.

When you are suffering from a cold, you have to save your voice whenever possible. Rest it at every opportunity. Don't talk to people on airplanes or while riding in a car. Stay out of noisy rooms where you will have to strain your voice to be heard. And on the air, cut down on your verbiage and rely on your analyst to help carry the broadcast.

Before game time, you should go through vocal calisthenics to loosen your voice so it won't crack on air. I will often warm up when doing the voice-over for the tease, reading the copy in different pitches to exercise my voice.

Even when healthy, you should avoid eating before or during a broadcast because it will affect vocal resonance and may even cause you to burp on air. What you ingest when ill is even more important. During the broadcast, I drink a lot of water, never Coke or anything carbonated. I also avoid coffee because the caffeine tends to make me hyper. If I'm really having problems, I will drink hot tea with lemon and honey.

In any case, what usually happens is, once the broadcast begins, once you get into the heat of battle, your adrenaline kicks in and you forget your ills.

Environment can also affect the voice. Bad weather— particularly very cold weather—can constrict your vocal cords causing your voice to tire more quickly. Appropriate clothing can alleviate the situation.

However, the worst environmental detriment to an announcer's voice is smoke. Smoking in the booth bothers everyone, including the spotters, the statistician, and the technical crew. I find my voice changes because of smoke, taking on a rasp, not to mention the irritation it causes the eyes. If your partner is a smoker, you need to set ground rules up front about smoking in the booth. I have always had an agreement that they can only light up at halftime or before the game and never in the booth proper.

Whatever personal problems the play-by-play announcer has, whether it be frostbitten toes, a monitor on the fritz, or a case of pneumonia, the audience is not interested. Just keep in mind what happens at a cocktail party when someone in a group says "My back is killing me" or "My divorce is going to put me in the poorhouse." The group will gradually disengage, looking for more interesting channels.

CHAPTER SEVENTEEN

# *Handling Controversy*

$S$ince "to err is human," controversy is bound to occur in any activity in which humans are involved. Some people relish controversy. Others would rather sports be perfect, an idyllic endeavor in which everyone competes, following the same high-minded principles. The fact is, controversy comes with the territory of broadcast journalism. Whether they like it or not, announcers have to be prepared for the inevitable.

When reporting a controversy, there are three rules of thumb play-by-play announcers should follow: (1) know the facts; (2) report the facts without bias; and (3) be decisive.

## Getting the Facts Straight

When the late Ohio State coach Woody Hayes threw his infamous punch at the Clemson football player running out of bounds, everyone watching ABC's coverage saw the moment. Everyone, that is, but ABC announcer Keith Jackson. For whatever reason, Keith was not watching his monitor when the camera caught the incident that ended Hayes' illustrious career. Because he didn't see it, he made no comment. The people at ABC's New York studio called the truck to find out why. Jackson's response, "Hey, I didn't see it. I'm not going to take somebody else's word for it because it's such a damaging story."

Though he was criticized for his lack of comment, Keith's stance was correct. Announcers shouldn't report controversy unless they have their facts straight. Reporting inaccuracies not only diminishes the professional stature of the announcer, but also adds fuel to the fire.

The most common area for controversy to arise is on the field as a result of an official's call.

Why anyone would want to be an official is beyond me. Call a good game and no one notices you. Make one bad call and everyone is on your neck. Why would anyone want to take that kind of abuse? Yet, most officials are very successful in other walks of life. They're school principals, corporation presidents, or leaders in the community. I respect these men. They have a tough job to do. But I also recognize that they can make mistakes.

Announcers can only bring calls into question if they know the rules. There is nothing more embarrassing than to say "that should be an automatic 15-yard penalty" only to have your analyst correct you moments later.

Football rules are the worst. They differ from level to level and are constantly being changed. Every year before the football season, the network brings its announcers together and has an expert update them on all the latest changes, illustrating them in storybook fashion. When I covered the Big Ten, Gene Calhoun, the supervisor of officials, even gave us a quiz of ten "what ifs" to test our knowledge of the rules.

Working with John Madden was always a treat, but particularly because of his knowledge of the game. John once told me, "Gary, the biggest thing I can help you with as a broadcaster is, I know the rules. Don't you ever worry about a rule. If there's something controversial, I'll take it."

It was reassuring to have John Madden's expertise next to me in the booth. But for every John Madden, there are dozens of announcers who are reluctant to go out on a limb because of the many twists and turns to football rules. And rightfully so. Rules are a mine field. You have to constantly study them in order to be at the ready. In a football game you do not have time to physically refer to a rule book between plays for answers to odd situations. Fortunately, referees are often miked for network television, therefore erasing any doubt about what they called. But without the mike, what they signal may not be explanation enough.

You and your analyst have to have an agreement on how to handle official rulings. Don't debate on the air. In most cases, it is the play-by-play announcer's responsibility to call the official's ruling and the analyst's responsibility to interpret it. In any case, you should never put your partner on the spot by asking, "What was that?"

Announcers have a maxim for handling officials' calls: If in doubt, lay out. Wait for the official explanation over the PA system or have someone in the truck follow up on it.

The same maxim also applies to calling injuries.

If you cover sports long enough, you can gain a reasonable knowledge of athletic injuries. You can usually tell a leg cramp, a knee injury, or a shoulder injury simply from the way the injured player is moving. However, it is dangerous to play doctor in the booth.

I've watched games on television in which the announcer and the analyst identify the injured party and guess at the extent of an injury, only to find after a commercial break that the injured player is not only someone other than the person first identified, but he is walking off the field under his own power. It has happened to me. What looked like an apparent leg injury turned out to be a shoulder injury. We didn't even come close to the right body part.

Because injuries force a break in the action, announcers have a void to fill. And the obvious story to focus on is what is delaying the game. Unfortunately, there is only so much you can say about the injury without speculating. If you do speculate, it's better to be on the safe side—call it a first-degree burn rather than a third-degree burn. It is easier to reverse yourself when later reports show the injury to be more serious than originally thought. But if you overreact, making the injury serious to begin with only to have to say it was just a false alarm, you are being needlessly cruel to the family and friends who are hanging on your every word.

During the 1989 baseball season, Minnesota's Gary Gaetti smashed a line drive that hit Seattle pitcher Billy Swift on the side of the head with such force it bounced into the seats along left field foul line on one hop for a ground rule double. Then Mariner announcer Rick Rizzs described his initial reaction this way: "It scared the daylights out of me. Your first thought is that he is seriously hurt. Billy had fallen to the front side of the mound like a sack of bricks. And you get this sick feeling down inside. It's a scary, sinking feeling."

Though Rizzs and his partner Dave Niehaus both felt dire concern for Swift, they knew they had a job to do. They knew they would have five to ten minutes of delay and that the game was now secondary. They redescribed exactly what had happened, going over each detail slowly and accurately—"It was a line drive off the bat of Gary Gaetti. It looked like it hit Billy off the side of the head and took his cap right off." They described where the ball landed. They described what was currently going on on the field, the position Billy was in, how he was being attended to, and who was attending to him. They described the atmosphere in the Kingdome, trying to capture the mood and emotion of the crowd. But never once did they speculate on Swift's condition.

If they had, they would have been wrong. Swift left the game, but walked off the field under his own power. His injury? A large bump on the side of his head. He spent the night in the hospital under observation, but didn't even receive a concussion. When his turn in the rotation came up again, he was back on the mound.

Remember, if in doubt, lay out. Wait for the injury report.

## Stating Opinion

It is an American credo that everyone has a right to an opinion. However, as a recorder of events, the play-by-play announcer is obligated to present both sides of an issue in a fair and unbiased manner when controversy arises. Does this mean that an announcer is not entitled to express a personal opinion?

If having an opinion means getting up on a soapbox to rant and rave, to hammer a point, the answer is no. But speaking out in a reasoned manner, presenting a case based on fact like a lawyer presenting a brief, is acceptable. The fact is, announcers are not your average fan at home watching television. Because of the preparation they do, they get close to the situation. Consequently, their comments frequently provide valuable insight.

Still, play-by-play announcers have to be careful when they editorialize. The key is knowing the facts.

When play-by-play announcers make editorial comments without knowing the facts, two problems can arise. First, by reporting a controversy inaccurately or stating an opinion based on erroneous information, announcers lose face as an authority, rendering their opinion invalid in the eyes of the audience. Second, in the absence of fact, emotion takes over. And basing an editorial comment solely on emotion can be very dangerous.

Let's look at a hypothetical situation. Say you're announcing a baseball game when, all of a sudden, Bill Batter, the on-deck hitter, jumps into the stands, tackles a fan, and starts fighting with him. You describe the incident for your audience just as you see it. But if you tack on the comment, "Throwing balls at fans. Attacking them in the stands. This kind of behavior by baseball players is deplorable. It's getting out of hand. The league office has to do something to stop it. Bill Batter should be suspended indefinitely," you would be stating opinion based on emotion. You would not have enough information to draw such conclusions.

In fact, you might have to offer Bill Batter an apology. Why? A little later word makes its way to the booth that the reason Batter attacked the fan was that the man was a purse snatcher. A lady had yelled for help, Batter had come to the rescue, tackled the fleeing robber, and was actually trying to subdue him.

One of the main responsibilities of the play-by-play announcer is to keep a cool head while others are losing theirs. Often when controversial situations arise, they catch everyone off guard. In such cases, announcers have to rely on their instincts, their experience, and the homework they've done. They have to capture the emotion of the moment without being drawn into it. Instead of stating an opinion, they should be honest and objective. In the above example of Bill Batter, the better response would be to say, "Like everyone here, I'm shocked by what has just happened. It has caught us all completely by surprise. My initial reaction is that no player should ever leave the playing field to confront a fan. However, I know Bill Batter and I have to think there had to be some kind of provocation. Let's hold off making any judgment until we find out more about what really happened."

The most common form of opinion offered by announcers is criticism of officials' calls. Pointing out a referee's or an umpire's mistake, based on a clear view on replay or an obvious misinterpretation of the rules, is one thing. Being dogmatic about it is another.

Announcers have to guard against referee bashing. Everyone sees things differently. If you are a network announcer who is supposed to be neutral, being adamant about a call will antagonize half your audience. If you are the voice of the team, you have to be especially careful about getting on the officials because it will be awfully tempting to blame it on those officiating when things are not going well for your team. After a while, referee bashing gets old to your audience. And, sooner or later, it will affect your relationship with the men in striped shirts.

Play-by-play announcers also have to be careful when criticizing the play on the field. The pro is paid to play the game and, therefore, should expect to be criticized for a dropped pass, an untimely foul, or a mental error. However, announcers should show some leniency to the student athlete. It is one thing for a pro quarterback to misread a defense, throwing it right into the arms of a defender, and another thing for a college quarterback to do the same. The pro quarterback has more time to study films to learn to read defenses while the college quarterback is often called upon to do more than just concentrate on his passing game.

You also have to be sensitive to "the old college try." Because they get so emotionally involved, college players often attempt to play beyond their capabilities which usually leads to mental or forced errors. Besides, a college player is less skilled than a pro. During the course of any college game, somebody is going to put a tremendous effort into doing the wrong thing. They should be recognized more for the effort than for its unfortunate result.

## Telling It Like It Is

In 1982, Pat Haden and I covered the Nebraska-Penn State game from Beaver Stadium, home of the Nittany Lions. Late in the contest, Penn State tight end Mike McCloskey caught a pass on the sideline that was ruled a completion. However, our CBS replay showed McCloskey failed to keep either foot inbounds. Pat and I commented that the catch should have been called incomplete. It was a crucial call because it enabled the Nittany Lions to continue a game-winning drive. The final: Penn State–27, Nebraska–24. The play became even more controversial at the end of the season when the Nittany Lions won their first national championship while Nebraska finished third. The difference? The Cornhusker's lone loss to Penn State.

The next year Haden and I were back in the Happy Valley to do Penn State's game with Alabama. Again, it went to the wire. Only this time, our replay showed Alabama tight end Preston Gothard getting his feet down in the back of the end zone on a pass that was ruled incomplete. Again, Pat and I commented on the missed call. And again, the call was crucial to the outcome since the negated touchdown eventually cost the Crimson Tide at least a tie. Penn State won 34–28.

Two controversial games back-to-back must have been too much for Penn State Athletic Director Jim Tarman. He was furious with Pat and me because, by focusing on the two calls, we had implied that the two Nittany Lion victories were tarnished. His thinking ran along the lines, "How could you say such things after we spent so much time with you, showing you around campus and buying you a meal?" He told CBS he would never allow Pat and me on campus again nor would we be allowed to do another Penn State game.

All has since been forgiven. But the story points out that announcers must report controversial situations without wavering. In the heat of battle during a broadcast, they cannot afford to anticipate what others might think of them. They have to be decisive and, as the old cliché goes, "tell it like it is." As Dick Vitale is fond of saying, "I'm often wrong, but never in doubt."

## Introducing Controversy for Controversy's Sake

Some people relish controversy. They are constantly looking for dirt to stir things up, to add spice to a broadcast. But announcers who want to be the Rona Barretts of sportscasting are probably not well suited to do play-by-play.

First of all, play-by-play announcers ordinarily don't have the time to do the in-depth research necessary for investigative reporting. And any time you try to stir things up with a story that hasn't been fully researched, you're only asking for trouble.

Second, there's no way to satisfy the public's insatiable appetite for juicy tidbits. Once you get in the habit of throwing morsels at your audience, that's what they'll come to expect. You become like King Midas: anything you touch turns controversial until you turn controversial yourself. Some controversial announcers have made names for themselves (like Howard Cosell), but their notoriety was better served by being a color analyst, a sports talk-show host, or an investigative reporter, not as a play-by-play announcer.

This doesn't mean that play-by-play announcers can ignore controversy. As a parent, I'm not always on the lookout for mistakes my children make. But, when my kids *do* do something wrong, it is my duty to get to the bottom of the problem. The same principle applies to announcers; if the controversy stares you in the face, you are obliged to address it.

Once before an Indiana-Michigan basketball game, Bobby Knight told me how much he disliked Michigan coach Bill Frieder because of the way he ran his program. Knight's animosity was so great, he did not intend to shake Frieder's hand before the game the next day, as was the pre-game custom.

I apprised our producer and the camera crew of what Knight planned so we could catch the moment, if not live, at least on tape. At the appointed time, we were right on top of the incident and fully prepared to address the controversy it instilled.

## When and How to Introduce Controversy

When controversy occurs on the field of play, play-by-play announcers have to address the situation. But when is it proper to bring up off-the-field controversy? If the controversy has no direct bearing on who wins or loses, should it be mentioned?

If everyone is talking about the controversy, there is no way the broadcast crew *can* ignore it. At the network level, the common practice regarding handling hot-potato stories is to discuss them in the production meeting where we decide when and how to bring the matter up on the air.

At the end of the 1990–91 college basketball season, I covered a key Southwest Conference game between Texas and Arkansas in Fayetteville. Just before we arrived on campus to prepare for the game, a major story broke about an alleged rape occurring in the athletic dorm. Razorback basketball players were among those said to be involved. Since it was the number one topic in Fayetteville, we were obligated to say something about it.

The problem was the story was so fresh (less than 48 hours old when we arrived on the scene), there were still too many unanswered questions. I tried to talk to Arkansas coach Nolan Richardson the day before the game, but he was unavailable because of the flu. We talked with his assistants, but they were tight-lipped about the incident.

Because the issues involved were so sensitive, we had to be careful what was said. I went to our producer, Jack Graham, and said, "Jack, I want to do this and I want to do it right. I know it's hard to say what has to be said concisely. So I think I'm going to write it out. You give me a spot in the broadcast where I can read it." When I finished writing what I wanted to say, I showed Jack. He agreed with it. He chose to put it in the program just out of commercial break after the first television time-out which occurred approximately four minutes into the game.

This is what I said:

"Arkansas was concerned about trying to maintain their focus for this game following an alleged incident involving five Razorback athletes, including basketball players. A Springdale, Arkansas, woman said she was sexually assaulted in the school's athletic dorm early Wednesday morning. Yesterday, the woman said she would not press charges. Arkansas officials indicated that there was no evidence to warrant charges anyway. Razorback athletic director Frank Broyles said the University would take disciplinary action if rules were broken. That's the distraction they've been working with all week long."

Cheryl Miller, my broadcast partner, then commented that the situation was not the kind of problem the team wanted to have hanging over its head going into the NCAA tournament. Beyond that, we didn't dwell on the issue. Until the situation had been legally resolved, it would have been inappropriate to do so. We played it like Joe Friday, the character Jack Webb portrayed in the old television series "Dragnet," who always said, "Just the facts, ma'am." We wanted to give the audience the facts, to be accurate and fair to everyone; to disclose, but not to destroy.

The Arkansas controversy made national news. It was a story the audience might have been aware of. But often in the course of doing their preparation, play-by-play announcers run into information that is not common knowledge, that would be interesting to the audience, but also damaging to some individual. Should they use the information on air or not?

Before a Notre Dame-Michigan State game in East Lansing, Dick Vermeil and I met John Heisler and Roger Valdiserri from the Notre Dame Sports Information Department in the lobby of the hotel where we were all staying. They were effusive about how happy Fighting Irish coach Lou Holtz was that we were doing the game and how he couldn't wait to meet and talk with us.

A short time later, Holtz entered the lobby. At that moment, Dick and I were standing off to the side, hidden from Holtz's view by a large pillar. When Heisler and Valdiserri told Holtz we wanted to talk to him, he flew into a rage. He went on and on about how "I've got to have some time" and how "I don't have time for those guys."

Then I walked around the pillar. Holtz saw me, came running over, and said, "Gary, how are you doing? Glad to see you." It was a complete about face. It was as though the last few minutes had never occurred. He gave us all the time we wanted and answered every question we asked.

The same weekend we also met with Michigan State coach George Perles. Talk about rolling out the red carpet. We couldn't do anything for ourselves. Perles followed us everywhere, physically opened doors for us, sat in the film room with us, and really bared his soul. He probably would have given us his firstborn if we'd asked. Dick was so taken by his cooperation, he bought him a fifth of Johnny Walker Black Label.

We had two stories to tell our audience: one bad, one good. We could have talked about Holtz, the Madison Avenue style dresser who was always on guard, whose mask in public was different than in private. And, we could have talked about Perles, a blue collar, Pittsburgh Steeler kind of guy, who sported white socks with everything and wore his heart on his sleeve. We could have used both; we chose to use only one. Why? Though Holtz's actions towards us may have seemed insensitive, they had no bearing on how his team played on the field. If anything, they illustrated the pressures of coaching one of the top programs in the country. Since Holtz was besieged by interviews, we gave him the benefit of the doubt.

In the course of working with coaches, announcers are often made privy to information even the press doesn't know. What are the guidelines for using that information?

First, how pertinent is the information? Is it really a major issue? Many dirt diggers operate under the assumption that where there's smoke, there's fire. It's been my experience that many times there might be smoke, but the fire isn't big enough to warrant air time. To do so would be to sensationalize a trivial incident.

Second, is airing a story worth damaging your relationship with people who have taken you into their confidence? Remember, to do your job as a play-by-play announcer you have to have a good working relationship with the people you cover.

Finally, is there a way to tell the story without putting someone in a corner? Often it's not what you say, but how you say it that makes the difference.

For example, take the case of Joe Smith, a real-life college coach whose identity I'd like to protect out of continuing respect for our working relationship. Smith made the jump from Smalltime College to Bigtime University, a member of one of the power conferences in the nation, and I was assigned to cover his first game. My analyst and I flew in early to watch practices and to talk to players and coaches. The day before the game, we decided to look at some more tape because Smith said it would be all right to come back any time. His door was always open to us. When we opened the door to Smith's office, thinking no one was there but Smith, we were surprised to find him surrounded by attorneys and investment counselors, discussing how to invest his newly increased income. We backed out of the office, closed the door, and went about our business.

Later we talked about how we couldn't believe what we had just seen. Here Smith had an opportunity of a lifetime, guiding a program with a rich tradition, one whose Bigtime boosters measured success solely on winning. And, on the day before his first game, he was showing more interest in his financial arrangements than what the other team intended to do. We both told each other, "He'll never make it."

A dirt-digging journalist might have taken that inside information and gone on the air like this: "The reason Bigtime U. isn't playing well today might be because yesterday Coach Smith was too busy investing his money to be concerned about today's game."

Instead, we handled it this way: "At Smalltime College, Joe Smith achieved great success with a hands-off style of coaching, delegating responsibility to others. However, here at Bigtime U., Smith may have to take a more hands-on approach to be successful." Our statement hit the central issue without embarrassing anyone or destroying any relationships. What we said made sense and Smith, if he heard it, probably wouldn't have argued the point.

# CHAPTER EIGHTEEN

# *Broadcasting Ethics*

*M*ost people are guided by a code of ethics regardless of their walk of life. But, because they are in the public eye, sportscasters have to be particularly cautious of how they conduct themselves.

One of the ethical considerations all journalists have to face is what should and should not be made public. Some broadcasters operate under the following rule: "If you don't want something broadcast, don't tell me. Anything you tell me is fair game." This rule might work for an investigative journalist, but it is very limiting for a play-by-play announcer. Once your sources understand this is your mode of operation, they become more defensive and less open. They either choose their words carefully, tell half-truths, or do not answer at all.

The better path for announcers is to develop a trust with their sources so they have confidence in what will or won't be said on air. When confidences are protected, information sources open up.

Some might argue, "Well, if it's not to be used on the air, why have it in the first place?" The answer is simple: the more information you have, the more accurate your call of the game. I take great pride in having created over the years a reputation that coaches can trust my ability to discern what can be used on the air. They can be candid with me and know I won't compromise them.

Compromising a coach's confidence is a very serious matter. For example, one of the most sensitive pieces of information a coach can tell an announcer is a team's game plan. Say John Cooper confides in me that Ohio State is going to run the wishbone for the first time. They've worked on it in secret, closed-door practices so the Buckeyes will catch UCLA off guard on Saturday. When I later talk to Terry Donahue about his game plan, I hint at what Cooper is planning. By violating Cooper's confidence, I not only potentially affect the outcome of the game, I also ruin my integrity: I certainly destroy any possibility of gaining similar advance information in the future from Cooper, and I will probably also damage my relationship with Donahue because he will not know whether he should trust me with like information.

Protecting confidential information isn't easy. In today's pressure-cooker, win-or-else sports scene, coaches sometimes overstep the bounds of propriety. What do you say when a coach asks, "I know you've talked to the other coach. What did he say?" or when a defensive coordinator asks, "I suppose those guys told you what they're going to do if we blitz?" In either case, the only correct response is to say, "I can't say anything about it." However, a blunt refusal to disclose information places the person who asked in an awkward and embarrassing position. I try to let the coach off the hook by adding the comment, "I'm not sure I understand it anyway" and laugh about it. Most of the time, coaches know they shouldn't have asked and are sorry immediately afterward.

Announcers also have to take care not to reveal confidential information in the questions *they* ask. Say you're covering an Ohio State-Michigan football game and you ask Ohio State coach John Cooper, "What concerns you most about the game?" He responds, "Well, first, we've got to stop Tyrone Wheatley." It just so happens that earlier the same day, you found out Wheatley is sicker than a dog. Even if he suits up, he will be too weak to be a factor. Though you likely won't use the answer on air, you have to play it straight and ask, "Why does Wheatley scare you?" You cannot say, "Hey, John. What if Wheatley doesn't play tomorrow?" Such a question indicates you have inside knowledge and apprises the opposing coach of that knowledge. As far as you are concerned, the information about Wheatley's illness is the same as inadmissible evidence in court. You can't use it.

A common saying in the military during World War II was "Loose lips sink ships." Sportscasters should heed a similar warning. Much of the information announcers pick up during their preparation might not only be useful to the opposing teams on the field, but to others off the field.

Before he decided to retire, former Phoenix Cardinal quarterback Neil Lomax was in terrible pain because of a chronic hip problem. I sat with Neil on the flight to a game when the condition first became serious and asked him, "Neil, are you going to be able to play?" He answered, "No way." Then after a brief pause, he added, "Ever."

What Neil admitted to me was privileged information. While the public was told the problem was a week-to-week kind of thing, insiders with the team knew Neil's career was over. Since quarterbacks are so critical to the outcome of an NFL game, gamblers would have paid for such a valuable insight.

Sports gambling is steadily growing. Newspapers and television regularly pick next weekend's winners and post the current point spreads. Its increasing prevalence in the public mind is scary. Even more scary is the accuracy of the people in Las Vegas who set the odds. It never ceases to amaze me how I'll look at a point spread of the game I'm doing, think to myself, "How can that be?" only to find out later they're right on, they've nailed it. Obviously these people are getting information the ordinary fan doesn't have access to.

The broadcast team—the announcer, analyst, producer, director, and the support crew—has to watch what is said in a public setting. They have to be continuously aware of who drifts onto a practice site, walks into a film room, or sits down at the next table at a restaurant. Discussions about injuries, game plans, and strategies could provide enough inside dope for someone to make a killing.

Compulsive gambling is a disease. It has negatively impacted sports figures such as Art Schlichter and Pete Rose. It has even taken its toll among those who broadcast sports.

Chet Forte was a top director for ABC Sports, winning nine Emmys, most notably for his work with "Monday Night Football." He was also a compulsive gambler. He bet on anything and everything, but particularly sporting events. Though

it was against ABC policy, he even bet on games he was working. Howard Cosell has written that Forte's gambling was common knowledge to the broadcast crew and his co-workers
kidded him, asking him who he bet on so they could bet the
other way.

Forte lost a fortune gambling. In 1990, his Saddle River,
New Jersey, home was sold at a sheriff's auction for $908,000
when Forte could not make payment on his mortgage. He has
since pleaded guilty to mail fraud, wire fraud, and income tax
evasion.

Though it may be tempting, broadcasters must refrain
from any form of gambling. It may seem harmless to pick winners in an office pool or to test your knowledge for a cup-of-
coffee wager, but the long-term damage it does to your image
and integrity is not worth short-term gratification. It's a form of
guilt by association: Once a sportscaster is linked to gambling,
even in a minor way, the potential exists for something much
worse.

# PART V

SPECIALIZING IN PLAY-BY-PLAY

# CHAPTER NINETEEN

# *Developing Add-on Skills*

*E*ven if your goal is to do play-by-play and you are gifted and fortunate enough to be able to specialize in it, your career in sportscasting will undoubtedly include other roles that require different skills. You may become the voice of the Los Angeles Rams, but unless you also do basketball or baseball or some other seasonal play-by-play, you are going to be left with a big hole in your calendar. Though sports seasons seem to be getting longer and longer, no sport is covered year round. To fill the void financially or simply to maintain sanity, play-by-play announcers have to be prepared to cross over, to do something that isn't their first love.

At the local market level, one of the likely jobs you'll be approached to do will be to host a radio talk show. The most challenging aspect of hosting a call-in sports talk show is the requirement to be knowledgeable about everything. For most sports announcers talking football, basketball, or baseball comes easy. But for a competent radio talk-show host, that isn't good enough. You have to be prepared to field questions from the person whose interest is the America's Cup, the guy who's into boxing, or the woman who loves volleyball. These fans have a passion for their sports and expect the talk-show host to be equally passionate. You might be able to field a question on occasion with "I don't know the answer. Let me get back to you on that," but you cannot respond that way forever and hope to keep your show.

It takes a special kind of person to host a talk show. I'm amazed how anyone can retain so much detail, how anyone can remember who batted in front of Ted Williams in the 1941 All-Star game just before he hit the winning home run. To do their jobs, talk-show hosts must have a ravenous appetite for information. Every waking moment must include some form of information gathering, be it from reading or from talking to people. I know I could handle a talk show devoted to football or basketball, but to do all sports requires a unique talent.

A common cross-over for play-by-play announcers is to move into the television studio as a host of a sports program or as the sports anchor in the news block. Studio work requires expanding some of the skills used in play-by-play. Instead of reading off-camera, you have to learn to read on-camera, which requires you to maintain a physical presence while reading. Instead of writing a brief tease or a two-minute opening, you may have to write the script for five, ten, fifteen minutes or longer. In addition, depending upon the kind of show you're involved in and the size of market, you may also be required to edit.

At the network level, once your special venue's season ends, you'll likely be assigned to cover lesser-known sports. Unlike the staples of sports television—football, basketball, baseball, golf, boxing, hockey, horse racing—most other sports rarely are seen live. Because of time considerations such as the event taking place overseas, networks tape the event and edit it to fit into a time slot. Most of what was shown on "CBS Sports Spectacular" and what is still seen on ABC's "Wide World of Sports" is taped.

Postproduction work for taped events requires long hours of building graphics, editing, and mixing sound. For the announcer, it means long hours of trying to recreate the event. One of the toughest jobs in broadcasting is to stand in a darkened studio with a monitor in front of you and try to recapture the emotion, the thrills and excitement that happened earlier that day or even weeks ago. Tape recreation is exacting. Every word must be precise, leaving almost no room for spontaneity. Yet, at the same time, it has to sound as though the event is happening as you speak.

CBS's coverage of the 1991 World Swimming and Diving Championships in Perth, Australia, was all done on tape. We worked in the recording studio sometimes till 2:00 in the morning to get each day's event right. In one race, the original call that John Nabor and I had done live was totally screwed up. It was so bad it was a good thing it was on tape. John and I had to go into the studio and redo the whole race. After reviewing the tape, we did everything over just as though it were live. We planned who would take it and where. Before the race, I set the lanes. I laid out for the starter's gun. I reestablished the swimmers to watch. Then John took over with his analysis of the start. And so on. In essence, we tried to relive the moment, capturing all the emotion we had originally conveyed, but this time using the right words.

Each cross-over job has its unique requirements, using a different set of skills. But regardless the type of announcing job you do, whether it is on-camera or in the course of preparation, you will also need to develop interview skills.

## How To Question

I've always admired Johnny Carson as an interviewer. He mastered the idea that it's the interviewee the audience wants to hear, not the interviewer. Therefore, Johnny's questions were short and to the point. Sometimes he could even elicit a response without asking a question at all, simply by using a facial expression.

We've all heard interviewers whose convoluted questions ramble on and on and on, seeming to never end. It's as though they can't find the period or the question mark to stop their sentence. Sometimes within the rambling are three questions, not one. Sometimes the question starts in one direction and ends in a totally different one. In any case, when the question is too complex, the interviewer risks losing the interviewee. The most embarrassing moment for all interviewers is to be asked by their subject, "What was the question?"

Interviewers should have a purpose to their interview. They should know whether the interview is to be a probing, investigative type or one which simply educes the subject's personal reaction to a set of events. In conjunction with their purpose, interviewers also need to know their time restrictions. Hosts of a half-hour talk show have leeway to be exploratory in questioning while play-by-play announcers interviewing a coach after a game have to be aware of the emotions of the moment, focus their questions, and get to the crux of the matter immediately.

During the 1988 All-Star game, Joe Morgan and I took turns interviewing players underneath the stadium after they had been taken out of the game. Since the producer called for the interviews during brief breaks in the game, we were severely strapped for time and were, generally, limited to two questions at most. Consequently, I chose to ask one question pertinent to the game and one pertinent to the player's season.

What do you ask? In developing questions, I've always used the rule of thumb—what would the average fan want to ask this person?

But even if you know what to ask, you also have to know how to ask it. Remember, the objective of the interview is to get a response from the subject. If the interviewer's questions evoke nothing but yes or no answers, the interview will go downhill fast. Instead, interviewers should make open-ended probes. By asking questions beginning with "Who," "What," "Where," "When," "How," and "Why," interviewers allow their subjects to expand their comments. Instead of asking "Was that the longest home run you've hit?" ask "How did that home run compare to others you've hit?"

You can also elicit a response from your subject without even asking a question, by using open-ended statements. You can say, "For the first three months of the season you struggled at the plate. Now in the last month, you've raised your average 30 points," and leave it at that. The statement shows your area of interest and implies to the subject that you are also asking "What happened?"

## Listening

Listening is the key to the best interviews. You may enter into an interview with questions you've prepared beforehand, with a clear idea of where you think the interview will go, but if you aren't flexible enough to deviate from your plan when your subject leads you elsewhere, you may miss a golden opportunity to develop a good story. Some of the most memorable interviews were based on pursuing the spontaneous reactions of the people being interviewed.

Good interviewers are good listeners. Through body language, they indicate their interest, encouraging the subject to respond. They keep eye contact with their subject. Nothing distracts interviewees more than answering questions while interviewers shuffle through notes or otherwise direct their attention away from the interviewee.

Listening means more than just hearing what was said. It also means being aware of the interviewee's body language.

Say you're interviewing a major league manager for a taped pre-game show prior to your call of the game. You ask questions about the last series, the way the season is going, the key to the pennant race, the pitching match-up for tonight. However, nothing you ask gets much of a response. The manager's answers are perfunctory. He's indifferent to you, ignoring the mike, his eyes gazing off toward the outfield. It's obvious he is tolerating the interview because you have a job to do, but he isn't really interested in it.

Then you change tack and get away from business. The team has just had an off day at home after a long road trip and you ask him how he spent the day. Suddenly he turns to you, all smiles, talking a mile a minute about the fish he caught. By his reaction, you should realize you've struck pay dirt. You've been given an opportunity to let the fans see more of the personal side of a major league manager if you just follow his lead.

A change in body language the other way can also be enlightening. For example, let's say you're interviewing Dean Smith. You begin by talking about Michael Jordan and his retirement, then move on to other players Smith coached who did well. His responses are expansive, full of feeling. He has a warm smile on his face.

Then you say, "Dean, you've coached at North Carolina 30 years. You've won two national titles and have had a very successful, full career. Many people say the only reason you remain in the business is that you want to surpass Hank Iba's record for most wins." Immediately, his warm smile fades to a set jaw. He responds, "I really don't think about that." He has sluffed off his answer, closing down his former openness. You should recognize he is uncomfortable with the direction of the interview. You have a choice of going on to another subject or continuing on the road you're on, realizing that there are potential land mines ahead.

The way I would handle this hypothetical line of questioning would be: "I sense you're uncomfortable when I mention you in the same breath with Hank Iba. I've talked with other coaches and gotten similar reactions. What's that all about?" Knowing Coach Smith, he would probably tell how he grew up in Kansas at the time "Mr. Iba" was winning the NCAA Championship at Oklahoma A&M in 1945 and 1946. He has always considered Iba the greatest coach who ever walked onto a basketball court. He is naturally uncomfortable comparing himself to his idol.

## Setting the Tone for the Interview

Regardless of whether it's a how-do-you-do, hand-shaking kind of interview or one that is serious and probing, whether on-camera or off, how interviewers act sets the tone for the interview. If interviewers have a smile on their face and a laugh in their voice, their subjects should not expect an inquisition. On the other hand, a furrowed brow and a voice of concern should indicate the interview is taking a more serious turn. Give interviewees mixed signals, and they become guarded and mistrustful.

If you are conducting an on-air interview, how you introduce a person adds to the tone of the interview. If your greeting is warm and friendly and filled with praise for the individual, you're telling your subject, "I'm on your side. Even if the interview turns serious, you can trust me." However, if you include in your intro a reference to something controversial regarding your subject, you are in fact saying, "Be prepared. I want to get down to brass tacks. This will be no-holds-barred."

Even when the topic of the interview is controversial, how interviewers phrase their questions also dictates the mood of the interview.

Say you're interviewing Bob Knight a few days after a game in which he tossed a chair onto the court. If you say,

"Bob, I tell you what. Everyone in the country is still talking about your chair-throwing incident last weekend," accompanying it with a smile and a chuckle, you would be indicating to Knight, "let's have a little fun with this. If you don't want to give a straight answer, I'm not going to pursue the point." Once Knight understands you aren't in an attack mode, he would probably respond like he did on NBC's "Late Night with David Letterman" when he was asked the same question: "I saw this little old lady without a seat, so I thought I'd give her mine."

If, instead, you have a concerned expression on your face when you say, "Bob, I was really shocked when you threw that chair on the court," Knight knows you're expecting some explanation. He may avoid answering—which means you have to do some more probing to get a response—but he is aware you really want to know what happened.

Spontaneity also affects the mood of an interview. As said earlier, the best interviews are the ones in which the subject's responses come from the heart, instantaneously. To ensure spontaneous responses, interviewers need to be cautious of two things.

First, be careful when the interview is taped, not live. Obviously, live interviews are preferable for spontaneity, since you can't go back and retract something said live. But even though taped interviews *can* be redone, you shouldn't make too big a deal about it, otherwise you shoot yourself in the foot. If you say to Coach Jones, "John, we have the ability in this show to stop at any time, because it's on tape. If we really screw something up, we'll just stop and start over," the next thing you know, Coach Jones will ask to stop whenever every little thing isn't exactly the way he wants it. Not only do you draw out the time it takes to do the interview, but the interview will end up sounding stilted and unnatural.

Second, be careful not to prompt your subject. You can relax an interviewee ahead of time by engaging in small talk as long as the topics discussed are more personal—Where are you from originally? Where do you live now? Are you married?—and not along the line of questioning you intend during the interview.

Often your subject will say, "What are you going to ask me?" It's a fair question, one you can answer without being specific. If Bob Knight wanted to know what I was going to ask him, I would summarize areas of questioning I intended to pursue: "We're going to talk about the Big Ten race. Then I'm going to ask you about some of your players. I also want to get your views on NBA players being eligible for the Olympics." By being general in your prompting, you not only set your subject's mind at ease, you also preserve the spontaneity of the interview and allow yourself room to change course if better avenues present themselves.

## Handling Difficult Interviews

Some of the most difficult interviews—and also some of the best—are ones that take place immediately upon the completion of an event when emotions are still at the surface. The best example is the interview in the loser's locker room.

In 1987, I had just finished doing a game between the Milwaukee Bucks and the Soviet national team when I was asked to do the post-game interview with the losing manager of the World Series. ABC chartered a flight for me to Minneapolis where I watched Game Seven between the Twins and the Cardinals in the truck with Curt Gowdy, Jr., and his crew, taking notes as the game progressed. When I realized Minnesota was going to wrap it up, I made my way to the St. Louis locker room and waited.

Doing a losing locker-room interview always provides some anxious moments, because you're never certain how people will respond to loss. This time was particularly unsettling for a couple of additional reasons. First, though I had followed the Series like most fans, my focus of attention had been preparing for the game between the Bucks and the Soviets. Second, I had not seen a single moment of the Series live. Like a vast majority of the country, my only contact with the Series had been via the tube. Even during the final game, I had watched the proceedings on monitors, not from the stands. When the Cardinals entered the locker room, it was an eerie, surreal sensation. It was almost as if the players had stepped out of the television screen into my living room, like Bo Jackson does in one of his TV ads for Nike.

Tim McCarver later told me the interview I did with the Cardinal's Whitey Herzog was one of the best losing locker-room interviews he'd ever seen. If the interview went well, it was because of factors other than having prepared for it. I had known Whitey in St. Louis and had done a couple of his games during the 1987 season. Consequently, when he saw me, he knew what I wanted, walked right up to me, and gave a very gracious interview. His recognition of and trust in me, which had developed over time, carried the interview.

Doing the winners' locker room can also have its challenges. The following year, I had just returned home from jogging when Executive Producer Geoff Mason called and asked me to come to Los Angeles to do the post-game interview with the Series champs. Again, I did not watch the final game live, but in the truck. Near the conclusion of the game, I sat in the Dodger clubhouse, deep in the bowels of Dodger Stadium, listening to Vin Scully's call of the game and the ever-building roar of the crowd above me.

Unlike my interview with Herzog the prior year, trust and recognition were not factors in the interview I conducted with Tommy Lasorda. In fact, I don't think Tommy even knew who I was since I had never called a Dodger game. This time, preparation was my best ally. I had researched Lasorda's comments at the beginning of the series and used them to start the interview. Lasorda reacted to my lead instantly and took it from there. Having a direction is a necessity in the winners' locker room because it helps keep you focused amid all the champagne spewing, the commotion, the celebration.

Some of the hardest interviews to do are those with non-professionals. Most college or high school athletes have not been interviewed very much. Consequently, they are ill at ease, particularly if the interview is for television.

I used to do a coach's show with the late John Jardine, former coach of the University of Wisconsin. John was an excellent interviewee. Even though we brainstormed before the show, John was good enough to wing it when we started taping. However, we had one segment called "The Player of

the Game" which was the most excruciating part of the program. Maybe one out of five kids had anything interesting to
say. Regardless the question, the answer was terse, a cliché
you'd heard 14,000 times with every word followed by "you
know."

About the only thing you can do when interviewing
young athletes with little experience in front of a microphone
or television camera is to put them at ease beforehand. Engage
in personal small talk. It will let them get to know you better
and you to know them. Also recognize that your subject will
likely run out of things to say long before you've run out of
questions. By finding out as much as you can about the athlete, you ensure having a reserve when the well dries up.

Of course, the toughest interviews are the ones that include the potential for discussing controversial topics.

To begin with, whenever you're faced with bringing up a
sensitive issue with your subjects, your goal would be better
served if you were not confrontational. Instead, you should
win over your subjects' trust, convincing them you are not out
to destroy, only to get their side of the issue. I've devoted a
good portion of my career to developing trust with people.
Because of that trust, they realize I won't be against them, and
they have been willing to answer hard questions.

Second, when conducting an interview that is bound to
lead to a controversial area, don't address the controversy out
of the blocks. What would happen if a radio talk show host
called up Bob Knight and started the interview, "Tonight on
the Newsmaker Line we have with us Bobby Knight, the basketball coach of the Indiana Hoosiers, considered one of the
outstanding coaches in the country. Bob, everybody here in
New York was just appalled when they saw clips of you throwing that chair last weekend. What's your reaction to that?" The
next two sounds the listeners would likely hear would be
"Click" followed by a dial tone.

Even when you have a time constraint, especially an interview conducted immediately after the conclusion of an event,
you should not jump your subject with controversy. Ask what
the turning point of the game was or who was the key player
so your subject can work out some of the emotions of the
moment. Then ask, "Bob, I'm sure everybody at home is won-

dering what was going through your mind when you tossed that chair on the court." You still may not receive a satisfactory explanation, but you have a better chance of getting a good response.

In a studio interview, you have more time to pave the way, to ease into controversy. Using my good friend Bob Knight as a guinea pig again, if I had conducted a hypothetical studio interview shortly after the chair-throwing incident, I might have started out saying, "It's been a pleasure to work with Bob Knight over the years. Even as a budding young sportscaster at CBS, he always treated me well. Bob, it's really good to be with you again. It looks like the Hoosiers are right in the thick of the Big Ten race this year." From there I might have directed the conversation toward his undefeated 1975–76 NCAA champs, comparing them to other great college teams of the past, then onto the people who influenced him such as Pete Newell.

To this point, all my questions would have been non-threatening. I would now be ready to open up the sensitive issue: "Bob, you've told me as a friend that you were always in control, that you always know what you are doing. What was the strategy involved when you threw that chair last weekend? Did it help your ball club?"

In similar situations, Bob has been known to respond with "I don't want to talk about it." But, because I have prepared the way, I would be able to follow up, "You talk about how much you admire Pete Newell, how he was your guru, yet Pete was such a mild-mannered coach. Mike Krzyzewski is one of your protégés and he's very calm. What makes Bob Knight so different?" I think it would be hard for Bob not to answer.

Whatever the adversity facing you, the best guide on how to conduct an interview is your instincts.

One of the best moments I've had in my network career occurred during the worst of circumstances. It happened at the 1988 Winter Olympics in Calgary where I covered the speed-skating venue. One of the most moving stories to come out of the games that year was that of the U.S. skater, Dan Jansen, a leading contender for multiple gold medals. Hours before his first race, Jansen received word his sister had died of leukemia. He fell during the 500-meters, admitting later that he was distracted, had lost his focus, and wasn't mentally prepared.

Instead of going home, Jansen remained in Calgary to compete. Three days later, he raced again. He was leading and on a gold-medal pace, coming into the final turn of the 1,000-meters, when he fell again. Eric Heiden and I reacted like every viewer at home, saying "Oh, no. I can't believe it." It was one of the most stunning, gut-wrenching experiences of my life. Everyone felt for the young man.

Shortly after the second fall, I was told in my earpiece to go down and interview Jansen. Considering the tragedy in Jansen's private life and the dual disasters on the ice, I knew it was not going to be an easy interview.

While the network cut to other venues, I raced down to the interview area. As I was about to enter, a Canadian policeman stopped me, saying I didn't have the proper credentials. I had conducted interviews there regularly for two weeks. I had my ABC blazer on. I had credentials running from my neck down to my toes. But for whatever reason, none of my credentials satisfied the policeman who blocked my entry to the interview area.

I had no time to argue so I dashed outside and ran around the world's largest skating arena in the snow and ice to the other side. There I gained reentry by way of the area under the arena where the TV trucks were located and, by a different route, made my way to the interview room.

I barely sat down with Dan and put my earpiece on when Jim McKay said, "Now, let's go back to the speedskating arena where Gary Bender has Dan Jansen."

It was obviously a tearful time for Dan. The mood was subdued. Under the circumstances, I simply let my instincts direct me. I put myself in touch with my emotions at the moment I saw Jansen's second fall, the ones I was sure the viewers at home also felt.

I directed my questions in two areas. First, I asked about the 1000-meters just completed: "Dan, we watched you come down the stretch, you were so close, I just can't imagine what you must have felt." Dan explained how the second fall was like reliving a nightmare.

Then I addressed what was on everybody's mind: "This has been an emotional drain on you, an emotional drain on everyone around you. I admire so much the courage of what you have done. People will never forget what you were able to do." At that point he opened up and talked about his sister. He knew some people thought he shouldn't have stayed to compete, but because he knew his sister so well, he was sure he had done the right thing. He was more focused for the 1000-meters. The reason he fell was because he had simply caught an edge.

Later, Prentice Rogers of the *Atlanta Constitution* wrote, "The sensitive handling of the Dan Jansen story will probably emerge as the high point of the coverage during the Games. It was reported with taste and poignancy when Jansen fell during the men's 500-meters speedskating event after learning just hours before of his sister's death. Gary Bender echoed the emotions of the nation with the anguish he expressed when Jansen fell again Thursday night in the 1000-meters."

I have since been told by friends and colleagues that the interview was the finest moment in my broadcast life. Their feelings are summed up in a letter I received from my former teammate in the booth, Billy Packer: "I just wanted to drop you a line and tell you how much I enjoyed your work at the Olympics. The interview you did with Dan Jansen was the finest I've ever seen under the circumstances. It was handled as only a person with great human feelings such as yourself could have handled it. Gary, it made me proud to know you as a friend and fellow partner."

# CHAPTER TWENTY

# *Career Considerations*

*I*t has been shown that people are happiest when what they do for a living coincides with what they enjoy doing most. Yet, most people aren't that fortunate. The lucky few who knew what they wanted to do early on recognized they had a special ability, a special skill to offer the walk of life they chose to follow. Because of that special skill, they also had a quiet confidence that they could do the job as well, if not better, than those who did it before them.

Knowing your strengths and weaknesses is a real asset toward choosing any career. However, many young people are not certain of their abilities or, if they are, are not sure how their abilities apply to a career field. Often they are guided by desire and not by practical considerations. That's why a "Broadcasting Skills Inventory Checklist" was included earlier in this book.

Even after choosing sportscasting as the career for you, there are other decisions to be made. In what area of sports broadcasting do you want to focus? Do you want to become a sports anchor, a sports talk-show host, a television journalist who does sports on the six- and ten-o'clock news? Maybe you want to do a variety of things. Or do you want to concentrate solely on play-by-play?

Choosing to be a sportscaster is one thing. Making it happen is another. Anyone who sets out on a sports broadcasting career path can expect a journey filled with many obstacles.

## Setting Goals

Bill Glass, a former all-pro defensive lineman for the Cleveland Browns and Detroit Lions, once said, "People who aim at nothing in particular usually achieve just that." If you didn't have a goal in a football game, you'd have utter chaos. Without a goal, there would be nothing to try to attain, nothing to drive you to succeed, and nothing to measure your success.

When I decided on being a sportscaster, I developed a three-stage mental image of my career path: first I expected to be the voice of the Kansas Jayhawks; I expected to work at KMOX radio in St. Louis; and I expected to work at the network level. Everything I envisioned happened. Was I a genius? Did I have a powerful crystal ball? No. Because I created career stepping stones in the back of my mind, I knew where I wanted to go. When opportunities presented themselves, I had a course of direction and didn't have to ponder my decisions very long. Being locked into a mental plan did two things for me: it gave me something to drive toward, to focus my efforts; and, when I did reach a level of my plan, I was not surprised or overwhelmed by it.

As you develop a mental career path, you should keep in mind your skill base. Among my strengths are my ability to communicate, to be extemporaneous, to describe things vividly as they happen in front of me. Among the things I do not do well is creating under the gun. It isn't easy for me to edit tape under pressure or write script under deadline and still pull myself together to go on the air, looking relaxed and not stressed out. Though I have had to do the latter in my career, I knew early on that my skills were best suited for play-by-play and not for reporting sports at six and ten.

Within your mental plan, you should also decide whether your ultimate job includes working in radio or television. Many play-by-play announcers prefer radio because it gives them more freedom. Yet, if you have success at it, somewhere along the road someone will ask you to cross over to television. Because of the increased income associated with tv, the offer will be tempting. In the back of your mind, you should have already decided which avenue you want to pursue. You can do both, but you still need to be aware of what is best for you.

Along those same lines, you need to know whether you want to reach the network level or not. Network announcers obviously get more exposure and higher salaries. However, there is also a down side. To get to the network, you have to be able to do the major sports—football, basketball, and baseball; in other words, you must have the flexibility to be a year-round, all-season announcer. You also have to expect to become involved with all those crazy different sports that no one else bothers to cover because of lack of money or interest or both. You cannot expect to do play-by-play in only one sport unless you are a great athlete who is hired on the basis of name value. Even then, you'll probably spend years as a color analyst as Pat Summerall and Frank Gifford did. Now Pat and Frank are capable play-by-play announcers who do other sports besides football. If you want to work in only one or two sports, you should probably set your sights as the voice of a team or a university.

When you set your goals, be specific enough to know what you want, but general enough so you don't limit yourself. My son Trey is also embarking on a career in sportscasting. After graduating from the University of Kansas, he got his first job as the play-by-play announcer for the Northwest League's Boise Hawks, a class A minor league baseball club for the California Angels. When I started out 25-plus years ago, Boise, Idaho, was off the planet. I was a Kansas boy who knew only Kansas. I would never have considered myself a candidate for such a position. That's how much things have changed. Many more opportunities are out there if you remain open to the possibilities.

Of course, to increase the opportunities available to you, you have to accept the fact that you may have to relocate many times in the pursuit of your career goals. It comes with the territory. Though Lawrence, Kansas, and St. Louis, Missouri, were on my career path itinerary when I started out, Hutchinson and Topeka, Kansas, and Madison, Wisconsin, were not. In order to overcome the roadblocks that will inevitably be placed in front of you along the way, you may have to make a detour here and there.

Once I set my goals, how do I attain them? Bill Glass once described three guidelines for achieving your goals.

First, you can't be afraid to make mistakes. There will always be somebody who is critical of what you do. When people criticize, you cannot draw in your horns. You cannot be continually afraid to step out and do it again. Remember, Babe Ruth was a legend who hit 714 home runs. But, in achieving that success, he was also a legendary failure, striking out 1330 times.

Second, you can't give up. In this business, it's very easy to get discouraged because of the tremendous drain physically and mentally. Your working hours are the worst. Often you are paid very little. Keep in mind the man whose first partner in business drank up all the assets and made him a business failure at 22 and deeply in debt. He refused bankruptcy and was still paying off his indebtedness at the age of 39. Besides being completely broke, he was further crushed by the death of the woman he loved. Ten years later, he tried politics and had initial success. But after two short terms, the voters threw him out. After a dozen more years of continual defeat, he was elected President of the United States. That man was Abraham Lincoln.

Third, don't forget those who believe in you and are counting on you. You are not alone. You have family and friends who will support you when you are down on yourself. In the 1929 Rose Bowl, California's "Wrong Way" Roy Riegles picked up a fumble and ran 69½ yards in the wrong direction before one of his teammates tackled him just inches from his own goal. Riegles was so upset with what he'd done, he took himself out of the game. At halftime, his coach told him, "Roy, you made a mistake that hurt us. But I believe in you. Go back in there and give it your best." Few remember that Riegles played one of the greatest second halves in his career.

## Measuring Success

What is success? It is a hard term to define. Some people view success as how high up the ladder of a company or a profession you climb or how large your salary. Yet, I've known people who never reached the network or never even worked in a large market and were still happy with their lot in life. The key to success is how you view yourself. If you achieve satisfaction from what you do, you are successful.

Defining success in this way, somewhere along the line in their career, everyone will experience success. A person cannot continually do the same thing day in and day out without enjoying some success.

Ralph Waldo Emerson said, "Man tends to become what he thinks most about." Earlier in this book, we talked about visualization, a concept many athletes believe in fervently. When the great Packer running back Jim Taylor ran 186 yards against the New York Giants, reporters asked him afterwards how he did it against such a vaunted defense. Taylor replied, "Gentlemen, all week long I imagined myself hitting off right tackle, imagined myself hitting up the middle, imagined myself sweeping left. So, when the game came about, I wasn't surprised because in my imagination I saw myself accomplishing everything that I did." When he knocked out Jack Dempsey, Gene Tunney said he pictured his "thundering left hook" dropping Dempsey 10,000 times before in his mind. If you see yourself doing something over and over again, you are more likely to do well when the time comes.

The opposite is also true. Worry pictures are success pictures in reverse. If you constantly worry about what might happen, figuring out the myriad of things that can go wrong, you condition yourself to fail.

A number of people have low opinions of themselves and are preconditioned to fail. They believe being humble is a virtue when, in fact, it is a vice because they carry a parachute with them in life. When they embark on a venture that doesn't work out, they are quick to bail out, presuming that they weren't meant to be successful.

To illustrate preconditioned failure, I've often told the fictional story of the basketball player whose coach comes up to him before the big game and says, "Michael, you're going to be a key to this game tonight. I want you to guard Jackson. He's just been wearing everybody out. No one has been able to stop him. But, with your defensive abilities, I think you can be the difference in this game. I don't expect you to shut him out, but I would like him to have to work for every shot. I want you to be in his face at every opportunity. Can you do it, son?"

Michael looks at the coach and says, "Yes, sir, coach. I'm ready to do it. I couldn't ask for a better challenge."

On the opening tip, the ball goes straight to Jackson who drives for an easy three-footer. There is nothing Michael could have done to stop him, but he looks at the coach as if to say, "Man, this guy is really good."

The next time down the court, Michael puts in a good defensive effort, but Jackson shoots over him and nails another one. From that point on, Jackson beats Michael at will. Why? Michael was ready to quit from the beginning. In the back of his mind, he was really saying, "Coach, I'll try it, but I don't really think I can do it." As soon as something went wrong, he was ready to fail.

To be successful, you have to be going somewhere. You can't stand still. Take riding a bike. At a standstill with the kickstand up, it is very difficult to maintain your balance. Gain a little forward momentum and balancing is easier. The more speed you attain, the easier it becomes.

It's an old cliché, but true: You never stay the same. You either get better or you get worse. If anybody says they're still doing the same kind of job they did two or three years ago, they aren't admitting it, but they've probably regressed.

To achieve your goals, you must frequently reevaluate yourself. In the broadcasting business, this is easy to do by simply reviewing tapes of yourself in action. You should see growth in the sophistication you've incorporated in everything from preparation to handling people in interviews to the credibility you've established. To be able to call Bob Knight a friend means, somewhere along the line, you have to grow to meet the professional standards that warrant his acceptance.

Because of the competitiveness of the sportscasting business, almost everyone wonders at some time or other whether their goals are attainable or not. I was driving to West Lafayette, Indiana, to do a Big Ten Game of the Week with Merle Harmon when Merle turned to me and asked, "Gary, what's happening about you getting to the network?" I had to admit there was nothing on the horizon. He said, "I don't know how to tell you this, but if you don't get there by the age of 32, I don't think you're going to make it." I never understood why the age of 32 was so significant—after having worked at the network level for nearly 20 years, I'm even more certain it was arbitrary—but, at the time, I was approaching 30. I had the panicky feeling that time was running out.

You have a family to support. The hours you work are long. You are making little money. You've mentally created this niche in the profession that is your ideal, but you haven't attained it. How do you know to stick it out or give it up?

One of the most impressive examples of stick-to-it-iveness has to be Detroit Tigers announcer Rick Rizzs. Rick spent an unheard of eight years in the minor leagues before finally making it to the majors as a play-by-play announcer for the Seattle Mariners. During that time, in addition to his play-by-play chores, he did everything from working as a clubhouse attendant to selling billboard space on the outfield walls. There were times when he had his doubts. But he also recognized, "in order to be successful in this business, you sometimes have to learn a little bit about failure because you're going to get rejected a number of times when you send out resumés."

Rick also realized up front that, to achieve success in the sportscasting business, you have to accept the fact that it will likely take time and years of low pay before it happens. However, "if you want it bad enough and want to work hard enough for it and set your goals high enough," says Rizzs, "in this great country, you can do anything you want. When you get to that first curve or that first obstacle, if you can't go through it, go around it because there's always an opportunity out there. You just keep trying till your heart says, 'It's not going to happen.'

"The barometer is, if you can feel yourself getting better, and if you believe in yourself that you're getting better, you always know you have a shot. If you have doubts whether you're improving, then you really have to look inside yourself and say, 'Maybe this isn't what I'm intended to do.'"

## Pitfalls for Beginning Announcers

In this book, most of the examples illustrating how to do play-by-play involve ideal situations while working at the network level. Beginning announcers will find their working conditions far less glamorous. When starting out, young announcers can expect to do without many things.

For example, whenever I broadcasted a game on my first job, I was my own engineer. I had to hook up my own equipment and monitor the VU meter to make sure it didn't go into the red. For someone who has no mechanical ability to fix anything if it fails, I found the experience threatening every time I did it. The most anxious moments came when I hooked up the terminals to the amplifier and called back to the station to see if they were receiving me. I prayed for the answer to be, "Yeah, we got you." Once I heard those words, half the battle was over.

Probably the biggest disillusionment for beginning sportscasters is that their first position will most likely not be devoted full-time to play-by-play. Most stations who hire first-time broadcasters usually cannot economically justify a full-time sports announcer. Consequently, budding play-by-play announcers have to learn to be jacks-of-all-trades just to do the one thing they want to do the most. They may have to spend Saturday afternoon spinning records, while everyone else is watching college football. They may have to sell their own advertising, host non-sports shows, or do anything management can think of to justify the few times they go on the air to do sports.

Though I wanted to specialize in play-by-play from the beginning, I also knew I wouldn't be able to right away. Looking back on my career, all the odd functions I performed early on—being a DJ, hosting a country western show, answering callers on a community call-in show—were necessary for my growth in broadcasting. I was able to learn the business from bottom to top much the same way the mail clerk at the network works his way up through program assistant to associate producer until eventually becoming executive producer.

Because their duties will not be dedicated to play-by-play, another frustration for beginning announcers will be the lack of time they have to do the kind of preparation they'd like to do. Station managers often don't understand the necessity of preparing for a game as has been described in this book. Consequently, budding play-by-play announcers will have to fight for every moment to prepare. KWBW used to have (and still has) a daily program called "Perky's Party Line" where people in the community called in to buy and sell anything and everything. I used to drive everybody nuts by working on my spotting boards while engineering the show. Because of the demands placed on me at the station, I was also never able to attend practices for the local teams. Instead, I made arrangements like the one I had with Hutchinson High School basketball coach Joe Krafels where I would call him every night at home and get the lowdown on how practice had gone.

Even if they find the time to prepare, rookie announcers will often find little material *to* prepare. When I worked the National Junior College Basketball Tournament for KWBW, I had 16 teams to prepare for and virtually no way to get any information on them since the participants often weren't known until the weekend before the tournament. I was lucky if I got a thumbnail sketch on every starter. In contrast, when I do major college games today, I have reams of material at my fingertips.

The point to all this is, just because you may have to do without many things in your first position, it does not mean you should lower your professional standards. Though it may require you to go through hoops to get information about a team, it shouldn't preclude you from trying to increase the knowledge you pass on to your listeners. You should always say to yourself, "I don't have enough. I need to find out more." As soon as you get by, thinking, "the information is too hard to get" or "no one cares anyway," then you become complacent and stop growing as an announcer.

Getting past that first job requires perseverance. But you can help your cause with a little creativity. For example, try to reduce the number of hats you wear. Because keeping score while calling a basketball game is very challenging, I once experimented by employing my wife Linda as a statistician. I had a high school basketball game to call on a Friday night and Linda wanted to go with me. On the drive to Wellington, Kansas, I taught her how to keep the score book. She was eager to help. Unfortunately, she wasn't very skilled at it. Throughout the game I kept repeating myself, "That was Ediger with the basket. Jay Ediger just scored," to give Linda time to catch up. It was the last time she acted as my statistician.

I didn't give up on the idea of getting some help in the booth, however. Somebody told me of an avid fan in town who loved to be around sports. I asked him if he wanted to go on a road trip with me, and he agreed. From then on, it became a regular thing. For meal expenses—our station manager, Fred Conger, barely allowed even that—Jerry Kershaw became my right-hand man in the booth, sharing driving time, keeping score, adding color, and providing much needed emotional support. Sometime after I left KWBW, Jerry switched chairs. He's still there in Hutchinson as the sports director at KWBW and the voice of the Hutchinson Salt Hawks and Hutchinson Blue Dragons.

## Dealing with the Brass

If your goal is to go into management one day, you would be better off starting in sales or programming. On-air talent rarely crosses over into management. The principal reason is that management looks at talent as having abilities limited to what they do on the air.

Generalizations are bad, but it's an old adage that management views talent as "a piece of meat." The typical management opinion of on-air personalities is that they are selfish egomaniacs who are oblivious to others, who would run over you in a second to further their careers. Not all members of management think that way, but most do. It is an attitude that has always upset me.

Consequently, I've worked long and hard to disassociate myself from that stereotypical reputation. My goal has always been to show management I was a dependable person who could represent the station or the network in any walk of life, whether it be in front of the Boy Scouts or the United Way. I wanted them to know I was capable of being more than just a sports announcer. If they wanted to bring me into a sales meeting to try to convince a sponsor to buy into a program, I wanted them to know I was the best salesperson they had. If they wanted me to speak at a gathering, they knew I would give them a powerful, motivating speech. I did not want them thinking I was some dumb jock or some prima donna who could only do play-by-play.

However, if you show your loyalty to management by doing all the extras they expect, don't expect the same type of loyalty to be returned. Broadcasting is cutthroat. You may have spent a month of Sundays on your own time to do promotions for management, but if the ratings aren't going well, all that hard work will be meaningless. When changes are made, don't expect management to stick by you.

Because of the precarious relationship between management and talent, announcers are faced with a dilemma: When management asks, can you say no? If you say no, will you ever be asked again?

The late Frank Glieber, one of the outstanding broadcasters of his day, was once called by CBS and asked, "Frank, are you a golfer?"

Frank replied, "Oh, yeah. I'm a golfer."

"Good. We're glad to hear that because we need somebody to be on the tower at the 17th hole at the Masters in Augusta in two weeks."

Frank said, "I'd love to do that. I'm glad you called me."

Promptly after hanging up, Frank raced to the local library to get everything he could get his hands on about golf. He had never played a round of golf in his life and knew virtually nothing about the sport. He responded the way he did because he was fearful the network would look unfavorably at his lack of versatility. A footnote to the story: Frank went on to do the Masters 19 straight years.

What happens if you say no? Take the case of Ray Scott. In the 60s, Scott was the top-rated announcer for CBS, doing everything from the lead NFL game to anchoring the network's coverage of the Masters Tournament. When Bob Wussler took over as president of CBS, Ray was asked to come in and visit. After a little small talk, Ray handed Wussler a sheet of paper.

Wussler said, "What's this?"

"These are the NFL games I'll do this year," said Scott. "In the past, I told management which games I wanted to work. They would assign them to me, then assign the rest of the games to others."

Wussler looked at Scott and said, "Well, that's not the way we do it here now."

"What do you mean?"

"We will determine two to three weeks at a time where you and the other people at CBS will work," said Wussler. "That will be our policy here."

Scott replied, "I'm not sure I want to do it that way."

Scott's ultimatum eventually cost him his job. As one astute individual once put it, "Don't throw the keys on the desk because management will take them."

# CHAPTER TWENTY-ONE

# Establishing a Play-by-Play Identity

## Style

What is style?

When applied to broadcasting, style is one's manner of expression on the air. In his book, *Sportscasting*, Carl Klages defined style as the "vocal fingerprints" of the play-by-play announcer.

In early May 1991, Bob Costas conducted an interview with Vin Scully on NBC's late night talk show "Later," during which they discussed Russ Hodges' famous radio call of Bobby Thomson's pennant-winning homer in 1951: "Branca throws. And it's a long blast. It's going to be . . . I believe . . . The Giants win the pennant! The Giants win the pennant! The Giants win the pennant! The Giants win the pennant! Bobby Thomson hits it into the lower deck of the left field stands! The Giants win the pennant! And they're going crazy! They're going crazy! High-Yo!"

"I would not have wanted to be remembered for that call of Bobby Thomson's home run," said Scully. "Admittedly, it's a great call. But, to me, Russ kind of lost it. He just went wild. I would have much rather have done probably what Red [Barber] did [during the simulcast on television] which was call the home run and shut up."

Costas rebutted, "And yet, for Russ Hodges, it seemed right. When I hear that—and I've probably heard it a 100 times—I don't think the man is hysterical as in unprofessional. I think this is the moment of this guy's life and, in his way, in a way that's right for him, he's equal to this moment. If I heard Vin Scully or Red Barber in that state, I would have thought the world had stopped spinning on its axis."

Style is very personal. *Webster's* says it is influenced by "a person's characteristic tastes, attitudes, and mode of behavior." Since no two individuals have exact personalities, no two announcers have exactly the same style. Vin Scully is eloquent. Harry Carey is boisterous. Jack Buck is laid-back. All have been successful.

Since style is a by-product of being yourself, the key to developing a distinct style of your own is knowing who you are, knowing your strengths and weaknesses.

Growing into a style of your own is an evolutionary process much like breaking in a new baseball glove. When you first purchase the glove, it is stiff. You have to oil it and wrap a ball in it to form the pocket you want. You play catch with it, experimenting with your finger placement inside. Some people put all their fingers inside. Some put one or two fingers out. Eventually, you work the glove into a shape and feel that is comfortable to you. The process is complete when the glove becomes an extension of your arm, when you're no longer conscious of it being a separate entity. That's why a professional baseball player does not like others using his glove. He worked long and hard to make the glove feel just right to him. He doesn't want to lose that unique feel.

Likewise, when you start out in the booth, you may be stiff and uncertain. As you gain experience, subtle changes occur. The enthusiasm level you express rises or lowers into a range that feels right at the right time. Your rhythm changes as you experiment, finding out what suits you. With experience, you reach a comfort zone in preparation, word usage on the air, all the facets of play-by-play. Finally, you reach a point where you're no longer running scared. You know exactly what's comfortable for you.

This process does not happen in a vacuum. Outside forces constantly influence your style development, even from the beginning. Like youngsters who buy the model glove of the star they most admire, young broadcasters often start out trying to emulate someone who has already achieved success in the business.

Today's youth has several advantages I didn't have when I was growing up. With the extensive sports coverage on television now, you can view a full range of play-by-play styles. When I was growing up, I had no idol to use as a starting point. I was not exposed to hours of sports on television. In fact, because of where we lived, I was even limited in what I heard on the radio.

However, there were individuals who influenced me as I grew in the business. Probably my earliest influence was Jim Simpson. I started watching Jim when someone told me he thought our styles were similar. Jim was a good conversationalist. He talked with his subjects, not at them. He wasn't flashy or memorable, just comfortable, flexible, reliable. He had the ability to make the mundane seem interesting.

Someone once said, if you take one idea from somebody and make it your own, you're a plagiarist. However, if you take three or four ideas from somebody, you're a scholar. Though my style is now comfortable to me, I'm still learning, still picking up new ideas.

The announcer I most admire, the one I'd probably try to emulate if I were starting out today, is Dick Enberg. Dick is the consummate wordsmith. He knows exactly how to capture the moment with just the right words, with just the right measure of emotion. I've also learned a couple of things from Pat Summerall. His laid-back style perfectly illustrates you don't have to talk every moment, there are times when the less said, the better. Pat is also a superb example of how to utilize your analyst, in his case, John Madden. Bob Costas' banty-rooster, opinionated style is probably 180 degrees opposite mine, but I've learned from him that it is all right to express an opinion because people expect it. And, watching the dry-witted Jack Buck work a major event like baseball's All-Star Game, I've come to realize it's important to retain a sense of humor amidst all the hoopla.

Incorporating various elements of style from others is an intelligent endeavor as long as those elements are then molded into a style that represents you. However, there is a difference between incorporation and imitation.

Often budding announcers start out copying their idols. For many years, a lot of young announcers were trying to sound like Vin Scully or Harry Carey. However, those who made it in the business didn't continue in that mode for long. Why? Scully and Carey are unique.

Imitation may be the sincerest form of flattery, but you can't build a career attempting to be somebody else. It is difficult to sustain something that isn't natural. For example, you may idolize Harry Carey, but your voice quality can't compare to his. You may be able to mimic his voice, but trying to do it all the time would be a strain. It would be like a baritone trying to sing soprano.

When CBS hired Terry Bradshaw as an analyst, John Madden was a hot item. The viewers loved Madden's effervescence, his off-the-wall mannerisms and comments. Terry tried to be the same way and bombed. Fortunately, Terry reevaluated himself, realized he couldn't be something he wasn't, came back as Terry Bradshaw, and is now enjoying a successful career.

Some people who have made it in the broadcasting business have been Jekylls and Hydes, whose on-air personalities differed considerably from how they acted in private. I knew one play-by-play announcer who was an extrovert in public or on the air, but at home was just the opposite. His wife said she could barely get a word out of him. I also know an announcer who is a competent, confident, interesting individual in the booth, but who is otherwise one of the most insecure, unpleasant people I've ever been around. One can only imagine the stress that predominates their lives. When your style is not an extension of your personality, you expend energy at a rate most people cannot sustain.

A clue that announcers are stretching beyond themselves is when they begin to rely on gimmicks, something out of the ordinary designed to draw attention. A gimmick can be a sound effect, a gesture, or, most commonly, a pet phrase such as "twine time" or "swisheroo for two."

Sometimes one person's gimmick is another person's trademark. The phrase "Holy Cow!" is synonymous with Harry Carey. Say "Oh my!" and you immediately think of Dick Enberg. And a football game called by Keith Jackson would not be the same if he didn't sprinkle in a few of his patented down-home descriptions like "hoss and a half."

The difference between a gimmick and a trademark is how the phrase came about. If the statement is not spontaneous, if it requires forethought, chances are it will sound manufactured, concocted, phony. When Dave Niehaus first used "My oh my!" he did not consciously set out to coin what is now his trademark. The expression is just what Dave says when he's excited, and with frequent use, it stuck.

That is the essence of style. When what you say is genuine, not fabricated, you have found your style.

## Criticism

Everyone entering the broadcasting profession can expect to receive their share of criticism. Whether they are listeners, viewers, columnists, colleagues, or members of management, critics abound. If you are thin-skinned, sensitive to anything negative said about your style or what you do and say in the booth, you will have a difficult time surviving. You will end up in a perpetual panic, bouncing here and there in a vain attempt to accomplish the impossible—trying to satisfy everyone.

The hardest thing for most people to understand about criticism is that there is no ultimate truth. Each critic has his or her own perception of an event which leads to constant disagreement.

After one basketball game I called, two different critics panned my performance. However, one said I was overdramatic, sounding as if I were narrating "Victory at Sea," and the other said I was plastic, unemotional, with little personality. Since the two perceptions were at such opposite poles, it would have been hard to be both. Who was right?

I first began to grasp the concept of individual perception after the 1982 Final Four. Throughout that year, a graduate student from the University of Michigan followed Billy Packer and me around to learn about our business. The culmination of her effort was to be a dissertation based on our call of the championship game.

The young lady was with us all Final Four Week, attending production meetings, following along as we interviewed coaches, did our sound bites, and walked through rehearsals. She was so unobtrusive, we hardly knew she was there. After the exciting championship game between North Carolina and Georgetown in which Dean Smith won his first national championship, we said our good-byes and asked her to send us a copy of her dissertation when she completed it.

Two months later I received her work at my home. At the time, I was too busy to read it and put it aside. It was several weeks before I ran across it again. I was shocked at what I read.

The dissertation was an analysis of the championship game with three columns per page. One column was the exact transcription of every word Billy and I said on the air. The second column showed all the camera angles, the mechanical aspects of the broadcast. In the third column, she had assigned an emotional or psychological reason for what Billy and I had said. What disturbed me was her interpretation of what we had said was often not what we had meant. Our words in black and white did not generate the same effect they had when we had said them aloud. It was such a cold, clinical observation that conveyed none of the excitement I felt we had brought to the millions of people watching the game.

I told Billy he should read it, we discussed it, and I finally came to the realization that other people see us differently than we see ourselves.

When you look in the mirror in the morning, the face you see is a familiar image, one you can control and alter to fit the expectations of others. But others see more of you than just your face. When you go into a clothing store to try on a suit, there are mirrors that show you from every angle, from the side, even from the back. You can see your profile, the back of your neck, the back of your torso. What you see is not the normal perspective you have of yourself, but one others see all the time.

In life, the portion of us that is difficult for us to see is not a part of our usual perception of ourselves. Yet, it *is* part of the total persona others see. It takes considerable effort and a series of additional mirrors for us to see ourselves as others see us.

Add in differences in social attitudes, beliefs, and values, and you see there is virtually no way you can see yourself as others perceive you. Through the years, I have received more than my share of criticism from the writers in New York. I'm convinced that part of the reason for their dissatisfaction has to do with the fact I'm a Midwesterner. People from the Midwest tend to be less cutting, less critical, less cynical compared to people from the East. For me to satisfy those critics, I would have to become somebody I'm not.

Politicians, professional athletes, and people in the entertainment and broadcasting industries have another aspect of perception to consider. The public's perception of an individual in the public eye is anything but accurate. It can be distorted by the press, by a critic, even by a good press agent. How can Kevin Costner be a king in Hollywood, an infallible Oscar-winning visionary for making "Dances with Wolves" and six months later become the typical success-has-gone-to-his-head star who thinks he can do anything and overreaches his abilities in trying to play Robin Hood? Did Costner suddenly change? Not necessarily. In fact, he completed his work in *Robin Hood, Prince of Thieves* before he received the Oscar and all the acclaim for *Dances with Wolves.*

People's perception of a public figure often takes on a life of its own, gaining momentum one way or the other. If the public image is good, critics will jump in your car on its rise to the top of the roller coaster. However, as soon as that perception turns negative, critics dive overboard before the crash at the bottom.

We tend to take our perception of others and ourselves for granted without considering why or how we form them and whether they are right. People hear what they want to hear. And once you don't like somebody, you can always find something to criticize.

Say you read in the paper that your favorite athlete has been suspended for drug abuse. The revelation comes as a complete shock to you. It doesn't fit the image you had of the individual. But now you start looking at that athlete in a different light. With the aid of a magnifying glass, you discover all sorts of things you weren't aware of. Since nobody's perfect, you can find any number of faults to pick at.

Lindsay Nelson once told me working as an announcer today is so much different from when he was at the top of the profession. Then, people appreciated his integrity, understood what he was trying to do, and respected his effort. However, if he were working nowadays, he believed he probably would not be able to survive in the business as long as he did because critics today are so analytical, so quick to tear down.

Professional critics are everywhere today. Often they have a forum not accessible to others who might have dissenting opinions. Consequently, they can wield considerable influence within the industry they critique. There are critics whose theatrical review can make or break a play on Broadway, whose movie review can affect a picture's box office revenues in certain cities.

Once, Doug Collins and I called an exciting, dramatic game between the Philadelphia 76ers and the Boston Celtics which was won on a last-second shot by Dr. J, Julius Irving. Immediately after the game, the producer, the director, and the crew congratulated each other, feeling everyone had done an outstanding job. Some members of the CBS brass were even in attendance and they, too, were very positive about how the broadcast had turned out.

The next day, Doug and I flew to New York City for a meeting. When we arrived we picked up a local newspaper and read that one of the columnists had panned our performance, focusing on a trivial mistake in particular. At the meeting, the network brass, who were so congratulatory 24 hours before, were now second-guessing the success of the broadcast, all because of that one article.

John Madden once said there is no democracy in coaching. If you want to succeed, you don't play the most popular players or the players whose personalities you like. You have to be objective and start the players who perform the best. The problem with the broadcasting business is that so much of it is subjective.

So how do you handle criticism?

First, listen to what John Maxwell said in his book *Be All You Can Be*: "The road to success is paved with critics that are ready and waiting to point out how imperfectly other people do what they themselves are unable or unwilling to do." Professional critics rarely engage in constructive criticism. They don't come out and say, "Gary Bender would be an outstanding announcer if . . ." If they were in the automobile repair business, no cars would ever be fixed. Since they are only held accountable to the publications that employ them, they're more likely to concentrate on negatives because controversy sells. Consequently, critics tend to be vultures, landing every once in a while to nip pieces of flesh off carrion.

Second, whether it is favorable or negative, keep in mind that it's only one person's opinion. Former Kentucky coach Joe B. Hall said, "Don't believe anything you read because paper will hold still, and you can write anything on it." Many actors make it a point never to read their reviews, regardless of whether they're good or bad. Their feeling is they are closer to the production and the profession than any critic can get and, therefore, are more capable of judging the quality of their own performance. The internal critic is far more accurate and meaningful.

Finally, we sportscasters probably take ourselves too seriously. We are not brain surgeons or rocket scientists. There are more people in the world who could care less how well we called a Saturday afternoon football game than those who do.

# EPILOGUE

During the 23 seasons Don Sutton pitched in the major leagues, only once did he win 20 or more games in a season. He never threw a no-hitter. In fact, he never led the league in any major statistical category except when he led both leagues with a 2.21 ERA in 1980. Yet, Sutton became only the 30th pitcher in major league history to win 300 games.

Don's analysis of his success is worth noting: "I'm a grinder and a mechanic. I never considered myself flamboyant or exceptional. But, all my life, I've found a way to get the job done."

I identify with that statement. I, too, have taken the bread-and-butter approach to achievement. I try to do the job without screwing it up. I believe you can count on me. I am reliable.

Reliable is an important word to me. "Liable" means responsible. "Re" means over and over again. That's how I've approached my work—in a responsible way, over and over again.

As I mentioned earlier, I've never called a game the way I wanted to. Yet, I strive to have that perfect broadcast. It has been said, "I'm not what I ought to be, not what I want to be, not what I'm going to be, but, praise God, I'm not what I used to be." The moment I quit trying, I quit improving. My personal challenge is to be prepared for my moment.

I think every announcer has his moment. Al Michaels had his in the 1980 Olympics when the U.S. hockey team unexpectedly won the gold medal. His pronouncement "Do you believe in miracles? Yes!" when the young U.S. squad beat the Soviets still sends chills through the people who hear it.

Jim McKay had his moment during the 1972 Olympics in Munich, when the world was glued to their television sets during the hostage crisis and eventual tragedy that befell the Israeli Olympic team.

I've covered some memorable moments—Roger Staubach's "Hail Mary" pass and Lorenzo Charles' "shot heard around the world." But I think *the* moment is still waiting for me. When it comes, I want to handle it so well, it will be indelibly imprinted on the minds of the listeners.

I'm still impressed with what I see in sports—the great athleticism, the emotion, the people I come in contact with. I will continue to work in this crazy business as long as I'm still impressed. As Albert Einstein said, "He who can no longer pause to wonder and stand wrapped in awe is as good as dead. His eyes are closed."

I assure you, I am not dead. My eyes are still wide open. When my life as a broadcaster nears its end, I hope to look back and be able to say what Abraham Lincoln said so eloquently: "I did the best I could, and I did the best I knew how, and I'll keep right on doing it up to the end. If the end brings me out all right, then what is said against me will not matter. If the end brings me out all wrong, then ten angels swearing I was right will make no difference."

# GLOSSARY

(The following definitions were provided in part by Turner Productions.)

**Chryon:** a computer character generator used to provide names, statistics, scoreboards, and credits that are electronically superimposed (keyed) over a live picture or a taped video.

**Cough switch:** an interrupt button that permits announcers to momentarily turn off their microphone in order to cough, clear their throats, or speak to someone without the sound being carried on the air.

**Isolation:** use of a camera to cover action or a person not shown live on the air. The scene captured can then be rerun as a replay or as part of an edited piece.

**Lay out:** a term used to describe when a producer asks announcers not to speak so the natural sound of the action can be heard. This strategy is often used at the end of a game to allow the audience to hear the sounds of a victory celebration.

**Marti equipment:** a remote broadcast transmitter that allows a sporting event to be transmitted from the place it is originating on a line-of-sight basis back to the radio station for broadcast. "Marti" refers to a noted brand name that has become the Xerox of broadcast transmitters.

**Mug shot:** a slang term for a head shot of an individual.

**Page (of graphics):** a full screen display of statistical, biographical, or other information. This term is commonly used when referring to a starting lineup display.

**Single shot:** a director's term referring to a camera shot of one person.

**Sound bite:** a short segment (usually no longer than 20 seconds) of an interview that is edited for playback during a program.

**Spotting boards:** tools used by football announcers and spotters to aid in quick identification of ball carriers, tacklers, blockers, or receivers during a play. They are sometimes constructed so that a team's offensive lineup and potential substitutes appear on one side of the board while the defensive lineup and substitutes appear on the reverse side and often contain additional player information that can be used by the announcer on air.

**Still-stores:** electronic equipment that is capable of storing and retrieving hundreds of individual frames of video, allowing the video to be played back a frame at a time. This equipment is mostly used to store head shots and full pages of graphics.

**Talk-back system:** an interrupt system by which announcers can press a button (the cough switch) and speak to the producer and director in the control room during a live telecast or a taping without the conversation going on the air.

**Telestrator:** an electronic device that allows an announcer to draw directly on a video screen. There are two types of systems: one in which the announcer utilizes a light pen for drawing and another which is heat sensitive requiring only the announcer's finger to draw.

**Train wreck:** a commonly used term in live television describing serious problems that make the telecast difficult.

**Two shot:** a director's term referring to a camera shot framing two people.

**Voice-over:** a term describing announcers' commentary added to a taped event or a feature after it has been edited.

# Index